Gospel Bo[...]

Mission, Evangelism and Prayer

By Rod Thomas

Copyright 2016 First Edition
Copyright 2019 Second Edition
Rod Thomas
Sendai Christian Publications

Contents

1. Introduction 1
2. From Bravery to Timidity to Trust - Moses 10
3. From Weakness to Strength -The Prophets 32
4. From Sadness to Boldness- The Little Maid from Israel 72
5. From Defeat into Victory - Daniel 81
6. The Boldness of Jesus Christ 97
7. Jesus teaches the Church 108
8. The Worshipping Witness - The Samaritan Woman 128
9. Peter and Pentecost 139
10. To Speak the Gospel with Boldness 152
11. The outstretched Hands of God 164
12. Prayer Request from Prison 172
13. A Spirit of Power and Love and a Sound Mind 185
14. Boldness in History 199
15. Boldness Today 233
Appendix I Why did John Mark leave the mission? 248
Appendix II Jonathan Edwards on False Boldness 252
Acknowledgements 258
Literature Cited 259

Quotes are from the ESV unless otherwise mentioned

1. Introduction

"...they were all filled with the Holy Spirit and continued to speak the word of God with boldness" Acts 4:31

I was sitting alone in the church in Sendai before the evening prayer meeting doing some preparation when two men entered. They introduced themselves as German Christians who had come to Japan in the wake of the tsunami disaster of March 2011. I assumed they were evangelicals who had come to assist in the relief effort. But they had come privately and not with a mission agency and they would not tell me their home church. I offered to put them in touch with a Christian volunteer organisation or set them to work in the relief and evangelistic ministry of our own church. But they declined and said they were prophets and that God had sent the tsunami to punish the Japanese for all their sins and that a larger tsunami was coming soon. One of them had a T-shirt with 'The Wrath of God' in large Japanese characters on the front and Romans 1:18 on the back.

I tried to find out what they intended to do and if we had any common ground. Would they distribute tracts, seeing they could not speak Japanese? How would they point people to Christ and explain the gospel? "Oh no", said they, "It is too early for that. The Japanese aren't ready yet". Then what did they hope to accomplish by coming to Japan? I told them that God is primarily glorified when sinners repent which they will not do unless Christ is preached. I said they had neither the means to evangelise nor the right attitude. They accused me of disobedience. After an hour I suggested they catch the first flight home and they left in a huff cursing me in God's name.

It is bad witnesses like these that put off many Christians from boldly telling the gospel. We do not want to be thought unfeeling or unsympathetic to people's needs like they were in the aftermath of the disaster that hit us in Japan. We Christians certainly believe in the wrath of God and impending judgement and that there is only one way of salvation. This message must be told. Yet we do not want to be like those two 'prophets' who were wild-eyed, angry, self-centred, Christ-less, unloving, and therefore ultimately disobedient, unevangelistic and ineffective.

For the past 40 years I have struggled in my own battle in telling the gospel boldly and faithfully to unbelievers, my conscience often accusing me of not using my opportunities to speak boldly, clearly and fully for Christ, or else for being careless and unloving to those I am supposed to reach.

We all know we should be more joyful, bold and evangelistic but are hindered by our timidity, worldly cares and spiritual depression. On top of that are various false reasonings and false teachings which reinforce our weakness so that days and weeks go by without us saying anything boldly about Christ at all. Gospel boldness is the most dire need in world mission today.

Gospel boldness is not mere courage. Courage, whether physical or moral, is a common grace which God gives to all men to overcome fear and do something unpleasant but necessary for self-preservation or the common good. Gospel boldness may resemble courage to an outsider but is like a fruit of the Holy Spirit shown only by Christians. It is closely related to our joy in the assurance of salvation and joy will always be present with gospel boldness. The Holy Spirit gives gospel boldness to his church to present Christ to the world clearly, fully, winsomely, and passionately. It is not the same as natural boldness: some people will be loud and brash in everything they do, whether it is telling the gospel or ordering MacDonalds, because it is a habit that they find that works for them, perhaps by cowering the opposition or hiding their own insecurity. However gospel boldness is not a habitual loudness, but behaves appropriately for each occasion. It is not self-centred but servant-hearted, which loves its hearers. Gospel boldness counts it, not an irksome duty but an immense privilege to present Christ. It is not satisfied with merely presenting the gospel for its own sake but is intensely concerned that the hearers believe. Gospel boldness is convinced of Christ's sufficiency, saving power, glory, love and necessity and recommends Him urgently to unbelievers as their only yet sure hope. Gospel boldness is not interested in self-preservation and reputation but the conversion of the lost to the glory of God.

The reasons for this book

1. There are few if any books on gospel boldness. John Piper lays a good foundation with his teaching on joy but does not quite get into it. MacArthur has a good book on Jesus' bold confrontations with the Pharisees but applies it to controversies with US quasi-evangelicals rather than evangelism or mission. Edward Welch has an excellent pastoral book exploring our reasons for the fear of man and the way to overcome this. Older writers have a high view of boldness but do not study it in detail or distinguish it from natural courage.

2. Timidity is a serious problem in mission and evangelism today. In Japan where so many pastors and missionaries are timid about the gospel it is not surprising if church members are not bold. In the days after the tsunami when the church had a golden opportunity to evangelise, many Christian groups did sterling relief work but very little evangelism. One pastor told us that we should not take advantage of people's weakness at such a time and that he and his church had made the decision NOT to do evangelism! On occasions when I have argued for bold evangelism people have commonly assumed that I am arguing for loudness, insensitivity and rudeness, or pressuring people through an evangelistic tool like the 'Four Spiritual Laws' or else they have countered that we must be wise. And

so timidity is not only a huge sickness which infects us, but we are suspicious of the cure. If this was only a local problem for us in Japan I would not write this book but I am convinced it is a weakness that threatens the mission of the church worldwide and as a result the visible church seems to be in retreat in many parts of the world.

3. The weight of scriptural teaching on boldness has to be recognised. 'Boldness' or 'boldly' occurs 11 times in the ESV Acts of the Apostles but even this underestimates its importance. For example in Acts 2 a completely-changed Peter displays boldness when he preaches his glorious gospel sermon and this will form part of our study in Ch 9. Yet the word itself does not appear in the text. So this is not a minor or novel teaching about an unimportant part of Scripture with little impact on the church. And yet it is completely sidelined today. For example I have seen more than one article or sermon on Acts 4 which praises the apostles' prayer and upholds it as a model for us but almost ignores the boldness that they were praying for.

4. This ignorance of the scriptural teaching on boldness means that we do not pray for it like we should. I can hardly remember ever hearing a prayer for boldness in any prayer meeting in any country I have been to. I hope your experience has been different but I doubt it. In any case prayer for boldness should be far more intense and frequent. This book is not primarily an exhortation to be bold, rather it is an appeal to see this teaching in the Bible and to pray intelligently, earnestly and always that God would grant us to speak the gospel with boldness (Acts 4:29).

Theological framework

Most of this material started off as sermon notes preached in Japanese. Of course it has been completely re-written for this book but most chapters are an exposition of a passage of

Scripture. This is in contrast to a topical method where many different texts would be used to support an aspect of the subject. In addition, the subject of boldness is one which lends itself to an exposition where the context of the storyline, character development and personal elements are important for gaining understanding of the subject. However the danger of this method is that chapters become an unrelated collection of stories about Bible characters. So in this section I am going to attempt a short 'systematic theology' of gospel boldness.

God's promise to be with his servants.

From the earliest times God has promised to be with his servants. As soon as it becomes clear that God speaks to hostile disobedient men through prophets, then boldness becomes an issue. Enoch and Noah walked with God (Gen. 5:24, 6:9). They were prophets and apparently spoke God's word to large groups of people (Jude 14, 1 Pet. 3:19-20, 2 Pet. 2:5) though we know very little about their ministry. The first great national prophet was Moses. It is significant for our study that boldness is dealt with in detail in the call and sending of Moses. When Moses shows unwillingness to go to Egypt, God simply says 'But I will be with you' (Ex. 3:12). The subsequent conversation shows that this promise includes at least three elements. Firstly God will give Moses the words to say. Secondly God will strengthen Moses' faith, enlighten him about his mission and give him boldness. Thirdly God will be Moses' ally and will work in Pharaoh, the Israelites and in nature and give him success. This promise of God to be with his servants is repeated throughout the Old Testament. As with Moses God's presence enabled the prophets in their ministry (eg Jer. 1:8, 19) and they show extraordinary resilience, power and boldness (Luke 1:17, Mic. 3:8). God was with Jesus Christ himself (Acts 10:38) and boldness was displayed prominently and gloriously throughout his Spirit-anointed ministry. The Father gave the Son His words to speak (John 3:11, 34, 8:28, 12:49, 14:10, 24, 17:8) though because of the unity between the Father and Son they are also the Son's words (John 8:51,

12:47). And Jesus, having no sin, no fear of man or other moral imperfection and loving God perfectly, always spoke boldly and clearly. He promised the apostles power to be witnesses (Acts 1:8) and finally in the context of the Great Commission said "And behold, I am with you always, to the end of the age." (Matt 28:20). How consistent with the Old Testament and all he had taught the apostles!

Boldness follows conviction that the Gospel is true

Boldness is a necessary result of saving faith and conviction of the truth. In Old Testament times the believers were bold because they were convinced that Yahweh was the one true God and all the rest were idols. In the New Testament the believers were bold because they were convinced Jesus was the only way of salvation and that there was "no other name under heaven given among men by which we must be saved." Acts 4:12-13. As JI Packer in the classic Knowing God says, "Those who know God show great boldness for God". The great inconsistency of our age is that we say that we believe and yet are timid in our confession before men. Bold confession can only be built on genuine faith. As Paul says 'Since we have the same spirit of faith according to what has been written, "I believed, and so I spoke," we also believe, and so we also speak' 2 Cor. 4:13.

A spiritual gift from Christ

Boldness comes from the Holy Spirit. Boldness is a spiritual gift, not a natural one. Boldness has one source only, the Holy Spirit. No one is born bold. Brave people are not necessarily bold Christians when they get converted. It is to be distinguished from any natural gifting, and is unrelated to age, gender, church office or social standing.

It is from Christ Before Jesus ascended into heaven he promised his apostles power from on high (Acts 1:8). Ten days later on the day of Pentecost He poured out the Holy Spirit upon the assembled disciples (Acts 2:4). Peter preached with great boldness. From then on the church was filled with power,

1. Introduction

enduring suffering for the sake of the gospel and speaking the gospel boldly.

<u>It is for all church members</u> Some gifts are for certain members only (1Cor. 12:7ff). 'Are all apostles? Are all prophets? Are all teachers?' Some but not all Christians would have these callings and appropriate gifting. That is Paul's whole point of using the body as an analogy. Different parts have different functions. But boldness is for all believers irrespective of their calling (Acts 2:17-18). For example Stephen was a deacon. His first task was to attend to the distribution for the widows to allow the apostles 'to attend to the ministry of the word of God and to prayer' (Acts 6:2). But this deacon showed remarkable boldness (Acts 6:10) and became the first Christian martyr. Another example are the women mentioned in this book (see chs 4 & 8) who though not called to preach or lead churches put to shame the men of their generation. So boldness is for all believers! However it is easy to see that the lack of boldness in those called to the speaking ministry is more devastating for the Kingdom than those in other callings.

Boldness is closely related to the fruit of the Spirit.

This power to speak the gospel boldly is not a power external to the heart and faith of the believer. In common with the fruit of the Spirit it is part of the believer's spiritual life. It depends in part on the believer's spiritual understanding (Gal. 3:2), assurance of salvation (2 Cor. 4:13), and joy (eg John 4:29). It can be cultivated. Those who sow to the Spirit (Gal 6:7-8), grow in understanding of the gospel and love to Christ will grow in boldness. As this study progresses I will show that boldness overlaps with love, joy, meekness and self-control (Gal 5:22-23).

Robert Haldane commenting on Romans 5:5 links gospel boldness with that fruit of the Spirit, hope.

"The experience of every Christian confirms this view. When is he inclined to be ashamed of the Gospel? Not when his hopes are high, his faith unwavering, and his impressions of future

glory strong. It is when His hopes fade and grow weak. Just in proportion as his hope is strong, will he make an open and a bold profession of the truth. Here, then, by a well-known figure, the assertion before us appears to import that, so far from being ashamed, believers glory and exult. Hope causes Christians, instead of being ashamed of Christ and His word (which without hope they would be), to glory and proclaim their prospects before the world, Galatians 6:14; 1 Peter 1:6-8, 5:1; 1 John 3:2. They glory in the cross of Christ through hope. This shows the great importance of keeping our hope unclouded. If we suffer it to flag or grow faint, we shall be ashamed of it before men, to which, from the enmity of the world against the Gospel, there is much temptation. Accordingly, our blessed Lord, who knew what was in man, has in the most solemn and awful manner warned His disciples against it; and the Apostle Peter enjoins on believers to add to their faith virtue — courage to profess it. "[1]

No Christian can throw up their hands and say 'this isn't for me, only the pastor has to be bold'. It is to be sought by all Christians and indeed importunately claimed (Luke 11:13). In the letters to the churches Christians are exhorted to be strong (1 Cor 16:13, Eph. 6:10) which includes at least being bold in proclamation of the truth as well as immovable in persecution. Christians are often exhorted to rejoice (Rom. 5:2, Phil 3:1, 4:4, 1Thess. 5:16, 1Pet. 1:6, 8, 4:13). Joy is a delighting and glorying in God and so joyful Christians will be bold. The apostles pray for the believers to be strong (Rom. 16:25, Eph 3:16, Col. 1:11) and joyful (Rom. 15:13, 2Cor. 1:24, Jude 24). And the joy of the Lord is a believer's strength (Neh. 8:10). Timothy and Titus are exhorted to be bold (1 Tim. 4:11, 2 Tim. 1:8, 4:1-2, Titus 2:1). And if Haldane (above) is correct 'virtue' in 2 Peter 1:5 refers to courage to profess our faith.

---

[1] Haldane p189-190

1. Introduction

The New Testament words for Bold Speech

The Greek noun for bold speech is *parrhesia* (31 times) and means freedom of speech, unreservedness of utterance, plain and unambiguous speech, the absence of fear in speaking boldly, cheerful courage and a commensurate deportment. The verb *parrhesiazomai* (9 times) means to speak boldly or freely. (All from Vine's Expository Dictionary of New Testament Words). There are other less common words which our English translations may sometimes translate as 'to speak out boldly', 'to have confidence' or 'to dare' etc. Unless otherwise mentioned the New Testament references use these words.

In this book I will explore this theme in its gradual development in the Old Testament, starting at Moses' preparation for ministry and the ministry of some of the other prophets, to Daniel and the church in the exile, through to the perfect example of Jesus in the Gospels, His signs, His preparation of the apostles for their mission to the world, His promises, the full flowering of gospel boldness in the book of Acts and its results and the subsequent apostolic teaching in the Epistles and the Revelation.

I will not be writing about boldness in prayer (Heb. 4:16). This is an important subject but has been covered by many authors.

2. From Bravery to Timidity to Trust - Moses

"Oh, my Lord, I am not eloquent..." Ex. 4:10
Please read Exodus 2:11- 4:17

You are a scuba diver 50m underwater and your air runs out. You jump out of a plane and your 'chute fails to open. You are doing a space walk but the tether breaks and you drift off into space. Imagine how helpless and desperate you'd feel in each of these situations. That is how you feel when you have to preach at an evangelistic meeting or tell the gospel to some friends and you know you cannot do it as you should. Getting us to that point is one of God's major tasks with each of us. We need to God's help to speak God's words. That is the main lesson that God teaches Moses here and Moses is ready to learn it. And it is vital for us.

About 25 years ago we were ministering in a church that was small even by Japanese standards. There were about 12 in the congregation. I was discouraged with how ineffective I was. Before becoming a missionary I had sought selection for the ministry in our home denomination, because I was sure that a missionary should not be less gifted than a minister at home. So my call was confirmed and I was ordained and sent to the mission field. And now here was I discouraged and convinced that I was a failure. I clearly remember praying, "I am not going to quit my post but I am now sure that I am NOT gifted to preach. Without your help I can do nothing". But the following Sunday something extraordinary happened. Instead of the believers staring at their bibles on their laps, every face was upturned and fixed on mine in rapt attention. Realising and feeling my total inability, and depending only on God was a lesson I hope I never forget.

The call and sending of Moses are very important for our

study. He was the first and greatest Old Testament prophet. He has the longest and most detailed call. Moses' weakness and failure are dealt with by God. This is very important for we may surmise I think with a high degree of certainty, that few if any of the subsequent prophets to Israel or Judah would have been ignorant of the apparent timidity of Moses and God's pastoral dealings with him in the story of the burning bush. So the teaching God gives Moses was intended for all future prophets as well.

Moses' early commitment to God

One day, when Moses had grown up, he went out to his people and looked on their burdens, and he saw an Egyptian beating a Hebrew, one of his people.
He looked this way and that, and seeing no one, he struck down the Egyptian and hid him in the sand.
When he went out the next day, behold, two Hebrews were struggling together. And he said to the man in the wrong, "Why do you strike your companion?"
He answered, "Who made you a prince and a judge over us? Do you mean to kill me as you killed the Egyptian?" Then Moses was afraid, and thought, "Surely the thing is known."
When Pharaoh heard of it, he sought to kill Moses. But Moses fled from Pharaoh and stayed in the land of Midian. And he sat down by a well. Ex. 2:11-15

Before we study the call of Moses in the passage about the burning bush, it is necessary to see what had happened 40 years earlier, because when Moses later shows reluctance to go to Egypt to confront Pharaoh it is not because of lack of commitment to God or his cause. There may be many reasons why men and women turn their back on God in times of stress, persecution or disappointment. Jesus specifies unbelief and love of the world in the parable of the sower (Mark 4:13-20) as reasons why people give up. Moses was never in this category at all.

The writer to the Hebrews, lists the young Moses as one of the heroes of the faith.

By faith Moses, when he was grown up, refused to be called the son of Pharaoh's daughter, choosing rather to be mistreated with the people of God than to enjoy the fleeting pleasures of sin. Heb. 11:24-25

These words mean that Moses had chosen God by the time he had grown up. He had repented from sin. Furthermore, he had already decided to reject the Egyptian court and to throw his lot in with the oppressed people of God.

Not only so but Stephen says that Moses already clearly understood that he was called to save Israel out of Egypt. He understood that he was God's chosen deliverer. Therefore he attempted to put God's plan into action by defending the oppressed Israelite and separating the two who were fighting.

And seeing one of them being wronged, he defended the oppressed man and avenged him by striking down the Egyptian.
He supposed that his brothers would understand that God was giving them salvation by his hand, but they did not understand. ..... "This Moses, whom they rejected, saying, 'Who made you a ruler and a judge?'--this man God sent as both ruler and redeemer by the hand of the angel who appeared to him in the bush. Acts 7:24-25, 35.

There is no evidence that Moses was acting outside God's will. Scripture has nothing but praise for Moses even at this early stage of his life. Rather, Stephen makes it clear that it was Israel that wasn't ready. Even at this stage Israel was hard and unbelieving. They rejected 'the ruler and redeemer' that God sent them that day in Egypt. Israel's rejection of God's chosen messengers starting with Moses and culminating in rejecting Christ is actually the whole point of Stephen's evangelistic speech. It was their habitual inveterate sin. Moses attempted to intervene and deliver Israel but he failed and the only conclusion we can draw is that God allowed him to fail.

No. Moses' reluctance to go back to Egypt when called by God at the burning bush was not because of lack of commitment to God or his cause. It was because of confusion at his previous failure.

40 years on the shelf

While Scripture praises the young Moses he still had a lot to learn and so after one 'speaking engagement' which did not go well, God puts him on the shelf for 40 years. Perhaps the words that God said to Hezekiah much later help us to understand why.

'God left him to himself, in order to test him and to know all that was in his heart.' 2 Chr. 32:31.

We can imagine a little what those 40 years were like for Moses.

1) 40 years to wonder if he had made the right choice. Was he right to have chosen the God of Israel over Egypt? Could he have done much better if he had stayed in Egypt and tried to ameliorate the working conditions of the Israelites from within the court, a sort of constructive engagement policy?
2) 40 years of testing his commitment. Did he still consider himself an Israelite and one of God's people? He was evidently popular and well-liked in Midian from the first (Ex. 2:17) and maintained a good relationship of mutual respect with his father-in-law Jethro throughout his life. He was not acquisitive and after 40 years he is still looking after Jethro's sheep rather than his own (Ex 3:1). He raised a family and yet he called his

firstborn son Gershom, which means "foreigner", because he knew Midian was not his true home. And although apparently he should be blamed for not circumcising him (Ex. 4:24-26) we conclude that his heart was still with his people in Egypt.
3) He had 40 years to intercede for his people, those people who had rejected him. Throughout that time he heard nothing but bad news as the conditions worsened in Egypt..
4) I believe in those 40 years Moses became very hungry for God. Perhaps during that time he wrote Genesis. Moses evidenced his hunger for God many times (eg Ex. 33:18).
5) And importantly for our study, those were 40 years to wonder what went wrong. He evidently came to the conclusion that he was not eloquent and he just did not have the gift of public speaking. He was dead right. And that is the Moses whom God sends back to Egypt.

Have I been describing you? You have sown much and harvested little. There are many years of prayers still not answered. You are wondering the reasons for not doing better, perhaps feeling a failure. And you have lost all confidence in the gifts you hoped you might have had at one stage. Realising one's weakness is essential to usefulness. It is a lesson that if God ever intends to seriously use us he will thoroughly teach us.

Burning Bush

Now Moses was keeping the flock of his father-in-law, Jethro, the priest of Midian, and he led his flock to the west side of the wilderness and came to Horeb, the mountain of God.
And the angel of the LORD appeared to him in a flame of fire out of the midst of a bush. He looked, and behold, the bush was burning, yet it was not consumed.
And Moses said, "I will turn aside to see this great sight, why the bush is not burned."
When the LORD saw that he turned aside to see, God called to him out of the bush, "Moses, Moses!" And he said, "Here I

am."
Then he said, "Do not come near; take your sandals off your feet, for the place on which you are standing is holy ground." Ex 3:1-5

After 40 years in the wilderness, the 80 year-old Moses met God in the theophany of the burning bush. There are three things God showed him about Himself, each of which is highly significant to his future ministry.

<u>God is Holy</u> Fire, often a symbol for God shows his purity and wrath. Moses was warned not to approach because he was on 'holy ground'. 40 years earlier Moses had fled from Pharaoh, but from now on Moses feared nothing except the wrath of God. He was permanently cured. We have to live above the fear of man if we are going to be faithful to God's word.

<u>God is Self-sufficient</u> The 'great sight' was not that the bush was on fire but that it did not burn up. This unearthly fire was self-supporting, independent, and didn't need any fuel to maintain itself. God himself is outside and above his creation and separate from it. He does not need it at all. He is not served by human hands as though he needed anything (Acts 17:25). He certainly doesn't need us or our service. A friend of mine Gareth Ayling was preaching at an OMF conference and said 'Mr and Mrs OMF missionary, God doesn't need you'. This is liberating and refreshing, for Moses, for the Old Testament prophet and for the Christian worker because it takes our eyes off ourselves and our work and fixes them on the sovereign God.

<u>God is Condescending Love</u> God came down to seek Moses. He appeared as the Angel of the LORD in a burning bush. It was a 'great sight' and a miracle but not terrifying in itself. In a few months the Israelites would sees the burning mountain. That WAS terrifying. But God had a different purpose here. He had come to draw alongside Moses and pastor this shepherd.

Many think that the angel of the LORD is the pre-incarnate Son of God come down to converse with Moses. God addresses Moses by his name, twice, and has a long conversation with him. It was not, as we might expect, a monologue with God giving instructions and then leaving Moses to follow them but a conversation where Moses was allowed to question God. The Israelites got the monologue a little later (see Ex 20) but God was here speaking to Moses face to face, as a man speaks to his friend (Ex. 33:11). In other words he was pastoring him.

This points to a much greater condescension later, when the Son of God as Jesus is born as a baby, humiliated and then crucified. God appeared to Moses in a bush, now to us on a cross. And he does not say to us 'Do Not approach' but 'Come near' and 'I will not cast you out.'(John 6:37)

Moses' Task

And he said, "I am the God of your father, the God of Abraham, the God of Isaac, and the God of Jacob." And Moses hid his face, for he was afraid to look at God.
Then the LORD said, "I have surely seen the affliction of my people who are in Egypt and have heard their cry because of their taskmasters. I know their sufferings,
and I have come down to deliver them out of the hand of the Egyptians and to bring them up out of that land to a good and broad land, a land flowing with milk and honey, to the place of the Canaanites, the Hittites, the Amorites, the Perizzites, the Hivites, and the Jebusites.
And now, behold, the cry of the people of Israel has come to me, and I have also seen the oppression with which the Egyptians oppress them.
Come, I will send you to Pharaoh that you may bring my people, the children of Israel, out of Egypt." Ex 3:6-10

God introduced himself as "God of your father" and of the three patriarchs. He then announced that he had come to save Israel. He would be the deliverer, saviour and redeemer. The implication was unsaid but strong. I am those things, not you, Moses. That God described himself as having '*come down*' showed that he was immanently with Moses, that he was ready for action and that something huge was about to happen.

God is the subject of all the main verbs. God would save the Israelites, but Moses only heard the last purpose clause *(that you may bring my people...)* and responds to God with five questions or complaints. Through these we see what is in his heart (and in ours too). And God answers these in a gentle pastoral manner. And from this conversation (for that is what it is) we learn that his reluctance to return to Egypt as Israel's 'Saviour' has deep complex roots in his heart and cannot be dismissed as mere timidity, nor can it be solved by just the exhortation, 'Get a grip on yourself Moses and get on with it'. And neither can ours.

1. I'm not fit
But Moses said to God, "Who am I that I should go to Pharaoh and bring the children of Israel out of Egypt?" Ex 3:11

Moses first objection was that he is not able or worthy or qualified either to confront Pharaoh or lead 600,000 people out of Egypt. Moses was quite right to feel this, though from a human perspective, Moses was eminently qualified. He knew the court, the learning of Egyptians and may have been personally acquainted with Pharaoh. Of all the Israelites, he was probably the most educated. We need to give Stephen's words their full weight.

And Moses was instructed in all the wisdom of the Egyptians, and he was mighty in his words and deeds. Acts 7:22

I understand this to mean that Moses was eloquent and could motivate men by his speech, also that he had accomplished great deeds perhaps on the battlefield or in some other public office in Egypt.

In addition, Moses now at age 80, knew the Sinai peninsular like the back of his hand and was the ultimate desert guide and wilderness survivalist.

All these qualifications, 40 years ago, would have given him confidence. But being qualified is not enough. The wonderful thing was that Moses felt it. God had taught him not to depend on himself. He felt lowly. That was good because God gives grace to the humble.

It is a major theme throughout the whole Bible that God uses the weak to accomplish his work that the glory may redound to him alone.

Moses's successors were weak in themselves. Considering the amount of encouragement God gave Joshua he was also in the same position as Moses (Josh. 1). Consider too the Judges, who were either weak or used weak methods, or both. Or David who said of himself. "But who am I, and what is my people, that we should be able thus to offer willingly? For all things come from you, and of your own have we given you". (1 Chr. 29:14).

Or the prophets who as we shall see put no confidence in their own ability.

Of course these Old Testaments types of strength-out-of-weakness point us to Jesus Christ who was born as a baby, laid in a manger, crucified in order to accomplish the great work of eternal redemption of all God's elect.

Since then the gospel has been preached in weakness. Gospel preaching is inherently a weak method in that the message of the cross is not attractive (it is repugnant to the natural man). But also the gospel is not preached by the strong, confident, gifted or qualified but those who readily admit they cannot serve him without his help. God uses the weak.

So how does God answer this objection of Moses?

He said, "But I will be with you, and this shall be the sign for

2. From Bravery to Timidity to Trust - Moses

you, that I have sent you: when you have brought the people out of Egypt, you shall serve God on this mountain." Ex 3:12

There is a wealth of comfort and power in those words for Moses. God is with those he sends. His presence is not merely subjective (I am rooting for you, I approve of what you are doing), nor is it only narrowly transcendental (I will keep my promise to you and take you to heaven when you die), but it is a dynamic promise to abundantly provide all the grace and power from beginning to end for the mission on which he sends him, despite him feeling weak and unworthy. It is a promise to both work in Moses internally and to work in the external situation, in Pharaoh, the Israelites and in nature.

These words point also to Christ, who is Immanuel, God with us. By the Son of God becoming a man, walking among us and being crucified for us God's presence with his people is assured. His last words before he ascended to heaven were, "And behold, I am with you always, to the end of the age." (Matt. 28:20). The context of these words is the great Commission- so in a fashion paralleling his words to Moses they mean that God will work both in us internally and dynamically giving us grace and in our external situation to accomplish his mission through us.

2. By whose authority?
Then Moses said to God, "If I come to the people of Israel and say to them, 'The God of your fathers has sent me to you,' and they ask me, 'What is his name?' what shall I say to them?"
God said to Moses, "I AM WHO I AM." And he said, "Say this to the people of Israel, 'I AM has sent me to you.'"
God also said to Moses, "Say this to the people of Israel, 'The LORD, the God of your fathers, the God of Abraham, the God of Isaac, and the God of Jacob, has sent me to you.' This is my name forever, and thus I am to be remembered throughout all generations. Ex 3:13-15

Moses was concerned about the Israelites' ignorance. It seems that Israelites had forgotten all about God except the fact the their ancestors worshipped him. They were ignorant of God's nature. Ezekiel tells us in fact that they had taken to idolatry (Ezek. 23:19). God would re-introduce himself to the Israelites, and would use the covenant name of YHWH revealed to Abraham but with its meaning spelt out as I AM WHO I AM' showing God's nature as the independent sovereign self-existent Creator. This also confirmed in words the object lessons taught by the burning bush that Moses was being sent on the HIGHEST authority by the holy, self-sufficient yet immanent God. Those who are sent do not go in their own authority, but in the name of the one who sends them.
And what is the message for us? It is that Christ is YHWH, the First and the Last who shed his blood for us (Rev 1:18). Before giving the Great Commission he says

"All authority in heaven and on earth has been given to me". Matt. 28:18

And so today the church is sent by the highest authority into the whole world to call its people to repentance and faith and to make disciples. The lowliest Christian, and the smallest weakest church in the most straightened circumstances is sent by this same authority. Let us realise this and stop being apologetic for our faith, and uncertain of our message. We can only be bold once we are certain of the authority of the one who sends us.

Go and gather the elders of Israel together and say to them, 'The LORD, the God of your fathers, the God of Abraham, of Isaac, and of Jacob, has appeared to me, saying, "I have observed you and what has been done to you in Egypt, and I promise that I will bring you up out of the affliction of Egypt to the land of the Canaanites, the Hittites, the Amorites, the Perizzites, the Hivites, and the Jebusites, a land flowing with milk and honey."'

2. From Bravery to Timidity to Trust - Moses

And they will listen to your voice, and you and the elders of Israel shall go to the king of Egypt and say to him, 'The LORD, the God of the Hebrews, has met with us; and now, please let us go a three days' journey into the wilderness, that we may sacrifice to the LORD our God.'
But I know that the king of Egypt will not let you go unless compelled by a mighty hand.
So I will stretch out my hand and strike Egypt with all the wonders that I will do in it; after that he will let you go.
And I will give this people favor in the sight of the Egyptians; and when you go, you shall not go empty,
but each woman shall ask of her neighbor, and any woman who lives in her house, for silver and gold jewelry, and for clothing. You shall put them on your sons and on your daughters. So you shall plunder the Egyptians." Ex 3:16-22

God gave Moses an overview of the plan of the deliverance from Egypt. The sovereign God told Moses exactly what he was going to do. Again God is the subject of most of these verbs and the salient point is that only God can do these things. They lie outside the sphere and power of man completely. Can Moses make the elders go to Pharaoh, or compel him with a strong hand, or strike Egypt with 10 plagues, or change the Egyptians' hearts so that they impoverish themselves giving away their valuables? Of course not. Only God can do these things. In promising this God was committing himself to be the Deliverer from Egypt, not Moses. It would have shown him how incapable he was of doing the task without God and yet assures him of God's assistance at all times.

Is the plan of salvation revealed to us in the New Testament any less grand? No. It is many times greater. God has provided a complete salvation in Christ. We are told in detail that it is God's work from beginning to end, from the predestination of his elect to the effectual call of lost sinners through the preaching of the gospel, to the final perseverance of the saints. While man cooperates in the work of salvation it is not dependent on his ability. God gives grace for man to complete the conditions he requires. If we cannot contribute to our own salvation how can we possibly produce it in others? Can we give the new birth? The hugeness of of the work of salvation compels us to lean only on God. This is far greater than the deliverance of the Israelites from Egypt. In addition we are sent in weakness, in the face of opposition to preach a gospel which the world counts as weak and foolish and yet are completely equipped by the Holy Spirit who will be with us unto the close of the age.

3. Israel's unbelief
Then Moses answered, "But behold, they will not believe me or listen to my voice, for they will say, 'The LORD did not appear to you.'" (4:1)

God had mentioned (Ex 3:18) that the Israelites will believe him. But Moses thought that God had a far too rosy-coloured view of the Israelites and proceeded to educate God about the problem. They were not only ignorant but stubborn and he had firsthand experience of their unbelief. As we have seen the New Testament application of Exodus 2 is Israel's rejection of the leaders God appointed for them (Acts 7). Israel's unbelief was habitual, inveterate and incorrigible. Moses could foresee God's whole plan falling apart because of this.

God then gave Moses three signs (Ex 4:2-9). Signs show authority and miraculous power and so encourage belief. We know however that unbelief is a sin in the heart and will not be solved by seeing miraculous signs. Faith must be generated internally in the heart by God himself. And so it seems that with respect to Moses' mission to Egypt God undertook to give the Israelites enough faith to get the job done, though this must have fallen short of saving faith in many of them.

Yet unbelief is a barrier we regularly underestimate. People do not just docilely believe when God shows his authority. Even seeing numerous and wonderful miraculous signs does not generate faith. Our Lord himself felt the full force of Israelite unbelief. No one ever did more signs than him and yet when John summarised his ministry he says,

'Though he had done so many signs before them, they still did not believe in him, John 12:37

People may hear the clearest apologetics for the faith communicated well. They may be in dire financial and physical circumstances and have all their needs met by loving Christians. They may be warmly welcomed into the embrace of a loving church. They may receive all these things and more and yet remain hard and unbelieving.

The apostles also did not spare Israel for its unbelief. It is common to hear the Jews of Bible times criticized as unbelieving in pulpits today because the New Testament describes them as such critical terms. But after 2000 years of world mission can we really conclude that Gentiles are any more believing than God's ancient people? The people who God sends us to today are also unbelieving. Indeed the hypocrisy, abuse of God's word, suppression of the truth, presumption, self-deceit, wilful blindness, and pride we see today when the gospel is preached matches anything seen in the Old and New Testaments. Moses was right. Unbelief is an insurmountable barrier in all people, and only God can remove it.

4. Not eloquent
But Moses said to the LORD, "Oh, my Lord, I am not eloquent, either in the past or since you have spoken to your servant, but I am slow of speech and of tongue." Ex 4:10

He said he cannot be Israel's deliver because he is not 'eloquent'. The NIV, KJV, ASV, RSV and ESV all use this translation. This objection by Moses is highly significant because it shows that Moses always saw his ministry as a speaking ministry. Stephen twice calls him a leader and redeemer (Acts 7:27, 35), but he was first of all a prophet and he led and saved by virtue of speaking God's words (Deut 34:10). He was not Israel's first president who gave his own decisions as laws to be obeyed or inspired by his authority. He transmitted God's words to Israel and for that he thought he had to be eloquent.

"I am not eloquent, either in the past". Moses remembered his previous failure to save Israel. This failure he blamed on his inability to motivate men by his speech.

"or since you have spoken to your servant"… Even after God had issued the command for him to go and save Israel, he felt no inner change. There was no eloquence buzzing round inside his head, no elevated emotion, and no flights of eloquent words forming in his brain. He was the same old Moses. I believe it is wrong to infer from Moses' objection here that he had a speech impediment (as Matthew Henry[2]). His objection was the normal response of anyone who is told that his speech is the key link between God and man.

Then the LORD said to him, "Who has made man's mouth? Who makes him mute, or deaf, or seeing, or blind? Is it not I, the LORD?
Now therefore go, and I will be with your mouth and teach you what you shall speak." Ex 4:11-12

Note first of all what God did not say. God did not say eloquence was unimportant. He did not say, "Say what you like any way you like and I will be with you'. Rather God confirmed Moses' high view of the spoken ministry and said he would help him. God spoke almost simplistically to Moses,

---

[2] Henry, Matthew 1710 Commentary on the Whole Bible, Zondervan, Grand Rapids pp1986

like to a Sunday school child. He told him that He was the creator and had total control over his faculties. 'Without me you can do nothing, but with me you can do anything. I can help you and I intend to.'

Moses here was promised the words to say and also the ability to say them. God promised him eloquence if he needs it, boldness as he needs it, poetry or prose as he needs, and nothing can or will stop him, because " I will be with your mouth". And, unlike 40 years ago, God's presence with Moses will ensure the Israelites will be motivated to follow him. God promised to give grace to Moses to speak and grace to the Israelites to believe.

What is real leadership? It is not a bureaucratic appointment. Being appointed to the directorship of a mission organisation or bishop of a denomination etc is only leadership in administrative terms. Leadership is not a matter of having an upfront, charismatic personality, and it is not the ability to forcefully communicate your 5-year vision. Leadership has always been teaching God's word to God's people in God's way so that they follow.

5. Send someone else
But he said, "Oh, my Lord, please send someone else." Ex 4:13

After God had repeated both his command to go to Egypt and his promise to be with him (v12), Moses pleaded that God send someone else. This seemed like surprising disobedience. Does this prove that Moses was basically disobedient and unwilling? I do not think so. All his life Moses had been the strong faithful determined servant of the LORD. But then God presented him with an entirely new playing field with new rules. He saw he must depend on God's ability not his own. He saw that God's presence with him was the only hope of power in his whole mission. And God's promise was the only guarantee that grace would not run out or fail him when he needed it. Anyone would baulk at this new arrangement, though of course there was an element of disobedience and weak faith in Moses.

Then the anger of the LORD was kindled against Moses and he said, "Is there not Aaron, your brother, the Levite? I know that he can speak well. Behold, he is coming out to meet you, and when he sees you, he will be glad in his heart.
You shall speak to him and put the words in his mouth, and I will be with your mouth and with his mouth and will teach you both what to do.
He shall speak for you to the people, and he shall be your mouth, and you shall be as God to him.
And take in your hand this staff, with which you shall do the signs." Ex 4:14-17

So God was angry. Moses should have trusted and obeyed and his failure to do so was blameworthy. But God did not dwell on his weakness. Instead He provided human support in the form of Aaron, who was on his way from Egypt to Midian, looking forward to see him. They will work together as a team, God being with both of them. Perhaps we can say the first action that God takes in keeping his promise to be with Moses is to provide this very practical help of the warm fellowship and support from his loving brother.

It is important to see the big picture. God has now laid out the arrangement and pattern he will have with all those whom he subsequently sends. All future Old Testament prophets are sent on the same basis as Moses. And ultimately this pattern points to Jesus as the perfect Prophet, Leader and Deliverer.

Jesus clearly was sent by his Father. He did not come of his own accord. One of his favourite self-designations is 'he who is sent', *(John 4:34, 5:36,37,38, 6:29.39, 8:18, 28, 29, 38, 49, 54, 55etc).*
His teaching too, came entirely from God, with no blockage or distortion caused by timidity, foolishness or mixed motives,

unlike us.

So Jesus answered them, "My teaching is not mine, but his who sent me. John 7:16
I have much to say about you and much to judge, but he who sent me is true, and I declare to the world what I have heard from him." John 8:26
And the word that you hear is not mine but the Father's who sent me. John 14:24

Of course Moses' unwillingness to go and deliver Israel contrasts with Jesus who had no hesitation about immediate obedience whatever the suffering and danger.

I have a baptism to be baptized with, and how great is my distress until it is accomplished! Luke 12:50

And Jesus did not flinch from obedience under the most dreadful terrors. When he foresaw the cross in the garden of Gethsemane he humbly submitted to his Father's will.

saying, "Father, if you are willing, remove this cup from me. Nevertheless, not my will, but yours, be done." Luke 22:42

And unlike Moses, Jesus was entirely alone, though surrounded by disciples who did not understand his mission and who fled when danger threatened.

And now Jesus who has fully experienced all it means to be sent, sends his apostles and us in a parallel sending to his own.

As you sent me into the world, so I have sent them into the world. John 17:18
Jesus said to them again, "Peace be with you. As the Father has sent me, even so I am sending you." John 20:21

Jesus promises His presence and His power to his church who

must speak the gospel relying on the power of the Holy Spirit.

For us today

We must speak God's word
If we are called to the ministry of the Word then this is our priority. Let us not get side-tracked by a host of good causes. Peter when tempted in this direction said "It would not be right for us to neglect the ministry of the word of God in order to wait on tables. We will give our attention to prayer and the ministry of the word." (Acts 6:2-4). God gives us his message and it is the gospel. What can be a higher calling? Bringing the word of God to unsaved men is a matter of life or death. It is the only means of grace for Christians to grow. So let us make this our philosophy of ministry and bring our activities to this test. "Am I speaking God's word?"

Make our speaking important.
This takes mental effort. Let us study God's word to rightly divide the word of truth. Let us look at the context and interpret scripture by scripture. And let us find out what the author really meant. Our aim is not to be just understandable but to easy to listen to and beyond that to be effective.

At Iconium Paul and Barnabas went as usual into the Jewish synagogue. There they spoke so effectively that a great number of Jews and Gentiles believed. Acts 14:1.

We must realise our own weakness
Many Christian workers go through these three stages like Moses. A) Zeal and commitment. They are full of excitement and idealism. They enter some area of lay or fulltime ministry expecting to make a difference. They have high ideals for themselves, for others and the work. B) But then they fail. Perhaps it is in the area of relationships, or in lack of success, or they burnout under the workload or have a breakdown because of stress. The result of failure is to conclude "I'm not

fit". The tendency then is to give up, or to become cynical or to search for some method that promises success or to look for a less demanding task than ministry of the Word. And yet the sooner we realise that God has been working in our life to show us our weakness the better. Recognising our inability and losing our self-confidence is progress not regress. C) Confidence in God's help. Few people go straight to this step. However, knowing God's way of working with his servants can prepare us for his lessons in ministry.

The calling of Moses teaches us that God does not just require our zeal and commitment. He requires our dependence as well. Let us recognise our total inability. Consider our lack of bible knowledge. We don't even understand the passage we are speaking on. We don't have the wisdom of life to apply it. We don't even have the IQ to cope with the facts, the spiritual discernment to weigh those facts or the speaking ability to communicate adequately. In the case of cross-cultural missionaries we cannot even speak the language properly. And then there is the whole issue of clarity and boldness. Our speech is skewed by our timidity, gloomy joyless attitude or some other sin. Even if we got it all together and spoke like the archangel nobody would be converted without God opening hearts. The Apostle Paul who was ahead of us all on all counts says of his own ability;

To the one [we are] the savour of death unto death; and to the other the savour of life unto life. And who [is] sufficient for these things? 2Co 2:16 KJV
Not that we are sufficient of ourselves to think any thing as of ourselves; but our sufficiency [is] of God; 2Co 3:5 KJV

We must express our anxieties to God

It is very comforting that Moses expresses his objections to God. Like him our timidity has deep roots. We are no stronger than him but we have stronger incentives than him to come to the throne of grace to boldly express them. We are sent by a Saviour whose ministry was characterised by suffering, who justifies us, who gives us full assurance of our salvation, who promises to fill us with his Holy Spirit and promises to be with us until the end of the age.

We must believe His promise to help
Let us come in humble dependence on Christ's help based on our desperate need and His promises.

And he said unto me, My grace is sufficient for thee: for my strength is made perfect in weakness. Most gladly therefore will I rather glory in my infirmities, that the power of Christ may rest upon me. 2Co 12:9 KJV

Moses' Best 40 years

In spite of his plea for God to send someone else, Moses did obey. We find Moses and Aaron boldly confronting Pharaoh (Ex. 5:1). When things did not work out and Pharaoh refused to let the people go he complained (Ex. 5:22), but God strengthened him by repeating his promise (Ex. 6:1-9). Moses again complained twice about his lack of eloquence (lit. "uncircumcised lips", Ex 6:12, 30), and again God repeated his promise to be with him (Ex 7:1-5). So for Moses the change from timidity to trust was a journey not a one-step jump to perfect submission or perfect trust. It was imperfect yet persistent trust. His boldness developed in parallel with his trust in the Lord. But at the end of the Ten Plagues you find Moses doing the speaking and Aaron in the background. God made him bold and he left Egypt *"not being afraid of the anger of the king, for he endured as seeing him who is invisible"* (Heb. 11:27). Finally when when the Israelites had their backs to the sea and were complaining to him, he forgot himself and encouraged them to trust in the Lord.

And Moses said to the people, "Fear not, stand firm, and see the salvation of the LORD, which he will work for you today. For the Egyptians whom you see today, you shall never see

2. From Bravery to Timidity to Trust - Moses

again.
The LORD will fight for you, and you have only to be silent."
Ex 14:13-14

Gone are his "uncircumcised lips". Now he is trusting in the Lord!
God also made him eloquent. The Song of Moses (Ex.15) is one of the most eloquent poems ever penned and forms the basis for many of the Psalms. Moses last sermon, Deuteronomy, is also eloquent and its intensity and spiritual power still can be felt by those who read it today.

We need God's help to speak God's words. This is the first lesson God teaches the first national prophet Moses. It was a lesson for all subsequent prophets, apostles, and ministers etc. We cannot do this work in our own strength. So we must confess our inability and pray.

"for when I am weak, then am I strong". 2 Cor. 12:10

Paul had learnt it well. Have you?

3. From Weakness to Strength - The Prophets

As an example of suffering and patience, brothers, take the prophets who spoke in the name of the Lord. James 5:10

The apostle James tells us to consider the prophets as examples of perseverance in their suffering. The suffering of the prophets was for the most part persecution brought on through their preaching. In each case if they had stopped preaching their suffering would have ceased instantaneously. They suffered in the course of their active obedience. Job, who James mentions in the next verse, was different. He suffered obediently but his was a passive obedience. So when James tells us here to consider the prophets, he is telling us to consider their boldness. In one chapter I cannot possibly do justice to each of the prophets. My intention is rather to briefly outline God's dealings with some of them. A common thread runs through them all. They were weak and yet strengthened and sustained by God, like Moses. If their perseverance and boldness seem supernatural, of course it was, because God was with them. As Israel descended into worsening apostasy and chaos so the pressure and loneliness of ministry became extreme for a prophet and yet their extremity was more than matched by the Holy Spirit's power.

Samuel

He was the last of the judges and after Moses the next great national prophet. As a young boy he was lent to the Lord and served in the tabernacle at Shiloh under the priest and judge Eli. Instead of being an idyllic spiritual upbringing it was traumatic. He witnessed the religious elite living in immoral hypocrisy, oppressing the poor, abusing their power, and despising God (1 Sam. 2:12-22). Little wonder that in later life he showed a short fuse when Saul exhibited the same tendency. He had almost certainly witnessed the ministry of a bold prophet (1 Sam. 2:27-36), though he himself did not know the LORD at that time (1 Sam. 3:7).

He was still a boy when God called him in the night. Thinking it was Eli he ran to him. After this happened three times, Eli perceived that the LORD was calling the boy, and instructed him to say those famous words, "Speak, LORD, for your servant hears." (1 Sam 3:9). He received a message of judgement on Eli, affirming the warning of the earlier prophet (1 Sam 3:11-14).

He lay awake until morning with a battle raging in his mind, the fear of man against the fear of God. And it was a battle he lost, because he made up his mind not to tell Eli the message of judgement. Only when threatened with this curse did he pass on the word of the LORD,

"May God deal with you, be it ever so severely, if you hide from me anything he told you." 1 Sam. 3:17

This catapulted Samuel into the spiritual leadership of Israel (1 Sam. 3:19-21) which he exercised faithfully and uncompromisingly until his death. However he was not fearless in himself. For example he was afraid of Saul finding out that he had anointed David (1 Sam. 16:2). His boldness was supernatural and was because "the LORD was with him and let none of his words fall to the ground" (1 Sam. 3:19).

The unnamed prophet against Bethel

After Israel separated from Judah, the king of Israel, Jeroboam, thought it would be a good idea to build rival places of worship so that the Israelites would not have to go up to Jerusalem to worship. So he built two, one in the north in Dan and the other in the south at Bethel. This was of course idolatry and God sent a prophet out of Judah to warn him (1 Kings 13). This prophet was also told not to eat or drink or return by the way he came (v8). He confronted Jeroboam and prophesied the destruction of the idolatrous altar at which he was worshipping (fulfilled 340 years later, 2 Kings 23:15). The king stretched out his hand against him which miraculously withered, Jeroboam pleaded for it to be restored which it was. The prophet refused Jeroboam's invitation and turned for home. But he was deceived by an old back-slidden prophet into accepting a meal at his house. And for his disobedience he was killed by a lion. The judgment of God in this case seems harsh. Had not this prophet accomplished his mission faithfully? Had not Jeroboam been impressed and in a sense received the Word of God (though he continued to disobey it)? Had he not gone in good faith believing that God had spoken through the respectable old prophet? Then why does God have his servant killed?

Perhaps it is easier to understand if we remember that his death was a further warning to Jeroboam to give up his recklessness in leading Israel to sin (as v33 makes clear). If God should treat his faithful servant thus for a minor infraction, how much more should those who force idolatry on God's people expect severe judgement? His death was ineffective to bring Jeroboam to repentance but in intention it was redemptive in that it was directed at the salvation of sinners. It is also a warning for all time that God demands obedience and faithfulness from his servants. Beyond that it teaches all future prophets that they are expendable and their wellbeing is subservient to the message. If their death can enhance the potency of the message then so be it; they must die. The message is everything.

Elijah

He suddenly burst on the scene.

Now Elijah the Tishbite, of Tishbe in Gilead, said to Ahab, "As

3. From Weakness to Strength - The Prophets

the LORD, the God of Israel, lives, before whom I stand, there shall be neither dew nor rain these years, except by my word." 1Kings 17:1

His call is not recorded, nor any anxieties, or doubts he may have had. He appeared without introduction to confront Ahab, the wicked king of Israel and to deliver the judgement of God which would be a drought lasting for 3 years.

He was phenomenally bold and the phrase "the spirit and power of Elijah" was used much later to indicate the spiritual power and boldness of John the Baptist (Luke 1:17). When Elisha knew he must succeed Elijah, he asked for a double portion (not twice as much but an exactly equal measure) of his spirit (2 Kings 2:9), showing that he recognised that Elijah's power was a gift of the Holy Spirit.

At the end of those 3 years, Elijah confronted the unrepentant Ahab again.

And he answered, "I have not troubled Israel, but you have, and your father's house, because you have abandoned the commandments of the LORD and followed the Baals. 1 Kings 18:18

Elijah commanded King Ahab to gather all Israel and the false prophets to Mt Carmel. Ahab meekly obeyed. The contest is well-known. The 850 prophets of Baal and Asherah danced and entreated their gods to answer and, of course, there was not a peep. Then Elijah gathered Israel and prayed briefly, humbly and directly to God who answered with fire from heaven. Elijah ordered the execution of all the false prophets and then prayed for rain and told Ahab to return to Jezreel. Elijah was in command of the nation.

And yet when Jezebel sent Elijah the message,

"So may the gods do to me and more also, if I do not make your life as the life of one of them by this time tomorrow," 1 Kings 19:2

all his boldness melted away and he escaped into the wilderness.

"Then he was afraid, and he arose and ran for his life ... 1 Kings 19:3a

What happened? Lloyd-Jones notes that he was tired and hungry and had an over-reaction to great excitement and was therefore open to depression[3]. However there was more going on than this. After the victory at Mt Carmel he was confused by the seeming failure of God's plan. Most likely Elijah expected the Israelites to follow him en-masse in a religious reformation. Ahab should have returned to the LORD. Jezebel should have been deposed. And yet he received no help either from God, angels or Israelites. How strange when he was fed by ravens and miraculously sustained in Zarephath! How strange considering the recent spectacular public miracle at Carmel! Also, he was shocked and depressed by his own failure, so much so that he asked to die. Like Moses before him, and Peter after him, Elijah was confounded by God not acting as expected. And in this confused state of mind he ran off. Unwarranted expectations are at the root of his failure of boldness. And yet, it is possible to see even in his failure a mercy, his flight saved his life and taught him that he also was in fact a weak sinner, no better than his fathers. Perhaps too Elijah was a more suitable mentor for Elisha, more humble, wiser and kinder, <u>after</u> he had failed than he would have been before. "The most experienced saint, if left to himself, is immediately seen to be as weak as water and as timid as a mouse"[4]. The "spirit and power of Elijah" were never actually

---

[3] Lloyd-Jones, p19
[4] Pink p201

3. From Weakness to Strength - The Prophets

his, but God's.

He journeyed on to Mt Horeb, and on the way the angels fed him. God there gave three terrifying experiences, a wind so strong that it tore rocks off the mountain, an earthquake and then a fire, but God was not in these things. Then Elijah heard "the sound of a low whisper" and he knew it was God and in deep reverence and humility went out to listen. I believe these three phenomena show God's power, and holiness and perhaps his wrath and yet the consideration of these will not restore Elijah. They will not heal him or restore to him "the spirit and power of Elijah". It was the gentle love of God communicated by words to his mind and received by faith, that restore to him the joy of his salvation, that send him back to ministry, refreshed and bold (Psa. 51:12-13). It is a paradox that the calm, rest-giving love of God should make a man as bold as lion. The power of this gentle love was embodied in Jesus, the friend of sinners, made explicit in what he taught (Matt 11:28-30) and is the experience of every Christian. Not the threat of the Law but the grace of the Gospel is the power behind gospel boldness.

God then gives him specific and limited instructions, encouraging him by assuring him that the work will carried on by Elisha and that He himself will preserve a faithful remnant.

Elijah appears again to condemn Ahab boldly for killing Naboth and stealing his vineyard (1 Kings 21:17-24) and to prophesy the death of his son, Ahaziah (2 Kings 1:3-16).

What do we conclude about Elijah's boldness? It was generated by the power of the Holy Spirit but also dependent on his own state of mind. Elijah had a high view of God (1 Kings 18:36, 42, 19:13) which explains why he had a low view of sinful kings. And yet he was a man with a nature like ours (James 5:17) and needed reassurance not to fear them, for example;

The LORD said to Elijah, "Go down with him; do not be afraid of him." 2 Kings 1:15

But as we have seen, when God acted in an unexpected providence with disappointing results and corresponding danger to himself, his boldness vanished away. Elijah was neither a brave man nor a coward. For most of his ministry he was filled with the Spirit and was immensely bold. But when the Spirit left him, he returned to normal and became timid, like the rest of us.

Miciah

It is trendy these days to have a philosophy of ministry. Miciah's was *"As the LORD lives, what the LORD says to me, that I will speak."* (1 Kings 22:14)
It was biblical, taken from Deuteronomy 18:18, and no mere slogan. He followed it rigorously. He was a contemporary of Elijah and lived in Samaria. He was hated by one king who slandered him to another, and was mocked and contradicted by false prophets and in constant danger of death; and yet he was faithful.

Isaiah - the forgiven sinner

Isaiah was called to the prophetic ministry in Judah by a remarkable vision.

<u>Isaiah sees God</u>
In the year that King Uzziah died I saw the Lord sitting upon a throne, high and lifted up; and the train of his robe filled the temple.
Above him stood the seraphim. Each had six wings: with two he covered his face, and with two he covered his feet, and with two he flew.

3. From Weakness to Strength - The Prophets

And one called to another and said: "Holy, holy, holy is the LORD of hosts; the whole earth is full of his glory!"
And the foundations of the thresholds shook at the voice of him who called, and the house was filled with smoke. Isaiah 6:1-4

Isaiah was terrified and awed by the sight before him. He saw the Lord, but cannot describe him. He could only give his relative position that the Lord was high and lifted up far above him. He saw the throne and only God's robe perhaps because he did not dare lift up his eyes to heaven. The name he used for "the Lord" is not YHWH but a word meaning sovereign ruler, further emphasising the separation between him and God.

God was surrounded by worshippers, seraphs (literally burning ones) who praise God in abject humility. They praised God to each other, saying 'Holy' three times (a Hebrew way of saying very, very holy) and acknowledging him as their own covenant LORD. So these seraphs were like huge flames flying around God and their praise, that the whole earth is full of God's glory was surely what caused pain to Isaiah. He was not like that! He could not praise God despite all the visible signs of God's glory! Rather, the shaking threshold and smoke showed that God was unapproachable because his wrath.

Woe is me!
And I said: "Woe is me! For I am lost; for I am a man of unclean lips, and I dwell in the midst of a people of unclean lips; for my eyes have seen the King, the LORD of hosts!" Isaiah 6:5

Isaiah was terrified and miserable. He was awed and very sad. He felt his sin. He felt filthy, especially in the area of his speech and in his lack of concern in right or wrong or in the company he kept. "I am lost" means "I am under the wrath of God and going to hell".

Forgiveness

Then one of the seraphim flew to me, having in his hand a burning coal that he had taken with tongs from the altar. And he touched my mouth and said: "Behold, this has touched your lips; your guilt is taken away, and your sin atoned for." Isaiah 6:6-7

How does God deal with sin? Objectively: Isaiah's sin was atoned for. How? By the sacrifice from the altar. Why the altar? Because a death by sacrifice was made there that worked redemption for Isaiah. This was not accomplished by animal sacrifice but looks forward to the cross of Christ.

Sent
And I heard the voice of the Lord saying, "Whom shall I send, and who will go for us?" Then I said, "Here am I! Send me." Isaiah 6:8

The atonement was objective and concrete. Isaiah was forgiven. And the announcement of this had an immediate subjective result. Isaiah was joyful. He was set free. He wanted to serve. And when God asked for a servant he joyfully volunteered. There was nothing Old Covenant about this, this was pure sovereign grace overcoming sin and driving out the saved as willing joyful servants for the Cause of Christ.

You received without paying; give without pay. Matt 10:8b

The Reality Check
And he said, "Go, and say to this people: "'Keep on hearing, but do not understand; keep on seeing, but do not perceive.' Make the heart of this people dull, and their ears heavy, and blind their eyes; lest they see with their eyes, and hear with their ears, and understand with their hearts, and turn and be healed." Isaiah 6:9-10

God then told Isaiah what to expect. People would not repent and believe. His prophecy though very clear (Repent.. turn to the Lord.. give up idolatry) would actually harden them. Why did God tell him this? So that he would have no illusions about worldly success in ministry leading to Judah's national resurgence. This reality check made him strong in the face of disappointment. It made him bold in confronting sin and it made him bulletproof against discouragement.

Then I said, "How long, O Lord?" And he said: "Until cities lie waste without inhabitant, and houses without people, and the land is a desolate waste,
and the LORD removes people far away, and the forsaken places are many in the midst of the land.
And though a tenth remain in it, it will be burned again, like a terebinth or an oak, whose stump remains when it is felled."
The holy seed is its stump. Isaiah 6:11-13

As Isaiah saw the people unrepentant and suffering under the attacks of enemies and shrinking in number, he would always remember these words when the LORD called him that these things *must* happen. But after all that there will be hope.

Jesus does the same with us. He describes how the gospel must be preached in the context of wars, rumours of wars, earthquakes, famines, worldwide powerful deception, apostasy, betrayal and especially in intense persecution. These things *must* happen too. And then he says,

See, I have told you beforehand. Matt 24:25

He tells us these things beforehand so that we will not be discouraged but get on with evangelism no matter the circumstances.

And yet despite this pessimistic forecast for Isaiah, there is in this chapter a promise-in-kind for the whole of Israel. Just as Isaiah the unclean sinner found forgiveness at the throne of grace and became an instrument in the hands of the Lord so may the whole of Israel.

Jeremiah, the fortified city, the iron pillar and bronze wall

He was the son of a priest, and was a prophet to Judah for 40 years (about 627- 587) until the destruction of Jerusalem, and then for a further period with the Jewish refugees in Egypt. He was bold and faithful and strong despite great pressure. What was his secret of his great strength? Let us look at his call in which God promised to be with him and how that promise was fulfilled.

His Call
Now the word of the LORD came to me, saying,
"Before I formed you in the womb I knew you, and before you were born I consecrated you; I appointed you a prophet to the nations." Jer 1:4-10

God's choice of Jeremiah was absolute. There was no discussion. It was unconditional and unilateral. God's choice was from eternity so there is no room for argument at all. And it is personal and affectionate. Jeremiah was chosen with love. And it would be an immensely significant ministry. Jeremiah would prophesy against the sins of nations which incur the destruction of entire nations and the restructuring of the world order.

Then I said, "Ah, Lord GOD! Behold, I do not know how to speak, for I am only a youth."
But the LORD said to me, "Do not say, 'I am only a youth'; for to all to whom I send you, you shall go, and whatever I command you, you shall speak.
Do not be afraid of them, for I am with you to deliver you, declares the LORD." Jer 1:6-8

3. From Weakness to Strength - The Prophets

Jeremiah complained that he could not speak eloquently or with authority because of his age. It is true that then as now, people are more likely to listen to an older man and that age does confer a natural authority. But God forbade him to dwell on this weakness and said that it was a matter of obedience ("go") and faithfulness ("speak"). God quickly exposed the real reason for his reluctance. It was fear of their faces. There is a natural timidity we have when young. But God will not have his servants trusting in their natural authority because of their age or giving in to natural timidity because of their youth. He demands obedience and promises power.

Then the LORD put out his hand and touched my mouth. And the LORD said to me, "Behold, I have put my words in your mouth. Jer 1:9

In similar wording to Deut 18:18 God put his words in Jeremiah's mouth and confirmed this by touching Jeremiah's mouth with his hand. Like Moses, and Isaiah and Ezekiel God promised to give him the actual words to say. And later this was pre-eminently shown in Jesus (Luke 4:13) and was what Paul prayed for (see ch 12).

Youth is not a problem for God, neither is any other weakness. The trouble with us today is that we think youthfulness is a strength! It is not. It is a weakness. And when recognised as a weakness can be turned into a strength. God delights to show his power by bringing strength out of weakness. Human inadequacy and confessed weakness is God's opportunity.

As God's voice on earth young Jeremiah was to receive enormous authority and power:

See, I have set you this day over nations and over kingdoms, to pluck up and to break down, to destroy and to overthrow, to build and to plant." Jer 1:10

This young priest was set over the nations, over their kings, governments, armies and citizens. He would change the world order. He would build and plant; destroy and break down. How? When God and Jeremiah spoke, those things would inevitably be fulfilled. For example God decreeing in heaven that the Babylonian army would smash Jerusalem is not effectually different to Jeremiah standing on a street corner declaring the same. And so Jeremiah as prophet was effectively ruling the nations under God.

God then gave two visions to Jeremiah (1:11-16), the vision of the almond branch which signifies that the prophecy will be quickly fulfilled (the almond was known as 'the tree in a hurry'[5]), and the boiling pot tipping threateningly towards Jerusalem from the north. Both these showed that judgement on Judah's idolatry was imminent and that the work of Jeremiah was urgent.

But you, dress yourself for work; arise, and say to them everything that I command you. Do not be dismayed by them, lest I dismay you before them. Jer 1:17

One might expect God's requirements to be reduced for a young man starting ministry in such a godless place, with so little support and with such a severe message to deliver. There was instead a command and a severe warning.

'Dress yourself for work; arise' Be ready! Wake up! *'Say to them everything that I command you'* Say everything. Leave nothing out. Do not mince words! Speak boldly. *'Do not be dismayed by them'*. Do not be afraid of them or embarrassed or ashamed into an ignominious silence or half-hearted timidity. *'Lest I dismay you before them'* If Jeremiah gave into the fear of man, God would bring on him what he tried to avoid; embarrassment, shame, and contempt. Unbelievers may

---

[5] Matthew Henry p936

persecute a bold believer but they will respect him. But no one respects the compromiser and a coward. Such a person loses out in both worlds. "A man who fears man also has God to fear".[6]

And I, behold, I make you this day a fortified city, an iron pillar, and bronze walls, against the whole land, against the kings of Judah, its officials, its priests, and the people of the land.
They will fight against you, but they shall not prevail against you, for I am with you, declares the LORD, to deliver you." Jer 1:18-19

And here is the promise that would enable Jeremiah to obey. *"And I, behold, I."* God said most emphatically that He would make Jeremiah strong. Jeremiah would be *"a fortified city"* unassailable and impregnable, *"an iron pillar"*, unbendable, immovable and the opposite of a reed blown by the wind, *"bronze walls"*, completely indestructible by any weapon or device known to man. God promised him great boldness and supernatural resilience, no matter how high and mighty the opposition. Note that his enemies would not be foreigners but fellow-Jews.

God also promised protection, *"I am with you... to deliver you"*, that his life would be spared until his work was done.

How God worked in Jeremiah

Let us look at how God was with Jeremiah. Of course God made him bold and resilient but God worked in Jeremiah and made him a man of God. His boldness did not arise in a vacuum nor was it super-imposed on his unchanged character. God changed him. God made him holy. And part of that holiness was boldness.

---

[6] Thompson p137

God made him pray for the people
"Though our iniquities testify against us, act, O LORD, for your name's sake; for our backslidings are many; we have sinned against you.
O you hope of Israel, its savior in time of trouble, why should you be like a stranger in the land, like a traveler who turns aside to tarry for a night?
Why should you be like a man confused, like a mighty warrior who cannot save? Yet you, O LORD, are in the midst of us, and we are called by your name; do not leave us." Jer. 14:7 -9

Jeremiah prayed for his fellow Israelites who were under the impending judgement which was his duty to announce. Even though they persecuted him and on many occasions tried to kill him he never gave up praying for them.

Jeremiah continued to pray for them even though God had said that judgement was certain. Some might repent! Some might be eternally saved even if they perished in the siege. Some might return to God even though they were carried into exile! This prayer came from God's heart. God himself stirred up Jeremiah to pray. Jeremiah could not stop praying for the people that God would turn from his anger (Jer. 18:20).

And yet in addition to the other obstacles God told Jeremiah NOT to pray for them!

Thus says the LORD concerning this people: "They have loved to wander thus; they have not restrained their feet; therefore the LORD does not accept them; now he will remember their iniquity and punish their sins."
The LORD said to me: "<u>Do not pray</u> for the welfare of this people.
Though they fast, I will not hear their cry, and though they offer burnt offering and grain offering, I will not accept them. But I will consume them by the sword, by famine, and by pestilence." Jer. 14:10 -12

Yet he continued to pray for them. It was very hard to pray for the people anyway without God telling him not to! And in a few verses we read that he was praying again.

Do not spurn us, for your name's sake; do not dishonor your glorious throne; remember and do not break your covenant with us. Jer 14:21

And yet in the next chapter God again told him not to pray for them.

Then the LORD said to me, "Though Moses and Samuel stood before me, yet my heart would not turn toward this people. Send them out of my sight, and let them go! Jer 15:1

Why did God tell Jeremiah not to pray for them? Obviously to frighten the people into repenting, and so that they should not trust in the prophet's prayers. Some commentators assume that God means he should not pray for their material welfare, rather than their saving repentance. While that may be the meaning in Jer 14:11 it is not so in Jer 7:16, 11:14, or 18:20. All of Jeremiah's recorded utterances were for the one aim of getting the people to repent so they could be forgiven (Jer. 36:3), even the command not to intercede. So God inspires the prayers which he himself obstructs.

Jeremiah is like the persistent widow (Luke 18:1-8) or the Canaanite woman (Matt 15:21-28) who did not give up despite the obstacles. But for marathon persistence in persevering prayer, Jeremiah takes the gold medal. He is like Christ. This fierce determination in prayer and spiritual violence came from God, so it is no wonder that we see the same wrestling struggle against all odds in our Saviour too when he was on earth (Matt. 26:36-44). Perhaps it is even true to say that the greater the obstacle the more intense and violent the prayers. It shows how far we have fallen when we pray so lethargically or not all for one of our greatest needs which is gospel boldness.

Because God was with him, he wept for them
Oh that my head were waters, and my eyes a fountain of tears, that I might weep day and night for the slain of the daughter of my people!
Oh that I had in the desert a travelers' lodging place, that I might leave my people and go away from them! For they are all adulterers, a company of treacherous men. Jer 9:1-2

Who was speaking? Grammatically it could be God or Jeremiah. Could God himself be saying that He wants to weep? That He Himself wants to escape? The cause of this wail of grief is human sin: adultery, betrayal, unfaithfulness and idolatry. God would like to go on holiday away from human sin. But he cannot. He will suffer long until the end of the world.

But if you will not listen, my soul will weep in secret for your pride; my eyes will weep bitterly and run down with tears, because the LORD's flock has been taken captive. Jer. 13:17

Here Jeremiah was speaking and showed the same attitude as God and wept for the people's pride and the punishment that results. Pride is the root sin and the cause of all false religions, disobedience, apostasy, hard hearts, envy, discontent, unforgiveness etc. Because God was with Jeremiah he imparted his own thinking and so Jeremiah wept not for himself but for Jerusalem like his Saviour after him (Luke 19:41).
And yet today the prouder the world becomes the church seems to grow more timid. But pride should be met by gospel boldness.

Because God was with him, Jeremiah was with God
Your words were found, and I ate them, and your words became to me a joy and the delight of my heart, for I am called

3. From Weakness to Strength -The Prophets

by your name, O LORD, God of hosts. Jer. 15:16

The words that Jeremiah received from God and had to deliver were a tough message. But they were the truth and he had come to delight in God's words. They were like delicious food to him. He preferred God's narrow road to man's broad one. So a manifestation of God being with Jeremiah was Jeremiah being with God. He was a friend of God. He had made God's cause his own. He sympathised with God. Jesus speaking to his disciples called them friends not servants because they know what he is doing. Paul later says he has the mind of Christ, meaning that to a certain extent God's thinking has become his. Whose side are you on, really? Is it the world or God? With whom do your true sympathies lie?

Because God was with him: God corrected him
Why is my pain unceasing, my wound incurable, refusing to be healed? Will you be to me like a deceitful brook, like waters that fail?
Therefore thus says the LORD: "If you return, I will restore you, and you shall stand before me. If you utter what is precious, and not what is worthless, you shall be as my mouth. They shall turn to you, but you shall not turn to them.
---And I will make you to this people a fortified wall of bronze; they will fight against you, but they shall not prevail over you, for I am with you to save you and deliver you, declares the LORD.
I will deliver you out of the hand of the wicked, and redeem you from the grasp of the ruthless." Jer 15:18 -21

We do not know what Jeremiah had done, whether it was just his petulant complaining (v18), or something more serious effecting his ministry. God warned him to return and repent and re-iterated his promise to be with his mouth, to strengthen and protect him.

Because God was with Jeremiah: Jeremiah was committed to

God

God forbade Jeremiah to marry, attend funerals or feasts (Jer 16).
He must not have a wife or raise a family because all the children would die in the siege and famine.

He must not mourn the dead because there would be no funerals in the sack of Jerusalem. The numerous dead would lie unburied.
He must not attend feasts because laughing and celebration would cease. These deprivations imposed by God on his prophet were like object lessons in his preaching (Jer 16:10-11) which enhanced his message and made it more pungent.

So Jeremiah gave up the 'right' to a normal life. He must endure these sacrifices for the sake of the word he preached. That is commitment. He points to Christ who came to serve and give his life a ransom for many (Mark 10:45). There is a movie called *The Expendables* but the heroes in it never get seriously hurt. If they get shot it is always a flesh wound and they can fall from great heights or have endless punch-ups with no ill-effects. It should be called *The Precious Ones* because they are always protected. But Christians, like their Saviour before them, are expendable, their health, finances, family and lives are at God's disposal. So Paul can say in the same breath that we are "accounted as sheep for the slaughter", and "we are more than conquerors through him who loved us" (Rom 8:36-39).

Because God was with Jeremiah, he loved his enemies

Behold, they say to me, "Where is the word of the LORD? Let it come!"
I have not run away from being your shepherd, nor have I desired the day of sickness. You know what came out of my lips; it was before your face. Jer 17:15 -16
Should good be repaid with evil? Yet they have dug a pit for my life. Remember how I stood before you to speak good for

them, to turn away your wrath from them. Jer 18:20

Jeremiah never desired the judgement on his people. He prayed for them and loved them even when they mocked him and planned his death. And so because God was with him he became like Christ whom he prefigured and loved his enemies.

Because God was with Jeremiah, he himself was affected by his message
Concerning the prophets: My heart is broken within me; all my bones shake; I am like a drunken man, like a man overcome by wine, because of the LORD and because of his holy words. For the land is full of adulterers; because of the curse the land mourns, and the pastures of the wilderness are dried up. Their course is evil, and their might is not right. Jer 23:9-10

Jeremiah was not a detached professional who passed on the message he had received from God in a lukewarm, take-it-or-leave-it fashion. Because God was with him he was deeply affected by his own message. He saw the holiness of God and felt the sin of the people.

And finally, because God was with Jeremiah, he was bold
God had told Jeremiah he would prophecy with supernatural boldness *"against the kings of Judah, its officials, its priests, and the people of the land." Jer 1:18*

While almost the whole book shows his boldness, let us look at very brief cross-section of his ministry to all these groups and see his consistent boldness.

<u>To all the people, concerning their sins</u>
Look at your way in the valley;
 know what you have done—
 a restless young camel running here and there,
 a wild donkey used to the wilderness,

in her heat sniffing the wind!
Who can restrain her lust?
None who seek her need weary themselves;
in her month they will find her. Jer. 2:23-24

To God the idolatry of the Israelites was as uncontrollable, tiresome and disgusting as an animal on heat! This is strong language.

Total destruction of their nation
A lion has gone up from his thicket,
a destroyer of nations has set out;
he has gone out from his place
to make your land a waste;
your cities will be ruins
without inhabitant. Jer. 4:7

He prophesied the complete depopulation of the cities and the destruction of the land. While this had never happened to them the inhabitants of Judah had witnessed recently the destruction of the northern kingdom. Now it was Jerusalem's turn.

Against the contemporary religion
The word that came to Jeremiah from the LORD:
"Stand in the gate of the LORD's house, and proclaim there this word, and say, Hear the word of the LORD, all you men of Judah who enter these gates to worship the LORD.
Thus says the LORD of hosts, the God of Israel: Amend your ways and your deeds, and I will let you dwell in this place.
Do not trust in these deceptive words: 'This is the temple of the LORD, the temple of the LORD, the temple of the LORD.'
Jer. 7:1-4

Then Jeremiah came from Topheth, where the LORD had sent him to prophesy, and he stood in the court of the LORD's house and said to all the people:
"Thus says the LORD of hosts, the God of Israel, behold, I am

bringing upon this city and upon all its towns all the disaster that I have pronounced against it, because they have stiffened their neck, refusing to hear my words." Jer. 19:14-15

The Jews trusted in their temple religion, their sacrifices without repentance and superficial recognition of God. But they would not give up their idolatry, immorality, oppression or sabbath breaking. Jeremiah stood in the temple precincts and pleaded with them to repent.

<u>Against the prophets and priests</u>
*An appalling and horrible thing
    has happened in the land:
the prophets prophesy falsely,
    and the priests rule at their direction;
my people love to have it so,
    but what will you do when the end comes? Jer. 5:30-31*

There was a destructive spiritual relationship between the false prophets who preached a false hope and made the people trust in a lie, the priests who maintained the corrupt status quo and the people who loved to be deceived. Only Jeremiah attempted to break the vicious cycle with his clear warning of coming judgement. (see also Jer. 14:15-16, 23:11-12)

<u>Against the leading priest</u>
"And you, Pashhur, and all who dwell in your house, shall go into captivity. To Babylon you shall go, and there you shall die, and there you shall be buried, you and all your friends, to whom you have prophesied falsely." Jer. 20:6

Pashur was a leading priest and had usurped to himself the role of prophet also. He had contradicted Jeremiah, had imprisoned him and suppressed his message to the people. By so doing he had invited God's judgement upon himself, his family, his friends and all his hearers. A fearful message!

<u>To king Jehoiakim</u>
"Therefore thus says the LORD concerning Jehoiakim the son of Josiah, king of Judah:
"They shall not lament for him, saying,
'Ah, my brother!' or 'Ah, sister!'
They shall not lament for him, saying,
'Ah, lord!' or 'Ah, his majesty!'
With the burial of a donkey he shall be buried,
dragged and dumped beyond the gates of Jerusalem." Jer. 22:18-19

No eulogies or funeral for this scornful king who had tried to silence the prophet on many occasions and burnt the scroll he had laboriously copied. His body would be treated as an inconvenient piece of trash and be dumped outside the city.

<u>And to Coniah (king Jehoiachin)</u>
"As I live, declares the LORD, though Coniah the son of Jehoiakim, king of Judah, were the signet ring on my right hand, yet I would tear you off
and give you into the hand of those who seek your life, into the hand of those of whom you are afraid, even into the hand of Nebuchadnezzar king of Babylon and into the hand of the Chaldeans. Jer. 22:24-25

Even though he was just 18 years old and reigned 3 months he receives the prophetic sentence of judgement.

<u>To the king of Judah, Zedekiah</u>
"I myself will fight against you with outstretched hand and strong arm, in anger and in fury and in great wrath.
And I will strike down the inhabitants of this city, both man and beast. They shall die of a great pestilence.
Afterward, declares the LORD, I will give Zedekiah king of Judah and his servants and the people in this city who survive the pestilence, sword, and famine into the hand of

3. From Weakness to Strength - The Prophets

Nebuchadnezzar king of Babylon and into the hand of their enemies, into the hand of those who seek their lives. He shall strike them down with the edge of the sword. He shall not pity them or spare them or have compassion.' Jer. 21:5-7

When he makes a show of humility by sending to Jeremiah asking if there any word from the Lord, Jeremiah prophesies not just defeat but that God would become his enemy, and with intense anger, fight against him and his army by pestilence, sword, and famine and then pursue those who survive.

<u>Against the refugees in Egypt</u>

"I will take the remnant of Judah who have set their faces to come to the land of Egypt to live, and they shall all be consumed. In the land of Egypt they shall fall; by the sword and by famine they shall be consumed. From the least to the greatest, they shall die by the sword and by famine, and they shall become an oath, a horror, a curse, and a taunt. Jer. 44:12

Jeremiah prophesied that the total destruction of the idolatrous Judeans who had escaped to Egypt in direct disobedience to God's command. God was determined that none would escape and would make them objects of disgust and shame.

So in this very brief overview of Jeremiah's bold ministry we see that he was absolutely consistent, unbending, unshakeable, from his youth until his mid-70s. God kept his promise and strengthened him by his Spirit. God worked in him and made him his zealous co-worker and as a result, sometimes despite himself, he was a faithful prophet.

> *If I say, "I will not mention him,*
> *or speak any more in his name,"*
> *there is in my heart as it were a burning fire*
> *shut up in my bones,*
> *and I am weary with holding it in,*

and I cannot. Jer. 20:9

And so God was with Jeremiah spiritually and internally: changing him and making him prayerful, weeping, obedient from the heart and with an intense personal relationship with God. God was with Jeremiah in his ministry also; giving him his word and boldness and endurance by his Spirit.

Jeremiah's suffering

Oh, my anguish, my anguish! I writhe in pain. Oh, the agony of my heart! My heart pounds within me, I cannot keep silent.
For I have heard the sound of the trumpet. Jer. 4:19

Jeremiah suffered spiritually and physically. We can only list them here but there is a story behind each.
The conflict with the false prophets (Jer. 14:13).
The agony of seeing the wrath of God poured upon his people (Jer. 4:11)
The rejection from Anathoth his hometown of priests (Jer 11:19-23)
His confusion at the Lord's ways (Jer. 12:1, 14:19)
His grief at the fall of Jerusalem (Lam 1-3)
His weeping because of their hardness (Jer 13:17)
His cursing the day of his birth (Jer. 14:19, 20:14-18)
His anxiety and confusion at the Lord's 'deceitfulness' (Jer. 15:18, 20:7)
The universal slander (Jer. 18:18)
Death threats (Jer 26:8)
Brutally beaten and imprisoned (Jer 37:15-16)
He is accused of being a traitor (Jer. 37:13)
He is misrepresented (Jer. 38:4)
He is lowered into a muddy well to die (Jer. 38:6)
He is accused of false prophecy (Jer. 43:3)

We do not read of any disciples, or any respectful listeners except his servant Baruch; there was only the constant opposition from all the people, priests, kings, the survivors of the siege. No wonder his suffering is proverbial. And yet in spite of it all he continued to faithfully and boldly declare God's word. No wonder James said, "consider the prophets" as examples for us.

We have seen God's promise fulfilled in giving Jeremiah boldness in the face of great suffering, but there was another element to God's promise to be with him which we must not overlook.

God protected him

At his call God promised to be with Jeremiah and protect him.

They will fight against you, but they shall not prevail against you, for I am with you, declares the LORD, to deliver you." Jer 1:19

This is emphatically re-iterated later during a period of discouragement for the prophet.

And I will make you to this people a fortified wall of bronze; they will fight against you, but they shall not prevail over you, for I am with you to save you and deliver you, declares the LORD.
I will deliver you out of the hand of the wicked, and redeem you from the grasp of the ruthless." Jer 15:20-21

Let us see how God delivered him from all his enemies.

God hid him

After Jehoiakim had burnt the scroll, he gave orders for Jeremiah and Baruch to be arrested , but the LORD hid them (Jer. 36:26). We do not how, whether they were protected by a kind believer or whether God limited the ability of those tasked with arresting them, but God was personally protecting them both.

Gospel Boldness

God provided a friend in need
Read Jer 38:1 -13
During the siege of Jerusalem by the Babylonians, Jeremiah prophesied to the people that the war and imminent defeat was a punishment from God and that *'he who goes out to the Chaldeans shall live. He shall have his life as a prize of war, and live.' V2.* The government officials went and complained to the king who was weak and gave into their pressure. Jeremiah was put into a well which was probably a slow way of killing him without actually shedding his blood. But God provided an unexpected friend, *'Ebed-melech the Ethiopian, a eunuch who was in the king's house'* who went to the king and protested on his behalf. He then got a 30 man team together and rescued Jeremiah. We know do not know any more about Ebed-melech except that he was a believer who survived the siege (Jer. 39:18).

On another occasion he was rescued by the elders while on trial for his life for false prophecy (Jer. 26:17-24).

God rules the hearts of men and can raise up friends for his servants, anywhere, anytime. At a time when having friends is more important than anything for many people, when even Christians will say nothing that might possibly alienate those around them, when being hated for the cause of Christ is a step too far for most of us, this truth, that God can provide helpers, friends, human saviours, providers under any circumstances should make us bold, and confident in the promise *'that if God is for us who can be against us'. Rom 8:31*

God turned enemies into friends
"Now, behold, I release you today from the chains on your hands. If it seems good to you to come with me to Babylon, come, and I will look after you well, but if it seems wrong to you to come with me to Babylon, do not come. See, the whole land is before you; go wherever you think it good and right to go.

3. From Weakness to Strength - The Prophets

If you remain, then return to Gedaliah the son of Ahikam, son of Shaphan, whom the king of Babylon appointed governor of the cities of Judah, and dwell with him among the people. Or go wherever you think it right to go." So the captain of the guard gave him an allowance of food and a present, and let him go. Jer 40:1-5

Nebuzaradan was captain of the guard. He was a senior enemy general, perhaps head of King Nebuchadnezzar's bodyguard. If so, he was like head of the SS to Hitler or the head of the NKVD to Stalin. Now this arch enemy of the Jewish people seeks out Jeremiah from among the captives, releases him from his chains, speaks kindly and with deep respect to him, even honouring the LORD, and gives him a free pass anywhere in the Empire with the further promise of provision if he should choose to go with him to Babylon. On top of that he gives him a food allowance and a present. It is difficult to see how Nebuzaradan could have been more friendly to Jeremiah.

This kindness was not a payment for Jeremiah's prophecies against Jerusalem. Jeremiah never chose sides. He had not minced words about about the coming judgement on Jerusalem but he said similar things about Babylon too (Jer. 50). He had just faithfully passed on God's word. And God protected him by making his enemies into friends. With Jeremiah and countless other believers after him, this proverb,

When a man's ways please the LORD, he makes even his enemies to be at peace with him. Prov. 16:7

has proven is true. God rules over the hearts of men. To buy your friendships by being mealy-mouthed about the gospel, to be timid to save yourself, to put your relationships with others before your duty to God will never work. Be bold in telling the gospel. Stop being ashamed. God will change people for your sake.

Gospel Boldness

God attacked Jeremiah's persecutors
These are strong words. Are they justified? When Jeremiah says a sad soliloquy in consideration of all his suffering and persecution, he remembers God's protection.

But the LORD is with me as a dread warrior Jer 20:11
How was God with Jeremiah? As a dread warrior! God went to war against Jeremiah's enemies. He hunted them down and killed them. Dread means frightening and terrible. Jeremiah's enemies did not view God as a dread warrior. No, they made light of God. Rather it was Jeremiah who viewed God as frightening and awesome as time and again God fought against those who opposed or persecuted him.
Let us look at four examples.

Hananiah
In the fifth month, God had told Jeremiah to make *straps and yoke-bars, and to wear them on his neck (27:2)*. This was an object lesson to show that his hearers would be enslaved by Babylon. But the false prophet Hananiah contradicted Jeremiah. He took it upon himself to break off Jeremiah's yoke and declare,

"Thus says the LORD of hosts, the God of Israel: I have broken the yoke of the king of Babylon. Jer 28:2

But,
And Jeremiah the prophet said to the prophet Hananiah, "Listen, Hananiah, the LORD has not sent you, and you have made this people trust in a lie.
Therefore thus says the LORD: 'Behold, I will remove you from the face of the earth. This year you shall die, because you have uttered rebellion against the LORD.'"
In that same year, in the seventh month, the prophet Hananiah died. Jer 28:15-17

So after two months God killed this false prophet who had opposed Jeremiah and contradicted his message.

Men of Anathoth

Anathoth was a city of priests and one of the cities of refuge in Benjamin (Josh 21:18) and was Jeremiah's hometown (Jer. 1:1). And yet far from supporting their most famous and worthy son they persecuted him. Specifically they threatened to kill him if he spoke in the name of the Lord (Jer 11:21). But God threatens total annihilation of all who threatened his prophet, and their families.

therefore thus says the LORD of hosts: "Behold, I will punish them. The young men shall die by the sword, their sons and their daughters shall die by famine,
and none of them shall be left. For I will bring disaster upon the men of Anathoth, the year of their punishment." Jer. 11:22-23

Pashur

We have already seen the judgement pronounced on this leading but faithless priest (Jer 20:6)

Shemaiah

Jeremiah had prophesied to the exiles in Babylon that their exile would be 70 years and they should make the most of it, settle down, get involved and seek the welfare of Babylon. Shemaiah was a false prophet among them who claimed to be the new high priest in Babylon and who contradicted Jeremiah and sent orders back to Jerusalem that he should be punished. But God rather orders *his* punishment,

therefore thus says the LORD: Behold, I will punish Shemaiah of Nehelam and his descendants. He shall not have anyone living among this people, and he shall not see the good that I will do to my people, declares the LORD, for he has spoken rebellion against the LORD.'" Jer. 29:32

And so God fought for Jeremiah the true prophet. God defended him and slew his enemies. Sometimes immediately, sometimes punishment was deferred. Sometimes perhaps these enemies repented when they heard of their doom in Jeremiah's prophecies and were forgiven (eg Neh. 7:27). We do not know. But certainly enough of Jeremiah's enemies died for him to say,

But the LORD is with me as a dread warrior Jer 20:11

Do not misunderstand. This was not Jeremiah taking revenge on his enemies. Nor was it Jeremiah praying down God's wrath on them (Jer. 17:16). No doubt the Jerusalem public did misunderstand and blamed Jeremiah for the judgements of God that followed his faithful ministry just as their forefathers had blamed Moses . (*"You have killed the people of the LORD." Num. 16:41*). Rather it was God ruthlessly and implacably fighting for Jeremiah and against his enemies.

It is a fearful thing to fall into the hands of the living God. Heb 10:31

One day, of course Jeremiah died, probably in Egypt, we do not know how but he was at least in his seventies. So he lived longer than all his persecutors, the kings, the priests, the officials and the people of the land. God kept his promise made on the day of his call, and delivered him. Any perceptive reader of the Old Testament will come to realize that to be called to be a prophet was effectively a death sentence. Jesus confirms this perception in Matt 23:29-37, and yet there is no contradiction. God will protect his servants until their work is done. And this may mean they live remarkably long as in Jeremiah's case.

What does this mean for us?
Consider the Christian church in the world at the present time.

3. From Weakness to Strength -The Prophets

Unless you live in N Korea or Iran or a few other places where the church is severely persecuted you live in relative peace and safety. In most places of the world you can worship God freely and even evangelise with the protection of the state. Do you stop to consider how utterly amazing that is? Christians are far outnumbered by unbelievers in all countries of the world, and according to the Apostle John, *..the whole world lies in the power of the evil one. 1John 5:19*

These unbelievers' thoughts and the currents and fashions of the world are largely controlled by Satan (Eph. 2:2-3). And so why then is persecution not intense and worldwide? It is because God is protecting his people. Not so that you can live a comfortable life and fulfil your dreams but so that you will be encouraged to be bold and tell the gospel. And when you start to boldly evangelise God will not suddenly withdraw his protection! The story of Jeremiah teaches us that the promise 'to be with you' includes the promise of protection. And so when Jesus in his last words to his church before his ascension says, *"And behold, I am with you always, to the end of the age." (Matt. 28:20)* he is promising his protection. What is the book of Acts except a record of Jesus being with his church and protecting it and what is the Revelation of John but a long apocalyptic showing God's presence with his church and protection of it until the end of time? And it is the fulfilment of Jesus' promise that we enjoy peace today. So, let us not abuse this divine protection but get on with the work of the gospel.

Ezekiel: A forehead harder than flint

Ezekiel was taken to Babylon with the exiles when he was about 26 and became a prophet when he was about 30 in 593 BC. He went on preaching until he was 52. So he was younger than Jeremiah and older than Daniel who was also in Babylon. One can only speculate what influence Jeremiah's ministry had on his young mind or how he may have interacted with Daniel who though younger rose to prominence in Babylon before

Ezekiel's ministry started and became well-known for his godliness before the final fall of Jerusalem (as Ezek 14:14 makes clear). It is fascinating to ponder how these three may have interacted throughout this ordeal.

Received the Word of God
And when I looked, behold, a hand was stretched out to me, and behold, a scroll of a book was in it.
And he spread it before me. And it had writing on the front and on the back, and there were written on it words of lamentation and mourning and woe.
And he said to me, "Son of man, eat whatever you find here. Eat this scroll, and go, speak to the house of Israel."
So I opened my mouth, and he gave me this scroll to eat.
And he said to me, "Son of man, feed your belly with this scroll that I give you and fill your stomach with it." Then I ate it, and it was in my mouth as sweet as honey. Ezek. 2:9-3:3

In his vision he saw a scroll extended toward him and then opened. Because we all have bibles on our bookshelves it might seem obvious to us that the Word of God should be represented by a book. And yet to Ezekiel and his hearers it conveyed an important truth: the Word of God was written and therefore unchangeable and non-negotiable. The written Law comes with great authority. By this image Ezekiel's message was given the same authority as the Law of Moses, indeed as the Ten Commandments, which were written by the hand of God himself. People did not listen to a prophet. They said he was speaking under pressure from others (Jer. 43:3). Or, they accused him of spouting his own imagination, as the numerous false prophets did (Jer. 23:26). Or, they despised a prophet because he was a familiar face among them, as Jesus says (Matt. 13:57). But no matter how weak or unlikely the messenger, Ezekiel's message was decreed in heaven and came with absolute unbending authority. We are so blessed to have the entire revelation of God in our Bibles. Let us treat the words in it not with the familiarity that breeds contempt but

3. From Weakness to Strength - The Prophets

with fear knowing that they were written by God himself. "It is written".

Ezekiel had to eat the scroll. This meant he must not just listen to his message and assent to it but he must receive it and inwardly digest it. He must make it part of him until he is one with his message. These were hard words "of lamentation and mourning and woe" but they were "sweet as honey" to him and he loved them. Ezekiel was in exile in Babylon. All the time he heard heard the incessant, noisy, optimistic lies from the false prophets. In contrast God's words were difficult and hard but true and pure. Even God's hard words are better than the world's lies, because love *"does not rejoice at wrongdoing, but rejoices with the truth".1 Cor 13:6*
Here we see the response of a true believer who is hungry for the true message from God. Truth is very sweet like honey.

Sent

And he said to me, "Son of man, go to the house of Israel and speak with my words to them.

For you are not sent to a people of foreign speech and a hard language, but to the house of Israel--
not to many peoples of foreign speech and a hard language, whose words you cannot understand. Surely, if I sent you to such, they would listen to you.
But the house of Israel will not be willing to listen to you, for they are not willing to listen to me: because all the house of Israel have a hard forehead and a stubborn heart. Ezek. 3:4-6

God commanded Ezekiel to be faithful and to speak with his words exactly. Ezekiel had no veto power over the words he spoke. And neither do we. We cannot just say what we like and leave out bits we do not like. God forewarned him of the unbelief of the Israelites. He was not going to foreigners. There were no cultural or language barriers to be crossed. If he was, they would have some excuse that they could not understand the prophet. But even though they can speak your own language they will not listen to you! Why? Because they are stubborn and will not listen to me, says the LORD.

So, Ezekiel, do not expect great success and an easy life.

And you, son of man, be not afraid of them, nor be afraid of their words, though briers and thorns are with you and you sit on scorpions. Be not afraid of their words, nor be dismayed at their looks, for they are a rebellious house. Ezek 2:6

Ezekiel's ministry would be difficult, uncomfortable and dangerous. Unavoidably Ezekiel was always with unbelieving Israelites. They were like constantly present 'briers and thorns' and 'scorpions'. But God commanded him not to be afraid. The reason for this command was because they are rebels. They were under judgement. They had set themselves against Almighty God. So even though they are against you, Ezekiel, God is against them. So cheer up. Ignore their threats. Get on with your ministry.

Boldness
Behold, I have made your face as hard as their faces, and your forehead as hard as their foreheads.
Like emery harder than flint have I made your forehead. Fear them not, nor be dismayed at their looks, for they are a rebellious house." Ezek. 3: 8-9

God here promised boldness to counter the Jew's stubborn 'heads'. Why heads and not hearts? Because prophetic ministry is a confrontation of wills and butting of heads as much as ideas. God made Ezekiel even more stubborn, bold and unbending as the proudest most rebellious exile. The name Ezekiel means 'God makes me strong' or 'God makes me hard'. So Ezekiel, like his predecessor, Jeremiah, would be an iron pillar. He would have a face and forehead of diamond. God would work this change in him.
A long time ago to be an atheist was to be an exception, now it

is the norm and people are proud of it. To live in open sin without shame, to be greedy and grossly materialistic, to take revenge and justify it, to purposely blaspheme and mock God and Jesus, all show a 'hard forehead'. As the world gets richer it gets prouder and harder… and in many countries the church gets more timid and softer. In Japan, I am told by many fellow missionaries and national pastors alike that 'soft and slow evangelism' and 'evangelism with restraint' is the way to Japanese hearts. It may well be the way to their hearts but it is not the way of the Holy Spirit which will lead to their repentance and conversion.

The more brazen the world becomes the firmer must be the church's will to confront. God can make us bold and give us the will to tell the gospel, clearly, boldly, repeatedly, lovingly and faithfully. So why do not we pray and ask for this?

Go and Speak
Moreover, he said to me, "Son of man, all my words that I shall speak to you receive in your heart, and hear with your ears. And go to the exiles, to your people, and speak to them and say to them, 'Thus says the Lord GOD,' whether they hear or refuse to hear."
Then the Spirit lifted me up, and I heard behind me the voice of a great earthquake: "Blessed be the glory of the LORD from its place!" Ezek 3:10-12

In this extraordinary passage, Ezekiel was sent, or more accurately transported, and emphatically told to speak. He was to hear God's words, receive them into his heart and speak all he was told. And he had to speak even if they refused to hear. He had to make himself unpopular by being urgent. Even if they say no thank you, no interest, I'm busy and accuse him of disturbing the peace etc he must be urgent. As Paul commanded Timothy,

preach the word; be ready in season and out of season;

reprove, rebuke, and exhort, with complete patience and teaching. 2 Tim. 4:2

Deeply effected
The Spirit lifted me up and took me away, and I went in bitterness in the heat of my spirit, the hand of the LORD being strong upon me.
And I came to the exiles at Tel-abib, who were dwelling by the Chebar canal, and I sat where they were dwelling. And I sat there overwhelmed among them seven days. Ezek 3:14-15

While being transported miraculously is a great miracle consider the miraculous work that God was doing inside Ezekiel. God was with him and the hand of the LORD was strong upon him. He feels 'bitterness in the heat of his spirit' and he sits 'overwhelmed' for a week. What is going on? Ezekiel was sympathising with God. God gave to Ezekiel his heart, his attitude and he became a friend of God. From then on Ezekiel's message was God's of course but it was also his own and came from his heart.

Responsibility - Severe Injunction to Speak
And at the end of seven days, the word of the LORD came to me:
"Son of man, I have made you a watchman for the house of Israel. Whenever you hear a word from my mouth, you shall give them warning from me.
If I say to the wicked, 'You shall surely die,' and you give him no warning, nor speak to warn the wicked from his wicked way, in order to save his life, that wicked person shall die for his iniquity, but his blood I will require at your hand.
But if you warn the wicked, and he does not turn from his wickedness, or from his wicked way, he shall die for his iniquity, but you will have delivered your soul.
Again, if a righteous person turns from his righteousness and commits injustice, and I lay a stumbling block before him, he shall die. Because you have not warned him, he shall die for

his sin, and his righteous deeds that he has done shall not be remembered, but his blood I will require at your hand.
But if you warn the righteous person not to sin, and he does not sin, he shall surely live, because he took warning, and you will have delivered your soul." Ezek 3:16-21

Ezekiel's unbending firmness and boldness was not just implanted in him without means. So what was the method that God gave him a 'diamond forehead'? By giving him a severe warning concerning his responsibility. This warning was effectual and changed his heart. He was like a watchman who stands in a tower far above the inhabitants, who sees the danger in the far distance, and can give warning of the approaching enemy raiders. Indeed he must give warning. Not to give warning would be a serious failure of duty, care and love. We must understand that as the Holy Spirit applied these words to Ezekiel he felt this duty in his heart as an internal compulsion, as Paul did later (*Therefore, knowing the fear of the Lord, we persuade others. ...For the love of Christ controls us 2Cor. 5:11-14*)

So the work of a prophet was to give warning. He had to warn the wicked to turn from his iniquity and the righteous not to sin. 'You shall surely die' echoes what God said in Eden and is what Jesus said to Pharisees.

I told you that you would die in your sins, for unless you believe that I am he you will die in your sins." John 8:24

If you do not warn him, you are responsible… We Christians today have good news of the gospel of Jesus Christ. We have a responsibility to our contacts: not to maintain our friendships with them at the cost of being irresponsible to their souls, not to avoid giving them some discomfort if it means speaking God's message of life to them, not to be so anxious not to waste their time when their real danger is that they may spend eternity in hell.

God was with Ezekiel. Jesus will be with us as he has promised (Matt 28:20). He will make us love him, love his word and write it on our hearts. He will give us gospel boldness.

Summary of lessons from the prophets

1. God promised to be with the prophets. This promise included God giving the prophet his word, the boldness to speak it, the endurance not to give up or grow weak, and protection.

2. God was with them because they were weak. They all in one way or another acknowledged their weakness. They were weak men dependent on God's help. They were crushed by persecution, Israel's hardness and sometimes discouraged. How hard it was for them to keep in tension the love and justice of the Lord, living that side of Cross. And yet God overcame their weakness and gave them boldness and endurance. Can he not also strengthen us? Our very weakness qualifies us for divine strength. Hear Richard Sibbes on this,

"Weakness with watchfulness will stand, when strength with too much confidence will fail. Weakness with acknowledgement of its weakness, is the fittest seat; and it is subject for God to perfect his strength in it; for being conscious of our infirmities drives us out of ourselves to the One in whom our strength lies. "[7]

3. God often told them to expect difficulties in the course of their ministry. Unwarranted expectations lead to sudden disillusionment and are greatly discouraging. But forewarned is forearmed.

4. Now if you take James' injunction seriously to 'consider the prophets' should you not be greatly encouraged? They worked

---
7 Sibbes p96

in the theocracy of Israel and Judah which was doomed to fail and fall apart, we work in an eternal kingdom which can only grow. We know about the cross and the death and resurrection of Jesus, they only saw these things dimly at best. We understand clearly the plan of salvation, the doctrines of grace, the salvation of the Gentiles and the free offer of the gospel. We live in the age of the Holy Spirit when all believers receive the fullness of the Spirit with all the joy, enlightenment, assurance of salvation and power and presence of Jesus that he brings. Each believer has more advantages than any of the prophets (Matt. 11:11). In fact in a sense we are all prophets (Acts 2:17-18). Should we then not as churches pray for the same boldness that characterised them?

5. The prophets "spoke in the name of the Lord". At any time the prophets could have made their sufferings cease instantly. How? By abandoning their ministry. To wake up each morning and to go out to the opposition knowing that the result could be slander, hatred, persecution and death shows their enormous endurance generated by the Holy Spirit. Of course they could not give up their ministry. God had changed their hearts and made them love him.

6. Finally, and most importantly, I can do no better than let Dietrich Bonhoeffer point us to Christ.

"It is infinitely easier to suffer in obedience to a human command than in the freedom of one's very own responsible action. It is infinitely easier to suffer in community with others than in solitude. It is infinitely easier to suffer publicly and with honor than in the shadow and in dishonor. It is infinitely easier to suffer through putting one's bodily life at stake than to suffer through the spirit. Christ suffered in freedom, in solitude, in the shadow, and in dishonor, in body and in spirit. Since then, many Christians have suffered with him."[8]

---

[8] Bonhoeffer, p17

4. From Sadness to Boldness- The Little Maid from Israel

Naaman, commander of the army of the king of Syria, was a great man with his master and in high favor, because by him the LORD had given victory to Syria. He was a mighty man of valor, but he was a leper.
Now the Syrians on one of their raids had carried off a little girl from the land of Israel, and she worked in the service of Naaman's wife.
She said to her mistress, "Would that my lord were with the prophet who is in Samaria! He would cure him of his leprosy." So Naaman went in and told his lord, "Thus and so spoke the girl from the land of Israel." 2 Kings 5:1-4

After the service Miss N was tearful. She had been teased by the men at work (again) because she was 30 years old and still unmarried. So she was unhappy, unwilling to go to her job on Monday and was in tears (again). My wife Glenda said firmly with some warmth, "O stop crying and tell them the gospel!". This was a new idea for N and so she did. The next Sunday two young men came with her to church. They came for about a month and then one went to a church closer to home and sadly the other stopped altogether. Her boss, who had been in on the teasing too, started reading his Bible everyday. Apparently his marriage was in difficulties. Perhaps this irony was lost on him (though not on us). Later also a young PhD student from her workplace started to attend our services and began to help out at the evangelistic events we were holding in the temporary housing sites for tsunami evacuees. Soon he believed and was baptised. All this because one young woman dried her tears and started to tell the gospel.

In the famous story of Naaman he journeyed to Samaria to be healed by Elisha the prophet. He was miraculously cleansed of

4. From Sadness to Boldness- The Little Maid from Israel

leprosy by bathing in the River Jordan and acknowledged that there is no other god but the God of Israel and he returned to Aram with the firm decision to worship Him alone.

The main point is that God will save the Gentiles. Jesus used this story as a warning to the Jews of his day that "no prophet is acceptable in his hometown" (Luke 4:24), and therefore that if they continued to reject Him and His ministry the kingdom would be taken away from them and given to others (Mark 12:9). For us Gentiles it is a story full of encouragement that it has always been God's purpose to save the nations.

But the story of Namaan's salvation starts with a young, zealous, Israelite girl in terrible circumstances. Let us consider her situation and how God was with her.

Her history
"Would that my lord were with the prophet who is in Samaria!"(v3) She had been brought up to know the God of Israel and respect Elisha as his true prophet. Probably she had godly parents and came from a home that had resisted the prevalent idolatry. This inveterate sin of the Israelites provoked God to send foreign invaders to discipline his people. This young girl was carried off in one such raid by the Syrians. "Carried off" suggests violence. Was she caught alone in the open field or was her family massacred? We do not know the details but she was captured and brought back as a slave. It is hard to imagine the devastation, sense of loss, grief, anger, sadness and loneliness that such cruelty must have caused.

Her circumstances
As a slave she had no rights and would have been liable to have been bought, sold or ill-treated at her owner's whim. While life in Naaman's household may have been tolerable while she worked hard and made no mistakes, it was a graceless and godless environment which would added to the trauma she had faced.

And yet God was with her
As he had promised Moses, God was also with this little girl. Her loving, earnest and faith-filled words can only be explained by the power and grace of God.

She said to her mistress, "Would that my lord were with the prophet who is in Samaria! He would cure him of his leprosy." 2 Kings 5:3

God sustained her faith while filling her heart with love resulting in her boldly introducing her master to the God of Israel.

So consider,

Her faith
God sustains her faith. She is far from Israel and other believers. She has no fellowship, scripture teaching, or encouragement. The sacrifices with their symbolism of the Son of God dying for our sins were denied her. And yet despite all these disadvantages she overcame her difficulties and grew in grace, and the seed that was sown when she was in Israel, blossomed against all odds. She believed in the Lord and coped with her disaster. At some point this young believer had to make a decision, whether to stay with God despite the terrible providence she had experienced, or to reject him and live for herself. Somehow, and it can only have been grace, the love and glory of God became real to her. God was with her. Perhaps she knew of Joseph (Gen 39) and how God was with him when he was sold as a slave into Potiphar's house and how he kept his integrity. Then after being falsely accused and thrown into the Egyptian prison he still maintained his faith in God because God was with him. Whether she knows of Joseph or not she mirrors his faith and obedience.

She believed also in God's true prophet. No doubt while in

4. From Sadness to Boldness- The Little Maid from Israel

Israel she had heard of Elijah and Elisha and their bold denunciations of Israel's idolatry calling them back to the one true God, their threats of judgement including probably the invasion, exile and enslavement by foreign armies which was the very thing that happened to her. To this young believer idolatry and turning away from the one true God would have been the worst wickedness possible. And through this fulfilment of prophetic warning her awe of Elisha as God's true prophet would have been strongly confirmed. The extraordinary miracles of Elijah and Elisha, the fire from heaven (2 Kings 1), miraculous ascent to heaven (2 Kings 2:11), the miraculous provision (2 Kings 4:5, 41) and raising of the dead (2 Kings 4:34-37), military victories (2 Kings 3:20) were subjects of conversation even by the unbelieving king of Israel (2 Kings 8:4). They would certainly been common knowledge among the believing remnant of whom this young girl was one and these miraculous signs would have confirmed her faith. However in one respect her faith was unique: Elisha had never cleansed a leper in Israel (Luke 4:27). And yet somehow this young girl receives supernatural assurance through the Holy Spirit that Namaan, a leper and Gentile, will be healed.

Her love
Along with her growth in faith, God enabled her to overcome her bitterness and resentment. No doubt her faith was severely shaken by the harsh providence she experienced and she probably went through a stage of hating the Syrians and especially the family that had bought her and enslaved her. Maybe she saw Namaan's leprosy as God's judgement on him and rejoiced in his suffering. Nevertheless she overcame all this evil with good and loved her enemies and kept Jesus' command,

> *"But I say to you who hear, Love your enemies, do good to those who hate you, Luke 6:27*

in a manner only surpassed by our Lord himself on the cross. Her love for Namaan was sincere and genuine. She wanted him to be healed. Really wanted him to be healed!

"Would that my lord were with the prophet who is in Samaria! He would cure him of his leprosy."

The NIV reads "*If only....*" as if it is her one great desire that he should be healed by Elisha. In both versions her words express ardent desire. God produced this love in her. Only by being with her in the cauldron of enslavement in Syria could such love flourish in such a trial.

Her boldness

Above all she was evangelistic. She wanted her master to know honour, love and worship God. She was a house servant waiting on Namaan's wife. No doubt she was to be seen and not heard and speak only when spoken to and yet when she learnt of her master's affliction, perhaps through the worries expressed by her mistress, she was bold and spoke out for her true Master in heaven. We only have a few verses on which to go on but it is as clear as daylight that there was no inhibition, mealy-mouthed timidity or lack of clarity in her words. They were impossible to misunderstand. So she was the best kind of servant. She was a servant of the gospel and ministered to Namaan and his wife the knowledge of the true God. None of this was rehearsed or forced: it came up out of a heart changed by grace. She loved God, and daily rejoiced in him and believed in His prophet. She was sustained by the Spirit though cut off from worship, instruction, and had no knowledge of the cross. He was present with her.

Her legacy

Let us consider the results of this young Israelite's boldness. The immediate result was that Naaman was miraculously healed and converted to the worship of the true God *"Behold, I know that there is no God in all the earth but in Israel."* 2

4. From Sadness to Boldness- The Little Maid from Israel

Kings 5:15

Consider too that, as a result, Elisha became even more famous and his influence was increased. In this way this slave-girl became a co-worker with the great prophet.

Also, the king of Israel (whose unbelief is challenged) and all the Israelites were warned that time was running out for them and that God would one day take his people from the Gentiles. Without her boldness, winsomeness and faith none of this would have happened.

In the mid-term, doubtless her example inspired Daniel and the other Jews who remained faithful in the Jewish exile that the same God would be with them too. Most scholars believe 2 Kings was written in Babylon by an unknown Jewish author around 550 BC who would have been contemporaneous with Daniel, or may even have been Daniel himself. It is intriguing that Daniel's attitude to King Nebuchanezzar is very similar to the slave girl's to Namaan (see the next chapter on Dan. 4:27).

Ultimately this servant girl points to Christ. who was sent to earth to serve.
Jesus was the ultimate servant.
She was sent from Israel to Damascus - Christ was sent from heaven to this fallen world.
She was torn from her family - Christ tore himself away from the Trinity.
She was forced into slavery. Christ made himself a slave. He became weak. He made himself poor. Why? So that the Gentiles and Jews might be saved freely by faith.

For I tell you that Christ became a servant to the circumcised to show God's truthfulness, in order to confirm the promises given to the patriarchs,
and in order that the Gentiles might glorify God for his mercy. As it is written, "Therefore I will praise you among the Gentiles, and sing to your name." Rom 15:8-9

Christ was the ultimate servant because he did the ultimate act of service: giving his life as a ransom for many:

But it shall not be so among you. But whoever would be great among you must be your servant, and whoever would be first among you must be slave of all.
For even the Son of Man came not to be served but to serve, and to give his life as a ransom for many." Mark 10:43-45

And Christ's own attitude now has become the model for Christian ministry. Paul expresses his philosophy of ministry;

For though I am free from all, I have made myself a servant to all, that I might win more of them.
To the Jews I became as a Jew, in order to win Jews. To those under the law I became as one under the law (though not being myself under the law) that I might win those under the law.
To those outside the law I became as one outside the law (not being outside the law of God but under the law of Christ) that I might win those outside the law.
To the weak I became weak, that I might win the weak. I have become all things to all people, that by all means I might save some.
I do it all for the sake of the gospel, that I may share with them in its blessings. 1 Cor 9:19-23

The gospel is often preached in weakness. The role of a servant is a weak one. The bold Christian is often misunderstood, persecuted, slandered and yet God is with them. So whether you are a slave-girl in Syria, a prisoner in the crucible of N Korea, a Christian in the vice of sharia law of Pakistan, a student in a sneering UK university or a patient in the cold desert of a Japanese hospital, God will be with you. God delights to come alongside isolated believers and strengthen their faith, love and witness. So seek His presence with confidence (Psa. 105:4). He has promised to never leave or forsake you (Heb. 13:5). His last words on earth were,

4. From Sadness to Boldness- The Little Maid from Israel

"Lo, I am with you always even to the close of the age." (Matt 28:20)

Some readers might think that boldness is inconsistent with weakness, but this is to misunderstand both words. The weakness spoken of here is the weakness of position, worldly status and of purposely taking the form of a servant. It is not the weakness of doubt or lack of conviction or lukewarmness. Also the boldness shown by this girl and her Saviour and inculcated upon us is not domineering or egotistical. Rather it passionately seeks the salvation of others whatever the personal cost and thus speaks boldly and clearly.

As soon as we express that Jesus is our Lord we immediately put ourselves in a position of weakness, because the world counts such as fools. And as soon as we seek their salvation, we become their servants for Christ's sake. It is a paradox but the humble servant who follows Christ is the one who boldly tells the gospel.

So let us be faithful to the gospel no matter how terrible our outward circumstances.

Let's pray for boldness to point passionately and clearly to the Saviour.

To do this let us also guard our hearts. Only get rid of the idols out of our hearts and cultivate our love for the Lord.

"If only my master would see the prophet who is in Samaria! He would cure him of his leprosy." - Slave girl
"Therefore, O king, let my counsel be acceptable to you:"- Daniel (Dan. 4:27)
"O Jerusalem, Jerusalem, the city that kills the prophets and stones those who are sent to it! How often would I have gathered your children together as a hen gathers her brood under her wings, and you were not willing!" - Jesus Christ

(Luke 13:40)
"Whether short or long, I would to God that not only you but also all who hear me this day might become such as I am—except for these chains." - The Apostle Paul (Acts 26:29)
"...do not harden your hearts..." - The Holy Spirit (Heb. 3:8)

5. From Defeat into Victory - Daniel

Don Cormack tells of a Christian Cambodian family massacred by the Khmer Rouge. They were gathered in a nearby rice field for execution when one of the sons suddenly escaped into the jungle. The father called out after him, 'Please come back. Let us die and go heaven together'. After a while he returned weeping.

'Now we are ready to go,' Haim told the Khmer Rouge. But by this time there was not a soldier standing there who had the heart to raise his hoe to deliver the death blow on the backs of these noble heads. Ultimately this had to be done by the Khmer Rouge commune chief who had not witnessed these things. But few of those watching doubted that as each of these Christians' bodies toppled silently into the earthen pit which the victims themselves had prepared their souls soared heavenward to a place prepared by their Lord.
The rapid spread of news such as this, of certain Christians boldly bearing witness to their Lord in death, was gossiped about the countryside. Eventually these reports were brought across to the refugee camps in Thailand; and not always by Christians but by typical Cambodians who until then had despised the Puok Yesu (ie the disciples of Jesus).[9]

A recent article in the periodical Evangelicals Now tells of a Boko Haram fighter in Nigeria. He had murdered Christians and was about to murder others when was struck with the weight of his sin, ran to a church and found forgiveness both from the Lord and from those who he had been persecuting.

Both these stories show the power of a Christian life that will

---

[9] Cormack p223

Gospel Boldness

not bow to pressure and that maintains its bold profession no matter what the cost. Any book on boldness would be incomplete without mentioning Daniel, because, even a superficial reader of this well-known Old Testament book cannot fail to be impressed by the boldness of Daniel and his three friends. I do not intend a detailed analysis but will draw out some of the salient points for our topic.

They were amazingly bold
Five famous incidents stand out.

The Refusal to eat the King's Food
But Daniel resolved not to defile himself with the royal food and wine, and he asked the chief official for permission not to defile himself this way. Dan 1:8
All meals served at the king's table were heathen feasts and were in honour of the gods. In this matter they had to take a stand. The great sin of Israel had been the worship of other gods. Of all the sins that Israel had committed the root sin that led to the others was idolatry. The godly remnant recognised this and loathed idolatry. Daniel was wise and gentle but utterly resolute. He politely made his request to be excused from eating such food. He did not get angry or provoke others to persecute him. He simply stated his case as objectively and as clearly as he could. He did not decide to refuse to eat only after the official was friendly, nor after he was given wisdom to speak to him about it. First came the resolution and then came the boldness and the wisdom and the words to use.

The results of this boldness were,

1. Favour *Now God had caused the official to show favor and sympathy to Daniel, (Dan 1:9)*
God rules hearts and can make enemies friends (Prov 16:7). The chief of eunuchs might have thought Daniel as difficult. Instead, God caused this court official to show "favor and sympathy" toward Daniel. We think we can make friends with the world and it will love us. We will be wrong. It will respect

5. From Defeat into Victory - Daniel

us if we stand for the truth. Here this heathen respected and favoured Daniel.

2. Wisdom. *"Please test your servants for ten days: Give us nothing but vegetables to eat and water to drink. Dan 1:12*
This was a wise and sensible reply. We need wisdom. But it is not given to double-minded men but only to those who commit themselves to obey. (James 1:5)

3. God answered their prayers *At the end of the ten days they looked healthier and better nourished than any of the young men who ate the royal food. Dan 1:15*

4. God gifted them in many ways. *To these four young men God gave knowledge and understanding of all kinds of literature and learning. And Daniel could understand visions and dreams of all kinds.* Dan 1:17
These were not trivial gifts, and they fitted these youths for responsible positions. To Daniel was given a very special talent in addition to the above: *"insight into every sort of vision and dreams."* Where such dreams or visions were divinely inspired or were to serve a special purpose Daniel had ability for seeing what they meant.

5. And so after three years when they stood before the king they passed with honours.

The Burning Fiery Furnace
King Nebuchanezzar set up a huge golden statue in the plain of Dura and commanded all his subjects who were present to worship when they heard the music.
And whoever does not fall down and worship shall immediately be cast into a burning fiery furnace." Dan 3:6
This image was probably not a regular Babylonian deity, because the king distinguished his gods from his image, rather it was probably of him, from a twisted understanding of the

dream in chapter 2. The king wanted total allegiance from all his subjects and he aimed to force this allegiance by religion. This has been tried many times since eg Romans with Caesar, Japan with Shinto.

This 'test' would have been easy for anyone except a true believer. The requirement was only to bow. Bowing is not a problem for idolaters who worship in form only, nor is it a problem for pantheists to add one more god. But for Shadrach, Meshach and Abednego it was an impossible requirement and they could not bow down.

I believe there is evidence in the text to show they were Nebuchabnezzar's prime target. He came to the 'worship' expecting opposition. The furnace was prepared. He wanted to eradicate from his kingdom all who followed Daniel. He openly challenged God. But "kindly" offered a chance of escape and a second chance to the three friends when they first refuse to bow. So where was Daniel? He was safely kept separate in the court of the king while this was going on (Dan 2:49). Daniel was valuable as a dream-interpreter but Nebuchabnezzar knew Daniel was passionate about his God and evangelistic and did not want his religion spreading. So other believers had to be weeded out. Shadrach, Meshach and Abednego were expendable. Above all Nebuchadnezzar feared that 'mountain that filled the whole earth' (Dan 2:35, 2:44-45) and rather like Herod after him who also thought he could fight against prophecy, all rival sources of power had to be eradicated. The world does not mind if we are Christians but it just cannot tolerate us insisting we are right, that we have the only way. And it doesn't like the word of God spreading. If one or two people become Christians it is OK. Or a few 100 may be. But not a few 10,000.

When Shadrach, Meshach and Abednego answer the king they do not give an apology for their faith, or a reasoned defence. If there was a possibility that the king's demand was based on a misunderstanding or the consequences were unintended then such a course would have made sense. But they knew they were the victims of deliberate targeted persecution and that is why they answer as they do.

Shadrach, Meshach, and Abednego answered and said to the king, "O Nebuchadnezzar, we have no need to answer you in this matter.
If this be so, our God whom we serve is able to deliver us from the burning fiery furnace, and he will deliver us out of your hand, O king.
But if not, be it known to you, O king, that we will not serve your gods or worship the golden image that you have set up."
Dan. 3:16-18

Note that they put no hope in the king changing his mind or in his mercy, they confess God's power to save them but submit to God's providence should he choose not to, and they confirm their resolution not to commit idolatry. This ringing response incenses Nebuchadnezzar who orders them thrown into the furnace. They are miraculously rescued and God appears as the fourth man.

Nebuchadnezzar answered and said, "Blessed be the God of Shadrach, Meshach, and Abednego, who has sent his angel and delivered his servants, who trusted in him, and set aside the king's command, and yielded up their bodies rather than serve and worship any god except their own God. Dan. 3:28

Nebuchadnezzar praises God for the miraculous deliverance. But what impresses him most is the youths' love for God. "They set aside *my* command... how marvellous! What a great God he must be to inspire such love in his servants!" Thus what impressed the king most was their boldness. This deep impression would have remained true even if there was no miracle and God had not rescued them. Even if they had died in the furnace, Nebuchadnezzar would still have been awed by

their love for God. Today in failed states, some Islamic countries and under totalitarian regimes many Christians out of love for Jesus "yield up their bodies rather than serve and worship any god except their own God". The story of their suffering may never hit the news but their witness has a powerful efficacy. Gospel boldness is never wasted. Poise in unjust suffering, devotion for God, a pure zeal for righteousness no matter what the cost, and boldness before hostile men are still what impress the world. The hardened centurion viewing the death of Christ at the crucifixion confessed,
"Truly this was the Son of God!" Matt. 27:54, Mark 15:39, and *"Certainly this man was innocent!" Luke 23:47*

Since the time of the apostles there have been those persecutors who have repented and become Christians themselves (from the Apostle Paul to Sergei Kourdakov who wrote '*Forgive Me, Natasha*').

The Apostle James was the first apostle to die for the gospel and yet immediately after this tragic loss to the early church we read *"But the word of God increased and multiplied." Acts 12:24*

Paul wrote that his imprisonment in Rome was not a disaster but had served to advance the gospel. Why? *"... most of the brothers, having become confident in the Lord by my imprisonment, are much more bold to speak the word without fear." Phil. 1:14* So then, persecution leads to gospel boldness and then to the conversion of the lost.

<u>The plea to repent</u>

"Then Daniel, whose name was Belteshazzar, was dismayed for a while, and this thoughts alarmed him. The king answered and said, "Belteshazzar, let not the dream or the interpretation alarm you."Belteshazzar answered and said, "My lord, may

5. From Defeat into Victory - Daniel

the dream be for those who hate you and its interpretation for your enemies! Dan. 4:19

..

it is you, O king, who have grown and become strong. Your greatness has grown and reaches to heaven, and your dominion to the ends of the earth. Dan. 4:22

...

Therefore, O king, let my counsel be acceptable to you: break off your sins by practicing righteousness, and your iniquities by showing mercy to the oppressed, that there may perhaps be a lengthening of your prosperity." Dan. 4:27

The main theme of this chapter is not Daniel's boldness. No, it is the amazing conversion of King Nebuchadnezzar. It is amazing because he was one of the greatest tyrants in history. He had destroyed Judah, laid waste Jerusalem, killed thousands of Jews, and persecuted and oppressed the few that remained. He was strong, proud, violent, easily-angered, mercurial and dangerous. And yet in God's hands he is turned into humble, zealous worshipper. Furthermore it is written by himself. You could say that it was the first tract, written by a Gentile, for Gentiles after his extra-ordinary conversion. It is arguably the most amazing chapter in the Old Testament. Yet Daniel plays an important role in this drama.

After the king had a frightening dream he called in all the wise men and astrologers. He did not call in Daniel despite his proven track record. He sensed correctly that the dream's interpretation was unfavourable to him and he wanted to hear a 'better" version. Anything to avoid the God who was hunting him down! When Daniel was called to interpret he was <u>direct</u>. "It is you, O king!". There is no beating around the bush, circumlocution or softening the blow. Daniel did not make the warning general, "This sort of thing could happen to someone like you", nor did he make it vague, "something unpleasant might happen". The meaning was absolutely clear because Daniel was bold. One is reminded of Nathan before King

David, *"Thou art the man!"*

And yet the blow *was* softened by Daniel's affectionate attitude. This was sincere and not faked. Although Nebuchadnezzar was an evil man Daniel loved him and had obviously been praying for him. So he did not rejoice at the bad news but showed his 'alarm' and 'distress'. He expressed the wish that the interpretation would be for someone else, not King Nebuchadnezzar. And after the interpretation had been given he pleads with the king to repent. He gives 'unsolicted advice' [10] which would have required great boldness. "O king, please listen to me. Stop sinning, show mercy, and perhaps God will delay the judgement or spare you altogether. Save yourself!" Daniel had been very bold. He was now in great danger. Unbelievers hate and fear bold believers with a demonic passion.

What was the king's response to this passionate plea? It seems he was not too pleased. There is no mention of Daniel being showered with honours or promotions, as had happened previously. And he did not take it to heart because in 12 months time the judgement fell upon him.

However, though the interpretation was ineffective in leading Nebuchadnezzar to repentance, its 'potential' effectiveness was much enhanced by Daniel's bold and warmly affectionate attitude. God's intent was Nebuchadnezzar's repentance, and it is for this that Daniel pleads. There is unity between God's message and his servant's attitude. The king dismissed the message, but it was not because Daniel was unfaithful in his delivery or because he was cold and academic. How often do people take our message with a pinch of salt, because we have no passion or urgency? Or, because we seem so timid? Paul says, *"Since we have the same spirit of faith according to what has been written, "I believed, and so I spoke," we also believe,*

---

10 Leupold, p193

and so we also speak." 2 Cor. 4:13. And eventually the king did repent, acknowledge God and believe. Daniel's consistent bold witness and passionate plea meant that he was a co-worker with God who struck the king with the madness that eventually saved him.

The Final Warning

Then Daniel answered and said before the king, "Let your gifts be for yourself, and give your rewards to another. Nevertheless, I will read the writing to the king and make known to him the interpretation.... Dan. 5:17
...
And you his son, Belshazzar, have not humbled your heart, though you knew all this,
but you have lifted up yourself against the Lord of heaven. And the vessels of his house have been brought in before you, and you and your lords, your wives, and your concubines have drunk wine from them. And you have praised the gods of silver and gold, of bronze, iron, wood, and stone, which do not see or hear or know, but the God in whose hand is your breath, and whose are all your ways, you have not honored. Dan. 5:22-23

Belshazzar now ruled in place of his father, and while the army of Media/Persia besieged the city, he put on a great feast for a thousand of his lords and concubines. The whole feast showed contempt for God and his providence. The fingers of a man's hand wrote in the wall and the king was at a loss for an interpretation. Finally the queen mother (evidently King Nebuchadnezzar's wife who was absent from the feast [11]) told him of his father's respect and dependence on Daniel for interpretation. Daniel was called. The attitude that Daniel showed to Belshazzar was different of that to his father. He refused his gifts with contempt.

---

[11] Leupold p225, Young p122

> *"These verses are the beginning of one of the finest sermons delivered by a court preacher under the most trying circumstances. The preacher is not found remiss in a single item. He tells the whole truth and tells it with unmistakable clearness. He cringes before no man; he uses no evasion or circumlocution; and he maintains a respectful attitude throughout. Withal he aims at the moral restoration of his hearer or hearers."*[12]

Belshazzar had sinned against the light. He had heard about his father's miraculous conversion and yet remained hardened. Nebuchadnezzar had written chapter 4 to the people in his kingdom to honour God, is it conceivable that he had not repeatedly and passionately told his son? Belshazzar is like many today who have heard the gospel and seen clearly the power of Jesus to save and yet rejected it all. He has no excuse.

The Lions' Den

With the accession of Darius, Daniel became one of three presidents who oversee the empire. After being trained in Nebuchadnezzar's court, Daniel had spent 60 years in government bureaucracy and was now 75-80 years old. In all that time he had been consistent and godly in all his behaviour. And because of his 'excellent spirit' the king planned to set him over the whole empire. This provoked to jealousy the other bureaucrats to plan his downfall. So they tried to 'dig dirt' on him. They assumed that he was corrupt as they were. When they found that he was completely different from them and they knew he would put a stop to their corrupt practices, they devised a trap for him, and got the king to sign 'an edict… that anyone who prays to any god or man during the next thirty days, except to you, O king, shall be thrown into the lions' den'.

---

[12] Leupold on v18-19, p230

5. From Defeat into Victory - Daniel

Now when Daniel learned that the decree had been published, he went home to his upstairs room where the windows opened toward Jerusalem. Three times a day he got down on his knees and prayed, giving thanks to his God, just as he had done before. Dan 6:10

Stuart Olyott in his excellent commentary points out that the real lion's den was his upper room[13]. Satan as the roaring lion no doubt tried his hardest to intimidate him from the duty of prayer "Give in - only a month. Don't throw everything away. Pray secretly, You are too strict" (1 Pet 5:8-9). The battle was fought, and won, there. To Daniel praying was not optional, and this was not mere duty for duty's sake. He had seen in the first year of Darius (Dan 9:1-2) in the book of Jeremiah that the exile would last 70 years. It was imperative then he intercede with God on behalf of his people concerning the return from exile, and so he continued to pray three times a day. A sample of Daniel's prayer life is given us in Dan 9:4-19. It is a penitent, Bible-based, faith-filled and God-honouring prayer (those other exiles Ezra and Nehemiah showed the same penitence before God, Ezra 9:6-15, Neh. 1:6-11). Chapters 7-12 show that Daniel had an intense and one might even say turbulent relationship with God. How could he then bow to pressure to give up praying! His boldness before Darius and at other times in his life is easier to understand in this context.

The end of the story is well-known. God sent his angel who stopped the mouths of the lions so that Daniel was not harmed and Darius issued a decree that all *"fear and reverence the God of Daniel"* (Dan 6:26).

They were underdogs
In the time of King Jehoiakim, Jerusalem fell and a few thousand of Jews were taken to exile in Babylon by King Nebuchadnezzar at the beginning of his reign. They were no

---

[13] Olyott p80

longer in a theocracy, but a minority in a pagan society. In the theocracy of Judah they had the framework of national laws and a culture shaped by the Word of God. To keep the Sabbath, to avoid idolatry, to keep ceremonially clean would not have been that hard or counter-cultural for most of Jewish history. But in pantheistic immoral Babylon all of these things and much more would have been unpopular, dangerous and would have required faith in the living God. In the days of the theocracy both before and after the exile there was always a tendency to despise Gentiles and this had become entrenched and codified by the time of Jesus. And yet during the exile, they were not only prisoners of war, with the status of slaves but were despised it seems beyond that status. For example when Arioch, Belshazzar and the accusers before King Darius use the term "one of the exiles of Judah" they do so with obvious contempt (Dan. 2:25, 5:13, 6:13). In this the Jewish believers resemble Christian believers today in most parts of the world believers, who are at best ignored, or treated with mild amusement, contempt or severely persecuted. And yet like the winter sun, believers shine brightest when they are lowest. When believers are in the majority or have political power somehow their witness to the world suffers.

God was with them

Despite their isolation in a pagan hostile land and the severe experiences of recent judgement on their nation, God was dynamically and remarkably with them in their weakness. Chapters 1-6 show a very important cycle: the believers boldly make a stand for the true God, who then works among the surrounding unbelievers. In Chapter 1 Daniel, Shadrach, Meshach and Abednego refuse to eat the king's rich food, in Chapter 2 God gives the king a disturbing dream. This dream was uniquely God's work. No man could get inside the king's head and once inside the king could not get God out. In chapter 3 the believers refuse to bow before his golden image and God reveals himself to the king as the Fourth Man in the furnace. In chapter 4 we have the remarkable and glorious conversion of

5. From Defeat into Victory - Daniel

King Nebuchadnezzar who had met the only true God <u>through</u> the boldness of Daniel and his friends. This cycle continues in Chapter 5 though the revelation of God leads to King Belshazzar's judgement rather than salvation and in Chapter 6 Daniel's boldness is followed by God revealing himself to Darius in the miracle of the lion's den. So in this divine cycle first comes the believer's boldness and then comes God's saving activity in the world. It is not that the boldness was manmade and God rewarded it with his activity. Rather, God empowered the boldness which then he responded to so the cycle could continue. This cyclical pattern shows both the necessity of boldness and its results.

Furthermore, this cycle was not hindered by a hostile environment but rather enhanced by it. The unbelief and threats of the king and the opposition of the court were essential elements without which the boldness of Daniel would have been tame and meaningless. God overcame both the timidity of the believers and the hostility of the world. (We will see the same cycle in the Acts of the Apostles).

There is a principle we see which holds good for the present day: when believers worship the true God, obediently stand firm and boldly witness for him, then He will work in the surrounding unbelievers. We cannot expect God to do anything if we dare not speak. When we stand firm unbelievers will meet Christ. When you and your church boldly tell the gospel then God will work in the surrounding unbelievers.

The Importance of Bible Reading, Prayer and Walking with God

Daniel seems supernatural in his boldness considering the enormous pressures on him. What was his secret? Can ordinary believers today expect to be like Daniel? Can they also be as bold? Is this even a legitimate question? Is "Dare to be a Daniel, dare to stand alone" a scriptural hymn to sing? Or is Daniel so unique that we should not even expect to be able to emulate him? Daniel of course is unique in that he points us to Christ. The book of Daniel should lead us to faith in Christ, because our real hero is not Daniel but Jesus. There are many pointers to Jesus in the life of Daniel. While Daniel was a prince of Judah who is sent from Jerusalem to Babylon, who stands before the king, undefiled; Jesus came from heaven to earth to gives us the righteousness of God so we may stand on the day of judgement. And while Daniel is put in the lions' den because of the law of the Medes and Persians; Jesus dies on the cross because of the inexorable law of God. And yet while Daniel points us to Christ he does not do so in a merely symbolic way. An example of such a symbol is the rock in the king's dream which grows to fill the whole earth (Dan. 2:44-45). Christ is like the rock cut by no human hand which destroys all earthly kingdoms. But this is a parable, a mere symbol. Daniel points to Christ in a different way. He was a man of God filled by the Spirit, living by faith and empowered from above who fulfils the will of God at his place and time. God was with Daniel. He points to someone much greater than him, the Saviour of the world. And yet there is an organic connection between Daniel and Christ, just as there is an organic connection between Christ and Christians. God was with Daniel. He was with Christ without measure and is with Christians through his Son by the Holy Spirit. So it is legitimate and indeed very instructive to draw lessons on the Christian life from the life of Daniel.

First of Daniel was consistent. His public life lasted about 60 years. From when he refused to eat the king's rich food to when he refused to stop praying at the king's command he was consistently bold. He was fiercely monotheistic, jealous for God's glory and eschewed idolatry (Dan. 2:20-23, 27-28, 5:23). The three kings he served under and the officials who were his colleagues recognised that God was with him (Dan. 4:8, 5:12, 6:20), that he was filled with the Spirit (Dan 5:11), that he was incorrupt and above reproach in every area of his life (Dan. 6:3-5). His boldness was part of his faithful walk with God of his entire life.

Second Daniel was prayerful. When he was in trouble he prayed with his brothers (Dan. 2:17-18). When he did not understand revelation he prayed (Dan. 10:12). When he read that it was time for the exile to end, he prayed, habitually and regularly (Dan. 6:10, Dan. 9:1-2, note the timing).

Finally Daniel fed on the Word of God. It was because he was awed by the God revealed in the Law of Moses, the inspired Israelite history and the prophets that he could not fail to be bold before kings. While the book of Daniel can be considered as prophecy Daniel and his 3 friends were not prophets with a defined call, national audience and a 'full-time' ministry but students and government employees who walked with God. Daniel received supernatural dreams, visions and revelation which affected him deeply (Dan. 7:15, 28, 8:27, 10:8) but the basis for his faith was previously-revealed revelation.

We Christians today need to learn that there are no short-cuts to godliness or to gospel boldness. Like Daniel no matter where you are, you live in a society which is tolerant of anything except a sincere faith in Jesus Christ. We must use the means of grace as Daniel did. We must use them intentionally not as mere habits to be kept. The means of grace (church-going, prayer, bible reading etc) are never ends in themselves but to *get grace*. Never be satisfied with less. We must be consistent and not have holidays from our bibles or vacations from church services or slacken off in our walk with God for our entire lives.

Let us hear what JI Packer in his classic Knowing God says. *"Those who know God show great boldness for God. Daniel and his friends were men who stuck their necks out. This was not foolhardiness. They knew what they were doing. They had counted the cost. They had measured the risk. They were well aware what the outcome of their actions would be unless God miraculously intervened, as in fact He did. But these things did not move them. Once they were convinced that their stand was right, and that loyalty to their God required them to take it, then. in Oswald Chambers's phrase, they 'smilingly washed their hands of the consequences'. We ought to obey God rather than men.' said the apostles (Acts 5: 29). "Neither count I my life dear unto myself, so that I might finish my course with joy,' said Paul (Acts 20: 24). This was precisely the spirit of Daniel, Shadrach. Meshach, and Abed-nego. It is the spirit of all who know God. They may find the determination of the right course to take agonisingly difficult, but once they are clear on it they embrace it boldly and without hesitation. It does not worry them that others of God's people see the matter differently. and do not stand with them. ... By this test also we may measure our own knowledge of God."*[14]

How do you measure up in his test?

---

14 Packer p24

6. The Boldness of Jesus Christ

Jesus was always bold
Jesus' boldness is displayed on almost every page of the Gospels. From the beginning of his public ministry Jesus spoke clearly, boldly, without fear of man or consequences. In the Sermon on the Mount (Matt. 5-7), Jesus attacked the religion of the Pharisees, their values (eg Matt 5:3-12), their disobedience to Scripture (eg Matt. 5:19), their hypocrisy and inconsistencies (eg Matt. 5:27-36), their religious practices (eg Matt. 6:3-7), and their worldliness (eg Matt. 6:24-34). John MacArthur says "The whole theme of the Sermon on the Mount was a sustained critique of the Pharisee's religion... and a systematic point by point critique of the Pharisees' interpretation of Moses' law" [15]. Jesus called them 'unsaved' and when a courteous if proud Jewish leader enquired of him he told him he could not enter heaven without starting at the very beginning and being born again (John 3:3,5,7). These men were the Jewish religious elite and respected by the whole nation and yet Jesus did not try to curry their favour nor did he shrink from exposing their sins. Jesus attacked the Pharisees as a group (Matt. 23) calling them hypocrites, white-washed tombs, blind fools and a brood of vipers. He unfavourably compared his Pharisee meal host with a woman of ill-repute (Luke 7:45-46).

Jesus never feared man or circumstances
He had no concern to fit in or to avoid offence to proud and ignorant religionists who took pleasure in being offended (Matt. 15:13). Jesus did not mind who he associated with, whether tax collectors, sinners, women or Gentiles. In the Pharisees' own estimate of Jesus, boldness was one of his chief distinguishing marks and they said rightly he did not regard the position of men (Mark 12:14). In contrast the chief distinguishing mark of the Pharisees, teachers of the Law and

---

[15] MacArthur, Ch 6

priests was timidity. They feared the crowd (Matt. 21:46), could not act without each other's approval (John 12:43) and could not reply except evasively (Matt. 21:27) and sometimes were entirely struck dumb by the fear of man (Luke 20:26).

Jesus did not operate within a comfort zone

He returned to Galilee after a popular visit to Samaria knowing that he would be rejected (John 4:43-44). Later to the horror of the disciples he set his face to go to Jerusalem knowing that he was going to his death (Mark 10:32-33). He frequently moved from where he was popular and had many admirers to where he would be in danger (Luke 4:42-44). He moved from the synagogue (Luke 4:44) where teaching was expected to a boat (Luke 5:3). That Jesus performed healings on the Sabbath is well-known, but there is evidence that Jesus especially chose the Sabbath for this (Luke records 5 sabbath healings, Luke 4:31-37, 38-39, 6:6-11, 13:10, 14:1) perhaps because he saw these miracles as signs of the same restoration (cf Acts 3:21) and release (compare Luke 4:18-19 with Luke 13:16, 14:4) which the Sabbath also signifies. And so he completely discounted the persecution leading to death to which this behaviour exposed him.

Jesus was consistent

Some men are bold in their sermons in church but too timid to evangelise their neighbours, while others are bold before strangers but melt before their families and friends, however Jesus was entirely consistent.

He had neither a set 'hostile face' toward outsiders nor a set 'friendly face' toward his allies. He called one of his favorite apostles, 'Satan' (Matt.16:23). When a large group of disciples gave up because of his 'hard' teaching (John 6:60) Jesus did not plead with the others to remain but asked, "Do you want to go away as well?" (v 67).

He was not intimidated by his family (Mark 3:33-35) and corrected his mother when she tried to manipulate him into doing a miracle (John 2:4).

6. The Boldness of Jesus Christ

The crowd heard him gladly because of his authority and boldness (Mark 12:37). The temple police could not arrest him because 'no man spoke like this man' (John 7:46). When warned of the danger of King Herod he called him 'a fox' (Luke 13:32).

At least twice Jesus 'cleansed' the temple, making a whip of cords, driving out the money changers, stampeding their animals and overturning their tables. Thus he attacked the centre of the hypocritical Jewish worship (John 2:13-16, Matt. 21:12-13). When on trial for his life, he continued to be consistently bold, clear and unconcerned for own welfare. He made the 'good confession' confessing that he was the Christ before the high priest (Matt. 26:64) and Pilate (John 18:37, 1Tim. 6:13) while King Herod got the silence he deserved (Luke 23:9).

Let us analyze Jesus' boldness and define it more clearly

1. Jesus wasn't habitually loud (Is 42:2, Matt. 12:19) though he could shout (John 7:37). Jesus was neither introvert nor extrovert. Habits such as these are for insecure sinners like us, who like to have patterns of behaviour which we feel work or which make us feel comfortable. Rather Jesus varied his words according to the needs of the hearers whether it was to Nicodemus, other individual Pharisees, Pharisees as a group, or to his mother. These responses were perfectly modulated to fit the occasion, were always appropriate, given in love and yet all displayed boldness.

2. Jesus never balanced timidity and boldness. Timidity is a sin. When Jesus spoke quietly without criticism to his hearers it was never because of timidity. A spectrum with timidity at one end and boldness at the other might exist for us but never for Jesus. Jesus was perfect and therefore perfectly bold.

3. Jesus never balanced gentleness and boldness, he was always perfect in both.

4. Jesus never balanced boldness and wisdom because they are not opposed to each other. Often the rejoinder to 'Let's be bold' is 'Yes but we must also be wise'. But Jesus was both wise and bold as was Stephen later (Acts 6:8). In fact true wisdom is bold. Worldly wisdom keeps quiet until another time, true wisdom speaks the gospel boldly in season and out of season (2 Tim. 4:2). True wisdom makes the most of the time, and is urgent about the gospel (Col. 4:5-6).

The Source of Jesus' Boldness: a Speaking Ministry empowered by the Spirit

God was with Jesus from birth and while he was growing up (Luke 2:40). As a result he grew up in favour with God and man. During his visit to the temple (Luke 2:49) he showed early signs of his integrity of heart, zeal for God and clarity of speech that was to characterise him as the Christ. Jesus, having no sin, no fear of man or other moral imperfection and loving God perfectly, always spoke boldly and clearly.

Yet from his baptism when he was anointed by the Holy Spirit he received power for his ministry as the Christ. We are to understand that Jesus did not draw on his divine nature as Son of God to give him special knowledge or power but relied on the power of the Spirit. Peter in his speech to Cornelius makes it plain that Jesus' miracles were accomplished by the presence of God in the person of the Holy Spirit.

...how God anointed Jesus of Nazareth with the Holy Spirit and with power. He went about doing good and healing all who were oppressed by the devil, for God was with him. Acts 10:38

Luke in Chapter 4:14-19 of his gospel makes it plain that not just the miraculous signs but Jesus' speaking ministry also was empowered by the Holy Spirit.

After his baptism he was tempted by the devil in the wilderness

6. The Boldness of Jesus Christ

and then he returned to Galilee.

And Jesus returned in the power of the Spirit to Galilee, and a report about him went out through all the surrounding country. And he taught in their synagogues, being glorified by all. Luke 4:14-15

Jesus spoke in the power of the Spirit.

And he came to Nazareth, where he had been brought up. And as was his custom, he went to the synagogue on the Sabbath day, and he stood up to read.
And the scroll of the prophet Isaiah was given to him. He unrolled the scroll and found the place where it was written, "The Spirit of the Lord is upon me, because he has anointed me to proclaim good news to the poor. He has sent me to proclaim liberty to the captives and recovering of sight to the blind, to set at liberty those who are oppressed,
to proclaim the year of the Lord's favor." Luke 4:16-19

No doubt because of the fame surrounding him he is invited to preach in the synagogue. And he reads from Isaiah 61. In Matthew's account of this event the incredulity of the crowd included this question 'Where then did this man get all these things?" (Matt. 13:56). And there are two answers to that question.

The first answer to the people of Nazareth would go like this. "Jesus got all this because he paid attention when he attended and the scripture was read and expounded. He never day-dreamed unlike the rest of you. While you were dead bored with some scripture passage it came alive to him as he recalled other scriptures and saw the connection between them, and the plan of Almighty God opened up before him. You went to meet your friends and be seen by them but he met his heavenly Father in his word. And unlike you who rebelled when you heard uncomfortable truths, Jesus was like a sponge who absorbed it all and applied it to his own heart. And when the preacher erred and went off at a tangent to please the rest of you, the young Jesus saw clearly the error, the sin that caused it and no doubt often he came away indignant that the text had been mangled, while glorying in its real meaning and longing for the day when his call would came. So where did he get "all this"? The same place you could have got it too! The Word of God!"

Jesus was in the synagogue every Sabbath. It 'was his custom'. And when the scroll of Isaiah was handed to him he knew exactly where to read from. Look at the long slow emphasis on 'The Book' in this passage. (The Book was handed to him... he opened it... he found the place... he began to speak etc). Jesus was a student of the Book. He honoured it and loved it. Jesus was the perfect church member, bible student and disciple. That which he calls us to he has done himself. And that which we find so difficult he can give us grace to do because he has done it himself.

The second answer is that the Holy Spirit was upon him. The quote is from Isaiah 61, a clearly Messianic passage which prophesies that the Messiah's ministry will be the ministry of the Word. He will "proclaim good news ... proclaim liberty ... proclaim the year of the Lord's favor." So it was a ministry of proclamation. For this ministry Jesus did not draw on his divine nature as the Second Person of the Trinity, nor was his pure human nature sufficient for this task. Rather the Holy Spirit anointed him for this ministry. When Jesus preached the Holy Spirit shone his light into the pure mind of Jesus, enlivening the word in his memory, giving him the words to say and the expressions to use, and the boldness and endurance to continue this work against opposition.

We err if we think that ministry was easy for Jesus because he was the Son of God. He had to feed on the Word of God and trust the power of the Holy Spirit, just like you. (see Ware for

6. The Boldness of Jesus Christ

an excellent explanation of the ministry of Christ in relation to his humanity[16]).

And he rolled up the scroll and gave it back to the attendant and sat down. And the eyes of all in the synagogue were fixed on him. Luke 4:20

When Jesus preached there was an absolute silence. Some churches are noisy with everybody chatting, others are quiet because everybody is dozing or dreaming. But nobody was asleep or chatting when Jesus preached. Their eyes were fixed on him and they hung upon his every word.

And he began to say to them, "Today this Scripture has been fulfilled in your hearing."
And all spoke well of him and marveled at the gracious words that were coming from his mouth. And they said, "Is not this Joseph's son?" Luke 4:21-22

Thus Jesus claimed to be the Son of God, the Redeemer of mankind, sent by the Father and anointed by the Holy Spirit. But Jesus' Holy Spirit-inspired speech did not result in faith. They praised his speech but could not accept his message. To them he was just the boy they grew up with, the son of Joseph the carpenter. Unlike the devil in the wilderness who, earlier in this same chapter, knew him to be the Son of God and tried to tempt him from his role as a Spirit-filled Messiah, the congregation in Nazareth considered him as just a man who could not possibly be the Spirit-filled Messiah.

And he said to them, "Doubtless you will quote to me this proverb, 'Physician, heal yourself.' What we have heard you did at Capernaum, do here in your hometown as well."
And he said, "Truly, I say to you, no prophet is acceptable in his hometown. Luke 4:23-24

---

[16] Ware p17

Jesus with the spiritual perception which came from the Holy Spirit, saw their attitude. It was pride. Yes the Nazarenes were proud that young Jesus had done so well and belonged to them. Now they expected to be treated accordingly as ones who were specially privileged. So they said in their hearts 'Perform the miracles and healings that we have heard about'. There was no sense of need, and no submission to him. They could not think of him as the Messiah in terms of Isaiah 61. And their unbelief showed in their attempt to control him. And in their hearts they judged him as one of themselves. 'Familiarity breeds contempt' and no prophet is accepted as a prophet in his own town. Jesus states a spiritual principle true today. Unconverted people 'judge according to the flesh' (2 Cor. 5:16) and cannot see spiritual realities (1 Cor. 2:14). It is impossible for them to understand that a person they have known can be empowered by the Spirit and sent back by God to minister to them. When they meet an outsider who has spiritual gifts and spiritual authority it is different. They ascribe any attributes of the Spirit to nature and respect him as a naturally gifted and dynamic person. This is why on a human level, it is harder to minister to your unconverted family, and to close friends who knew you well than to anyone else. But in reality, whether your family despises you or strangers admire you, all ministry can only be accomplished by the Holy Spirit.

But in truth, I tell you, there were many widows in Israel in the days of Elijah, when the heavens were shut up three years and six months, and a great famine came over all the land,
and Elijah was sent to none of them but only to Zarephath, in the land of Sidon, to a woman who was a widow.
And there were many lepers in Israel in the time of the prophet Elisha, and none of them was cleansed, but only Naaman the Syrian." Luke 4:25-27

So Jesus saw that the people in Nazareth were proud. But Jesus did not accuse them of pride or warn them of the consequences of unbelief. That would have been good but what he did was more devastating, much bolder and exposed him to much great danger. With great boldness and wisdom that could not be argued against he demolished the basis for their pride by showing that it had always been God's plan to bypass the privileged and the entitled to go to the 'poor', as per God's programme in Isaiah 61. Thus he smashed their idol of national pride. He told how in Elijah and Elisha's day he revealed his salvation to a Gentile widow and Gentile leper and left the Israelites to continue in their unbelief. There was an implied warning here that God would leave the Nazarenes unless they swiftly let go of their idol, their national pride.

God protects Jesus

When they heard these things, all in the synagogue were filled with wrath.
And they rose up and drove him out of the town and brought him to the brow of the hill on which their town was built, so that they could throw him down the cliff.
But passing through their midst, he went away. Luke 4:28-30

The Nazarenes understood exactly what Jesus was saying, that is why they reacted with such fury. And they rejected their most famous son who adorned their backwater town with his grace and glory, all because their pride was injured. How foolish to throw away so much good when all they had to do was to humbly agree with God's word. Did people from Nazareth really have anything to be proud about? Only that Jesus was raised there! And that was enough to damn them.

And they tried to kill him. They were a microcosm of their compatriots in Jerusalem who crucified him, and of all future persecution. Christians are not usually persecuted because people do not understand the gospel but because they do understand at least some aspects of it which injure their pride. But the mob in Nazareth could not kill him. Somehow he passed through them unharmed. God protected him. Earlier in this chapter the devil quoted Ps 91 to tempt Jesus to abuse God's protection. Jesus refused. Later when Jesus was in ministry his Father in heaven protected him so that *he did not strike his foot against a stone*. This protection was consistently afforded Jesus until his time came (eg John 7:30).

So the elements we have seen concerning the presence of God with the prophets and Old Testament believers were true in Jesus' life too. God gave him the words to speak. God gave him boldness. And God gave him protection.

The significance for us

1. We should admire and adore Jesus and worship him. As the Son of God he had infinite power and knowledge but while he was on earth he chose to live as a human believer, a disciple and as an apostle. His great boldness was entirely supplied by his Father. He did not internally generate it by depending on his divine nature as Son of God. He had to pray and depend on God for it. He was so alone! So misunderstood! So unjustly hated! So cruelly treated without cause! And yet he never flinched, never gave up, never weakened in his resolution, never lost direction or compromised. He was consistently bold.

2. Let us not despise the regular study of God's word. Do you have daily personal devotions? A Quiet Time? Do you attend a mid-week bible study? Do you make an effort to attend a faithful bible-teaching church? Are you a man or woman who honours and loves The Book? This does not seem hard work and tedious to a real believer.

3. When Jesus ministered he depended on the power of the Holy Spirit and not on his divine nature as Son of God. He did not depend on himself. The mission to evangelise the world which he gave his apostles and which the church continues today is on the same basis. The mission is conducted in the

power of the Holy Spirit. We are not to depend on ourselves but he who gives the Spirit.

Jesus said to them again, "Peace be with you. As the Father has sent me, even so I am sending you." John 20:21

Let us pray with confidence for the Holy Spirit according to his own promise (Luke 11:13, 12:12)

4. Do you find confessing Christ before men impossibly hard? Do you find that you cannot say one intelligent thing about God to your friends? Do you find that you cannot articulate the love you have for Jesus? Is preparing a Sunday school talk or telling the gospel to a group of adults beyond you? Apply to Jesus the sympathetic Saviour. He has had to stand on the same level ground on which you now stand (minus your sin, which he forgives). Because he has gone through all these struggles and received help from his Father, he is perfectly qualified to give you the same help (Heb 2:18, 4:15-16).

7. Jesus teaches the Church

Jesus came to save the world. For that, most importantly, he had to die for sins, but secondly he had to prepare the twelve to be the foundation of his church, to be apostles and to evangelise of the world. What a task! Each disciple had a headful of wrong ideas. They were prejudiced and slow to believe. He had to train these men to be bold witnesses. How did he do this impossible task? In this chapter we will look at one of Jesus' signs and Jesus' teaching of the disciples as it relates to gospel boldness (we will look at John 4 in Chapter 8).

The sign of the dumb speaking

Looking ahead to the Day of Pentecost, the disciples were filled with the Holy Spirit. Three signs accompany his coming; the sound of a mighty rushing wind, tongues as of fire upon each of them and speaking in other languages. But the most important sign was that the disciples were no longer dumb. Of course before they were not physically dumb. They could argue with each other about who was the greatest etc and Peter especially had a healthy tongue and vocal cords. He was always speaking! But the disciples were spiritually dumb. They could not praise God. Not in public anyway. They could not be witnesses. Until the day of Pentecost they were locked in the upper room for fear of the Jews. But when the Holy Spirit came upon them they praise God, publicly and loudly. This great change was the culmination of 3 years of Jesus' ministry to them, intercession for them and was enabled by the Holy Spirit. This was what the Messiah died for! A boldly witnessing church!

Jesus did many healing miracles. What do you think was the greatest? Probably the raising of Lazarus or the widow of Nain's son or the giving of sight to the man born blind. We answer thus because we measure the greatness of miracles by medical science. And truly these miracles show the great creative power that only God has. But in the Gospels the miracles are termed signs and are not just miracles of power but signify an aspect of the Messiah's salvation. For example the sign of giving sight to the blind signifies that Jesus is the Light of the World (John 9), and the raising of the dead signifies that the Messiah will raise the dead (John 11) and therefore that Jesus is the Christ.

So perhaps we should measure the importance of a miraculous sign not by medical science alone but by what it signifies. Now the Old Testament prophets looked forward to a Messianic age when the nations of the world would praise and sing with joy to the Lord (Ps 107:1-3, 138:4, 148:13, Is 35:5-6, 43:20-21, 51:3). And so they spoke of the Messianic sign of the dumb speaking. For example we have a beautiful prophecy such as,

then shall the lame man leap like a deer, and the tongue of the mute sing for joy.
For waters break forth in the wilderness, and streams in the desert; Is. 35:6

It was because of such messianic expectations that the Galilean crowd were amazed by Jesus healing a mute man and said *"Can this be the Son of David" Matt. 12:22-23.*

I do not want to make too much of this but it seems to me that healings of the dumb (or the driving out of a demon causing dumbness) attracted more than the usual amazement (compare Matt 9:33, 12:22-23, Mark 7:31-37, Luke 9:43, 11:14). Why the particular amazement of the crowd in these instances? It seems disproportionate. Greater miracles of power have been recorded and in fact healing from muteness may not require any physical change in the human body at all. Perhaps rather it was the messianic significance of this sign which caused such a reaction from the crowd as well as the words of praise to God that the healed man said, or shouted or sang afterwards.

Note too the importance given to such a sign in Matt. 15:30-31.

*And great crowds came to him, bringing with them the lame,
the blind, the crippled, the mute, and many others, and they put
them at his feet, and he healed them,
so that the crowd wondered, when they saw the mute speaking,
the crippled healthy, the lame walking, and the blind seeing.
And they glorified the God of Israel.*

The crowd bring many sick to Jesus among them those who are mute (v30) but when they wonder at the healings the first sign mentioned is the dumb speaking (v31).

Note too that that the most vicious attack of all from the Pharisees, when they called Jesus possessed by Beelzebub, prince of demons, was occasioned by Jesus healing a mute man (Matt. 12:22-24, Luke 11:13-15). Presumably because *they* understood its significance.

The Evangelists were preachers to young Christians in the early church and were concerned to teach the true significance of these miraculous signs. When dumb sinners praise God to the world then the kingdom of God has come with power! We Christians are no longer spiritually dead, blind, deaf or lame but we are remarkably dumb. It is true that the Christian church is a living church. We are alive to God. We pray to him and seek him. We love him and hope only in him and are dead to sin and the world. We are truly no longer deaf. We have heard the voice of the Son of God and we have repented and believed and follow him as our shepherd. And when we read and hear the Bible we recognise it for what it is; the Word of God. It is true too that we have spiritual eyesight. We see with the eye of faith the glory of Jesus and understand and glory in substitutionary atonement, justification by faith and the mediation of our Saviour. All these things are true but we are still tongue-tied when it comes to articulating our faith. We can speak loudly about football, natter away endlessly about new recipes, make small talk about the weather or complain eloquently about the bad habits of our neighbours but when it comes to telling the Gospel to the lost we are as silent as if we were dumb. Can the Gospel stories help us? Yes they can.

The very first sign in the Gospels is the striking dumb of Zachariah (Luke 1:21) and his subsequent healing (1:63). He did not believe the words of the angel Gabriel concerning the birth of his son John the Baptist and was struck dumb as a result. He remained dumb and only recovered his speech by being obedient in faith when he wrote on a tablet "His name is John". So we learn that faith and speech are connected. We can only speak for God when we believe his word. So then perhaps we are not as spiritually alive, and seeing and hearing as we flatter ourselves. If we believed as we should then we would speak as we should. But if our faith is dormant so will our tongues be.

So what should we do? We should pray! When Jesus and Peter, James and John descended from the Mount of Transfiguration they found a crowd gathered around the rest of the disciples (Mark 9:14-29). The problem is a demon-possessed boy and his anxious father, and the disciples are totally powerless to drive out this demon. The demon in question is a "deaf and dumb" demon (9:25). The word is *chothos* and can mean either deaf or dumb but the meaning here is dumb, as 9:17 makes clear. Jesus says "This kind cannot be driven out by anything but prayer." (v29). Two things are immediately noteworthy in this saying. Firstly this dreadful spirit which caused the disciples so much grief can only be driven out by prayer. And secondly Jesus tells the disciples that they will meet this "kind of" demon again. It seems there are many like this. And the only recourse is prayer.

So what have we learned from the sign of the dumb speaking?

1. A bold witnessing church is the particular result and crowning glory of Christ's work. 2. It requires a miracle of healing grace for sinners to praise God. 3. Bold witness comes from faith. 4. We need to pray for gospel boldness.

The Duty of Evangelism

If the aim of the Messiah was to build a boldly witnessing church then we would expect Jesus' instruction of his disciples to reflect this. The gospels are filled with teaching about evangelism. In Matthew 10 Jesus chose 12 apostles and sent them out as evangelists. He gave them many instructions. Some are timeless and can be applied directly to the present day. Some of these are specific for the time and place but nevertheless teach principles that are timeless. And subsequently on later occasions like any good teacher Jesus repeated these instructions and built on previous teaching he had given them. Some things Jesus expected the apostles to remember (see for example Luke 22:35). Other things the gospel writers leave to be understood by us. For example when Luke describes the mission of the 12 he says that Jesus "gave them power and authority over all demons and to cure diseases, and he sent them out to proclaim the kingdom of God and to heal" (Luke 9:1-2), but when he describes the mission of 72, he leaves it to be understood that exorcism was included in their commission (as Luke 10:17 makes clear). And so the Gospels' teaching on evangelism is cumulative in the sense that previous teaching informs later teaching. So for example we should understand the Great Commission (Matt 28:18-20) in the light of the commission of the 12 (Matt 10), the commission of the seventy-two (Luke 10:1-17), the prophecy about the end times (Mark 13) and the work of the Holy Spirit (John 14-16) etc. This is just good exegesis but it is worth repeating because today nothing suffers from pragmatism so much as evangelism. Does Jesus send us into the world to evangelise? And if so what is it? What are the priorities? What does Jesus teach? So in this section we will look at the commission of the 12 in Matthew 10 but refer forward to subsequent teaching of Jesus as well.

1. The main Work is Proclamation
And proclaim as you go, saying, 'The kingdom of heaven is at hand.'
Heal the sick, raise the dead, cleanse lepers, cast out demons. Matt 10:7-8

Jesus' own example was to prioritize the preaching of the gospel (Mark 1:15, 38). The kingdom of heaven refers to the rule and authority of God. This is God's world. The gospel is God's message. People are rebels against God and repentance is urgent. And the signs that Jesus performed signify the healing effects of believing the gospel. The gospel proclaims freedom from sin and its consequences. It is common today to argue from this text and others like it that the work of the church is two-fold, preaching the gospel and doing works of mercy. And in addition we are told that works of mercy are to be done first so that we have the 'right' to preach the gospel afterwards. But is it not more accurate to say that healing of body, mind, society (and yes even the environment) follow the preaching of the gospel, rather than prepare people to receive it as is commonly argued today? Putting the gospel second always leads to loss of boldness and is not the leading of the Spirit. It is also a waste of precious time.

2. Avoid Acquisitiveness
You received without paying; give without pay. Acquire no gold nor silver nor copper for your belts,
no bag for your journey, nor two tunics nor sandals nor a staff, for the laborer deserves his food. Matt 10:8b-10

Jesus gives succinct clear commands concerning possessions. The apostles and the apostolic church should always have an attitude of giving and eschew the love of money. Grace in hospitality, generosity with money, effort and time befit those who have been forgiven much. We are just passing on the grace we have received. Think of our Lord dying for our sins. Think of those who told us the gospel: the sacrifices they made and the time they spent and the prayers they said for us. We are not being generous when we do relief work, or diaconal work or pastoral work, we are just passing on grace. And if people praise us we should vehemently confess that we are sinners in need of a Saviour, just like them. How often Christian workers disobey this command! We serve and we give and inwardly creeps a feeling of self-righteousness, and after a time this turns into self-pity, which if we are not careful turns into self-serving and corruption. Throughout church history leaders have served themselves rather than the Lord. Let us rather remember the love of the Lord who bought us and avoid acquisitiveness.

3. Be Singleminded
And whatever town or village you enter, find out who is worthy in it and stay there until you depart.
As you enter the house, greet it.
And if the house is worthy, let your peace come upon it, but if it is not worthy, let your peace return to you. Matt 10:11-13

Our human relationships too must been determined by gospel priorities rather than our own advantage. Who is a worthy person? Someone who believes the gospel and supports the Lord's work with zeal according to knowledge. Thank God for them! The evangelistic and mission-minded Christian is the best kind of person: as friend, as marriage partner, or as a co-worker! Jesus had Mary and Martha. Peter had his mother-in-law. Paul had Priscilla and Aquila.

Jesus tells the twelve not to upgrade if they find another home offers a better breakfast or room. Value a person by their gospel character rather than what they can give you!

4. You are sent
And if anyone will not receive you or listen to your words, shake off the dust from your feet when you leave that house or town.
Truly, I say to you, it will be more bearable on the day of judgment for the land of Sodom and Gomorrah than for that town. Matt 10:14-15

The purpose of Jesus' words here is to impress on the disciples their great responsibility. They have been sent with an urgent message of life or death. They were sent by Jesus himself who had received all authority in heaven and earth (Matt 28:18). The apostles were not just to have a sense of urgency but to warn to unbelievers that they face judgement if they reject the gospel and its messengers. Do you think that Sodom and Gomorrah have already been judged when God destroyed those proverbially wicked cities by fire from heaven? No, that was just how they died. Their real judgement is still to come! It will be terrible. But it will be worse for the towns of Jesus' day who heard the apostles' preaching and saw the miraculous signs. If the degree of judgement depends on the goodness of the message that is rejected, what about people today who reject the cross, the love of God, the promises, the bible stories, miracles of Jesus, and eternal life. So keep the day of judgment before you. And keep it before those you are trying to reach!

5. Be wise and innocent
"Behold, I am sending you out as sheep in the midst of wolves, so be wise as serpents and innocent as doves. Matt 10:16

Picture in your mind a sheep. It is weak and defenseless and yet steadily walking toward a pack of wolves. The wolves are ravenous and rapacious and think only of satisfying their greed. What are you doing little sheep? Are you blind or stupid? Why are you going into such danger? No! He is obeying his Shepherd. He has faith in his Shepherd. He may be weak and defenceless, but he is sent.

The unconverted are compared to wolves. They have no mercy or love, think only of their own appetites, and are dangerous. The amazing aim of the gospel is to make wolves into sheep by sending sheep.

But the foolishness of many of us is that we do not recognise the true nature of the unconverted. They are wolves, not sheep who have not yet realised it. So Jesus counsels us to be as wise as serpents. Be aware of your circumstances, your danger, and remember you are among wolves. Pray for strength to be bold and faithful. Pray for guidance and protection.
'Innocent as doves' means not responding to your danger with harmful or worldly self-defense mechanisms (eg lying, gossiping, manipulation etc) but with trust in God.

Jesus tells his Church to be wise. True wisdom is to fear God and tell the gospel. It is worldly wisdom to 'wait for a better time' or say ' it is not time to tell the gospel'. Calvin says about such worldly wisdom,
"Take note, they are wiser than God, who, speaking by St. Paul, tells us that Jesus Christ must be preached as is fitting, and men must not proceed to bury him any more, for seeing he is risen in glory, he will have the sound of his gospel ring out loud and clear, without any dissimulation, as I said before. "[17]
Christ is now risen and those of you who are timid about proclaiming him, act like he is still buried, says Calvin.

6. Be prepared for persecution
Beware of men, for they will deliver you over to courts and flog you in their synagogues,
and you will be dragged before governors and kings for my sake, to bear witness before them and the Gentiles. Matt 10:17-18

---

[17] Calvin, p695, sermon on Ephesians 6:19-24

The connection with verse 16 is clear. Why 'Beware of men?' Because they are wolves. We are very stupid sheep if we expect wolves to love us. Jesus looks right forward to the time of Acts and beyond, and warns that a boldly witnessing church will be persecuted. Jesus expands on this in his farewell address to the apostles in John 15:18-16:3. However there is not much chance of the church of today being persecuted. We are too quiet. We give up at the slightest growl from a 'wolf'. How we need to cry for boldness!

7. Do not be anxious, rather trust the Spirit
When they deliver you over, do not be anxious how you are to speak or what you are to say, for what you are to say will be given to you in that hour.
For it is not you who speak, but the Spirit of your Father speaking through you. Matt 10 :19-20

The situation is still persecution. Jesus foresees the disciples in a hostile persecuting court-room. They have been 'delivered over', showing their helplessness before powerful persecutors. Their fate hangs on the defence they give. One mistake could result in a death sentence! How often this has been repeated in history as governments have taken the lead in persecuting the church! Who would not fear and panic? Yet Jesus says, 'Don't be anxious'. Specifically, do not be anxious about how you speak (in a clever, worldly-wise way) or about your words (a carefully prepared, legally water-tight defence). Jesus wants believers who are even on trial for their lives to be more concerned with evangelism than survival. But if you are anxious about these things then you are still concerned about saving your life instead of prosecuting the mission Jesus has sent you on. Why not be anxious? Jesus says that the Holy Spirit will give them the words to say. For the apostles these words may have included direct revelation but for believers today 'these words' from the Holy Spirit will be the written word of God. Either way, for the apostles or for us today it is the gospel of Jesus.

When will these words be given? 'In that hour', and not before. This help will be given at the time of need. So dependence and trust is needed.
What is exactly promised? The Spirit of your Father speaking through you. This is an amazing Trinitarian promise. And there is no reason to limit this to the apostles. An apostle, and a present-day believer in the apostolic gospel may speak the same spiritual words.

So control yourself. And do not panic. Realise that this evil thing that has happened to you is a 'time for you to bear witness' (see below). Do not depend on your words. Speak what you know of the Bible, with love to Christ, with zeal for the salvation of your hearers and with boldness. Hold nothing back. And that is the Spirit of your Father speaking through you.

Two similar passages
Luke 21:12-15 *But before all this they will lay their hands on you and persecute you, delivering you up to the synagogues and prisons, and you will be brought before kings and governors for my name's sake.*
This will be your opportunity to bear witness.
Settle it therefore in your minds not to meditate beforehand how to answer,
for I will give you a mouth and wisdom, which none of your adversaries will be able to withstand or contradict.
Jesus emphasises the same elements: the disciples being delivered up, government persecution, and the promise of divine help to speak. Jesus makes it more explicit that this is 'an opportunity to bear witness'. If this most extreme form of persecution is 'an opportunity to bear witness' then surely Jesus expects us to use all of life's situations as opportunities for evangelism. How far are we all from this attitude!
John 15:20- 16:11

Jesus amplifies the Promise of the Holy Spirit's help in his last supper address in John 14-16. The Holy Spirit will be the power the apostles' need to be Christ's witnesses to the world. In 15:20-25 he warns the apostles of persecution for the sake of the gospel. In 15:26 he promises the Helper "whom I will send to you from the Father, the Spirit of truth, who proceeds from the Father, he will bear witness about me." Then in 15:27 he says the apostles will also bear witness to Jesus. So Jesus envisages a dual witness: the Holy Spirit bearing witness through the apostles.

In John 16:8-11 Jesus describes the results of this witness of the Holy Spirit: he will convict the world of sin, righteousness and judgement. This work of conviction is not independent of the apostles' preaching, as if the Holy Spirit goes off on his own to convert people. Given the context it is through the apostles bearing witness to the world that the world is convinced of the truth of the gospel. And to "convict the world of sin, righteousness and judgement" bold witness is required, because these are unpopular truths. Bold witness and the convicting work of the Holy Spirit must always go together. We see an example of this in Paul in Acts 24:25 *And as he reasoned about righteousness and self-control and the coming judgment, Felix was alarmed and said, "Go away for the present. When I get an opportunity I will summon you."*

But today the church avoids these 3 subjects, sin, righteousness and judgement like the plague. Can we really expect that Holy Spirit will do his work if we timidly disobey the truths he has on his heart?

8. Opposition even from Family
Brother will deliver brother over to death, and the father his child, and children will rise against parents and have them put to death, Matt 10:21

It is amazing that opposition should arise from one's own nuclear family. Why is this so common? Relationships within the family are so close, and often they feel they own us and that we should be loyal to no one else but them. So when we love Jesus more, they feel jealousy. Yes, people become jealous of God. This is very common. Of course your family members will not say 'We are jealous of God' but rather 'you are spending too much time at church', 'you are ungrateful to give up the religion of your parents' etc. This jealousy can turn into anger and rage leading to persecution to death. Even family members are 'wolves'.

But there is comfort in these realistic words of Jesus. He has told you beforehand to expect persecution not just from governments but even from your close family, so do not be surprised or stumble when it happens. Also Jesus himself experienced rejection by his own brothers who did not believe in him, so he can give you 'help in time of need'(Heb 4:16).

9. Endurance
and you will be hated by all for my name's sake. But the one who endures to the end will be saved.
When they persecute you in one town, flee to the next, for truly, I say to you, you will not have gone through all the towns of Israel before the Son of Man comes. Matt 10:22-23

We must endure. It is because we are hated for Jesus' sake that we must endure. Opposition and persecution will never stop until the end of the world. It will always be with us. Jesus says that it is OK to move to avoid persecution but it is never OK to stop evangelising. What does he mean by 'you will not have gone through all the towns of Israel before the Son of Man comes'? Any town where there are true Israelites is a town of Israel. Sendai, Japan where I live and work is a town of Israel. This is not an unnatural interpretation. The uniform teaching of the whole New Testament is that a true Israelite is a Christian (Rom. 2:29, 9:6-8). So wherever God's people may be found is a town of Israel.

But the important thing in this text is that, You MUST endure to the end to be saved. This shows that without Christ you cannot be saved. You must believe in Christ until the end. And also enduring in the faith is to keep confessing him even though you are threatened.

"A disciple is not above his teacher, nor a servant above his master.
It is enough for the disciple to be like his teacher, and the servant like his master. If they have called the master of the house Beelzebul, how much more will they malign those of his household. Matt 10:24-25

Our master is Christ and he was hated and abused. They called him Satan. Has anyone called you too busy? Strange? Overzealous? Crazy? Satan? These labels are embryonic persecution. For if the world can label someone as crazy or strange or satanic then it becomes acceptable to persecute and kill them. In fact it is viewed as a righteous necessity. Does anyone like the devil? So the inevitable precursor to persecution is evil speech.

There is also comfort in this warning. Jesus has told us beforehand so when it happens we will not stumble but remember his words and be strengthened instead.

10. Fear of Man
"So have no fear of them, for nothing is covered that will not be revealed, or hidden that will not be known.
What I tell you in the dark, say in the light, and what you hear whispered, proclaim on the housetops. Matt 10:26-27

Jesus is speaking of the day of judgement. All people will be judged, and this universal judgement means that man must not be feared. Everyone's secrets, their gossip, their thinking, their true motives will be revealed. We need to wear these glasses that Jesus provides for us. Then those big, strong, rich, confident people of whom we are naturally afraid will shrink and appear less terrifying when these are applied.

I was serving in a small church in Mitchell's Plain on the Cape Flats in South Africa, when one Sunday Peter came to the service. He had just been let out of prison. He had been stealing cars since he was 15, and he was now 35 and had been in and out of prison for most of that time. And he told us his story. Early on he had joined one of the notorious prison gangs, and had endured much from them. During his latest stint he had decided that he would leave the gang. The penalty for leaving a gang was death but he had decided that he could not stand the abuse any more. One day when he was alone they came for him. Gang members, knives in hand, came to attack him. Peter sat down, closed his eyes and prayed the Lord's Prayer over and over again. After a while he opened his eyes and they had gone. Afterwards they came up to him and 'we came to kill you but something stopped us'. Realising that God had protected him, Peter then and there praised God, repented, and came to faith in Christ. From then on he did his best to evangelise his fellow-prisoners, becoming known as 'The Pastor'. He also lost his fear of man. He said that before he was converted other people seemed so big and tall, and afterward they all seemed so small. This is to see the world through Jesus' eyes.

Because of the universal day of judgement, all sins will be revealed and men judged, so Jesus is training his disciples to lift their eyes off people to God.

And do not fear those who kill the body but cannot kill the soul. Rather fear him who can destroy both soul and body in hell.
Are not two sparrows sold for a penny? And not one of them will fall to the ground apart from your Father.
But even the hairs of your head are all numbered.
Fear not, therefore; you are of more value than many

sparrows. Matt 10:28-31

Another reason to fear God rather than man is that God is infinitely more frightening than man. The knowledge of the existence of hell adds ballast to the Christian's worldview making him stable and is a corrective for a host of sins especially the fear of man. God is infinitely more scarey than man but <u>infinitely more loving.</u> He is our loving heavenly Father who has forgiven all our sins and who cares for us. He cares for the sparrows and the hairs on our head. Who cares for us to the extent of numbering our hairs?! This argument from less to greater means that God cares for you more than you do yourself. The personal, detailed, and faithful care of God should make us bold and cheerful in the face of persecution. 'Fear not', says Jesus. In life and death you are surrounded by God's love.

Jesus taught the disciples not to be overly concerned at the necessary offence caused to proud hearts by the gospel.

Then the disciples came and said to him, "Do you know that the Pharisees were offended when they heard this saying?" He answered, "Every plant that my heavenly Father has not planted will be rooted up". Matt. 15:12-13

In effect Jesus says 'Too bad, can't be helped'. Why? 'They and their whole system will be destroyed on the Day of Judgement if not before.'

11. So keep confessing Jesus
*So everyone who acknowledges me before men, I also will acknowledge before my Father who is in heaven,
but whoever denies me before men, I also will deny before my Father who is in heaven. Matt 10:32-33*

From the context this acknowledgement of Jesus means a public recognition and confession before hostile men. We cannot be silent: the endurance of v22 is a public and verbal confession of faith. There is a double confession; one on earth and one in heaven. The confession of Christ by his people on earth is reciprocated by Christ in heaven before his Father. For those who confess Christ on earth will be acknowledged in heaven. I believe that it is unwarranted to limit this is to only future judgement, but believe it refers to the present advocacy of Christ on behalf of his church. Here we have Christ pleading before his Father on behalf of his small persecuted but boldly witnessing church! What a great privilege to be recognised (confessed) by Jesus before his Father! This is glory: to have Jesus praise you before his Father. Even today when the Christian confesses "I believe in Jesus": Christ stands before his Father and confesses "This one is part of my body! Give him grace!" Viewed from this perspective the fear of man is a very small thing indeed.

12. Not Peace but a Sword
"Do not think that I have come to bring peace to the earth. I have not come to bring peace, but a sword.
For I have come to set a man against his father, and a daughter against her mother, and a daughter-in-law against her mother-in-law.
And a person's enemies will be those of his own household.
Matt 10:34-36

The Jews thought that the Messiah would restore Israel to prominence and national glory and that for them, at any rate, peace would reign on earth. But the peace the Messiah brings is first of all peace with God, and then peace of heart and mind and then peace with others who are brought to the same salvation. And so by these words Jesus is bomb-proofing his disciples and his church for continual opposition on earth. Yet today we expect everything to go our way. Somehow we feel it is our right to have an easy life, success, and most of all for everybody to love us. Jesus has been preparing his disciples for the opposite. The unconverted are wolves (v16), so beware of them (v17) for they even betray their own families (v21). The new element in this saying is that this hostility is actively brought about by Jesus. We must not be surprised at this. God promised a war between good and evil. The first gospel promise is Gen 3:15 when God said to the devil, "I will put enmity between you and the woman, and between your offspring and her offspring…" and now Jesus fulfils that promise of a division between God's people and the devil's. That is why even your own family will oppose you. It is the 'sword' brought to earth by Jesus to refine and extend his church.

13. Jesus as Number 1
Whoever loves father or mother more than me is not worthy of me, and whoever loves son or daughter more than me is not worthy of me.
And whoever does not take his cross and follow me is not worthy of me.
Whoever finds his life will lose it, and whoever loses his life for my sake will find it. Matt 10:37-39

Jesus tells his disciples to love him more than their closest natural tie ie their families. Intense, sincere and genuine love for Jesus is the only power that will enable the disciples to overcome persecution and to continue to boldly evangelise the world. It is impossible to over-emphasise the importance of love for Jesus. This is why he says it so strongly here and even more emphatically in Luke 14:26. There is no other engine that will drive world evangelisation, not money, human energy, cooperation, or evangelistic programmes. Without love for Jesus these other things are just empty shells.

It is worth drawing out the distinction that is evident in Jesus' words: love for our families is to be distinguished from love for him. Perhaps a misunderstanding sometimes creeps in amongst us. We think that we are quite good Christians because we love our families. But family love is not particularly Christian. Drug lords and Mafia bosses love their families! If I love my children I am actually loving myself, and if I love my parents that is an entirely natural affection and not a sign of Christian grace at all.

The themes here in Matt 10 such as the importance of the preaching of the gospel, divine assistance in speech, intense, violent persecution etc are repeated in Mark 13. Jesus speaks about the siege of Jerusalem and the end of the world. There is a small controversy about how much applies to each scenario [18], but in practice it makes little difference because the mission of the church is the same. And the whole prophecy in Mark 13 is sandwiched between the stories of two women: there is the widow in temple (Mark 12:41-44) and the woman with nard (14:3-9). The similarities between these women are too great to be coincidental: 1. Both are women. 2. One gave something very small (2 lepta), other something very expensive (worth a year's wages). But both give sacrificially. 3. Both act from love to do something which from our perspective seems an unwise extravagant sacrifice but to them seemed quite reasonable. 4. Both ignore the opinions of those around. 5. Worldly people ignore one and criticise the other 6. Both are commended by Jesus. 7. Both stories make us uncomfortable. Surely these women symbolise a Church which loves Jesus and serves him with joy. This love is the only attitude with which to cope with the pressures and opportunities of Mark 13, and mission of Matt 10, or the Great Commission. Loving Jesus is the root of all evangelistic or missionary endeavor, and the only soil in which gospel boldness will grow. Anything less is 'not worthy' of Jesus.

The next verse (v38) also ends in 'is not worthy of me'. To Jesus the cross meant death. So the disciples' cross is his path as a disciple. The Christian life is way of the cross. But notice the motive for this life is given in the previous verse. It is

---

[18] Storms

7. Jesus teaches the Church

"Love to Christ" which will be visible as the disciple chooses the cause of Christ more than his family ties and more than his comfort and safety.

14. Rewards for disciples
"Whoever receives you receives me, and whoever receives me receives him who sent me.
The one who receives a prophet because he is a prophet will receive a prophet's reward, and the one who receives a righteous person because he is a righteous person will receive a righteous person's reward.
And whoever gives one of these little ones even a cup of cold water because he is a disciple, truly, I say to you, he will by no means lose his reward." Matt 10:40-42

In these 3 verses there are four little chains. In each God rewards those who welcome or help disciples. Again the motive is love to Christ. The main point is clear. God is the ally of all who receive Christ's servants. Christ is a friend to all their friends. And he is a rewarder of all who serve from true motives. So in these short verses Jesus is comforting and encouraging the disciples with the stupendous assurance that all of God's providence in the world of men is aligned to assist them.

8. The Worshipping Witness - The Samaritan Woman

"Come, see a man who told me all that I ever did. Can this be the Christ?" John 4:29
Please read John 4:27-42

The climactic verse of this passage is the final one,
They said to the woman, "It is no longer because of what you said that we believe, for we have heard for ourselves, and we know that this is indeed the Saviour of the world." John 4:42

This confession that Jesus is the Saviour of the world and not just a Jewish Christ must rank as one of the greatest confessions of all time, of the same order as Peter's confession in Matt 16:16. Not just Jews but Samaritans also (and therefore all peoples of the world) may be saved through Jesus Christ. It is not just the conclusion of John 4 but also of Ch 3 as well. Then Jesus told the Jewish leader Nicodemus (one of the most educated, cultured, decent and religious men in Judah), that he is an unbeliever and he needed to start over, be born again and believe in him for salvation. This spiritual new birth is the only way into the kingdom, for God so loved the world...

And so the stories of the educated Jew and the immoral woman of Samaria both converge to the same conclusion; there is only one saviour for the entire world. Yet within this story in ch 4 Jesus is also teaching his disciples about how they should go about world evangelism. They needed to start think correctly. Nationalistic Jews who despise all gentiles, selfish men who only think about the next meal, or proud men who claim credit for the work done by others are hardly fit to evangelise the world.

8. The Worshipping Witness - The Samaritan Woman

First Step: Deal with your prejudices

Just then his disciples came back. They marveled that he was talking with a woman, but no one said, "What do you seek?" or, "Why are you talking with her?" John 4:27

Jesus and his disciples had arrived outside the Samaritan town of Sychar (v5). Jesus stayed by the well while the disciples went to shop for bread (v7-8). A lone Samaritan woman who comes to draw water meets Jesus and has the most amazing conversation with him. He showed that he knew all about her moral failure (v18) and yet he continued to teach her about eternal life. He said that while the Jews were entrusted with the word of God, God seeks worshippers who worship him in Spirit and in truth (v20-24). She perceived he was a prophet (v19) but Jesus clearly told her that he was the Christ (v26).

At the end of this short conversation the disciples returned. But God in his mercy kept their mouths firmly shut so that they said nothing either to her ("Go away") or to Jesus ("Why are you talking to this worthless person?"). In this way God prevented them from quenching a smoldering wick. They did not yet have Jesus' attitude because they had not yet understood the gospel. It is always a blessing when Christians do not complain, judge, criticise or mind other people's business. When we have prejudice and pride etc our hearts it is better to be silent. Better yet is to ask God to deal with our bad attitudes. Do you secretly feel some people are more valuable than others? Do take you a dislike to others and become judges with evil thoughts (James 2:4)? Despising the poor, the ugly, the unemployed, the old etc will vitiate your evangelism. 'Lord, help me not to put people off or let down the Cause' is a biblical prayer (Ps 69:6) and is the first step to an evangelistic mind. And learning to shut up instead of expressing your opinion is an essential step to gospel boldness.

From worship to boldness

So the woman left her water jar and went away into town and said to the people

"Come, see a man who told me all that I ever did. Can this be the Christ?"
They went out of the town and were coming to him. John 4:28-29

Notice her boldness. She who had come to draw water at midday to avoid contact with others because of her shame started speaking clearly and openly. Gone was the downcast look, and the inability to look one in the eye and the mumbled words. She was not shy, embarrassed, or timid any longer. She told all. She was bolder than Nicodemus. But where did this boldness come from and how did it arise in her heart? She was bold because she was excited by Jesus. The short conversation with him had thrilled her with hope. And although she knew so little she was absorbed and intrigued by Jesus himself, his teaching and his attitude. In short she had become a spiritual worshipper of the Son of God and v23 had been fulfilled in her. Your purpose in life is to be rescued! And when you are you will worship! Because she was bold she was credible. She had a bad reputation and was doubtless despised and unpopular but her zeal, boldness and the impact of a changed life made her impossible to ignore. A long time ago the disciples had also worshipped Jesus and invited others to him, (John 1:41,45), but that zeal had worn off. As future apostles they needed to recover this worship and maintain it. "The Father is seeking such people to worship him." The Apostle John surely recorded all this for our learning, that we might be bold witnesses like this woman.

Nothing has changed since those times. If we really love Jesus, are excited about him and are joyful because we are assured of our salvation we will be bold, credible and more effective. Conversely a lukewarm Christian is hard to believe. There is no other path to gospel boldness than heart worship of our Lord Jesus Christ and rejoicing in Him.

This chapter started with Jesus asking the Samaritan woman

8. The Worshipping Witness - The Samaritan Woman

for a drink. You could say that Jesus' thirst brought salvation to Samaria. Perhaps this foreshadows the fact that his suffering brings salvation to the whole world! 'I thirst'. Worship him for his sacrificial death for you and sing his praises among the nations!

Lloyd-Jones in his classic book *Spiritual Depression* says that the main reason why people are put off becoming Christians is that our despondency makes us weak and bad representatives of the gospel. Why on earth would anyone want to become like us?![19] Like the Samaritan woman who only became bold when she became joyful, joy in the gospel is our key need. How can we be joyful, bold witnesses if we are so gloomy and miserable? So then the greatest enemy to gospel boldness is not so much our natural timidity but inability to worship and our spiritual depression.

I suggest to you that the evidence of this spiritual depression is our lack of gospel boldness. The joy of the Lord is a believer's strength (Neh. 8:10). From the point of view of the joyful angels in heaven we are probably all marginally depressed but have just stoically got used to it and plod along to heaven with a gloomy countenance. Fight depression with all your might. I know there are many causes for depression and I have no wish at all to add to the burden of those who through no fault of their own have fallen into depression. But do not submit to it. Fight the onset of depression with all your might. Force yourself to praise and discipline yourself to sing (Eph 5:18-20).

I am not prone to depression but have experienced it. From time to time I feel like a dark pit has opened up beneath me and I have to fight not to fall in. 11 days after the tsunami in NE Japan, the hard work, the difficulty of living with the cold, no

---

[19] p12 in David Martyn Lloyd-Jones 1964, Spiritual Depression: Its Causes and Cure William B. Eerdmans Publishing Company pp300

electricity or running water, and constant ministry had taken their toll on Glenda and me. We were both tired and the adrenalin had worn off. The petrol gauge of our car (which I used to give lifts to tsunami victims) was creeping toward empty and our mission leaders 300 km away in Tokyo showed no sign of sending the practical help we needed. So when I got in the car that morning I just felt down and dejected. But I knew I couldn't minister in that state and forced myself to sing. I could only think of 'Guide me O thou great Redeemer'. Soon I was bellowing it out over the steering wheel and tears were streaming down my face. Your situation is different. But if you feel depression creeping over you, fight it, and if you must go down, go down worshipping. Know that if you allow the black cozy blanket of despair to wrap itself around you it will greatly weaken your ministry. (Later that day some young men in a truck swung by and said 'we are from a church in Chiba - we have brought you some gasoline!' God had sent his angels to help!).

Jesus teaches the disciples about zeal
Jesus corrected the disciples' lukewarmness by pointing to his own heart's desire which they must make their own.

Meanwhile the disciples were urging him, saying, "Rabbi, eat." But he said to them, "I have food to eat that you do not know about."
So the disciples said to one another, "Has anyone brought him something to eat?"
Jesus said to them, "My food is to do the will of him who sent me and to accomplish his work. John 4:31-34

Jesus was not just tired and thirsty (v6-7) he was hungry, that was why the disciples had gone to buy bread. But Jesus told the disciples his real hunger was not for food, but to do God's will. What gives you strength, satisfaction, joy and comfort? A good meal! Now what has the same effect on our Saviour? Speaking to this woman and seeing the change in her had evidently given him great satisfaction and joy. Jesus was zealous to do his Father's work! And not just to start it but to accomplish it. Here Jesus was referring to the cross. It is an amazing insight into the zeal of our Saviour. See also Luke 12:50. We should worship him for this! If we really worship him then we will want to have the same heart's desire as him.

Calvin has an interesting comment on this section, *"The earnestness and promptitude of the woman are so much the more worthy of attention, that it was only a small spark of faith that kindled them; for scarcely had she tasted Christ when she spreads his name throughout the whole city. In those who have already made moderate progress in his school, sluggishness will be highly disgraceful. But she may appear to deserve blame on this account, that while she is still ignorant and imperfectly taught, she goes beyond the limits of her faith. I reply, she would have acted inconsiderately, if she had assumed the office of a teacher, but when she desires nothing more than to excite her fellow-citizens to hear Christ speaking, we will not say that she forgot herself, or proceeded farther than she had a right to do. She merely does the office of a trumpet or a bell to invite others to come to Christ."* [20]This woman was not called to be an apostle but unlike the Twelve her zeal and boldness are 'worthy of attention'. How often women put to shame those men whose office of preaching demands boldness. Which one of us preachers has not been convicted by the boldness of an Amy Carmichael or a Mary Slessor? It seems Jesus in this passage is purposely shaming the disciples by comparing them to a woman.

Do not put off until tomorrow what can be done today
Do you not say, 'There are yet four months, then comes the harvest'? Look, I tell you, lift up your eyes, and see that the fields are white for harvest. (John 4:35)
It seems that Jesus quoted a common proverb which he then

---

[20] Calvin, John 1553 Commentary on the Gospel of John 4:28

said was quite inappropriate for evangelism. Worldly proverbs no doubt had authority for the disciples. The proverb Jesus quoted came from agriculture and means 'don't be impatient to get the harvest in, wait for the right season", and then from that origin, to "it is OK, no rush, put it off until convenient".
Jesus says that is not the right proverb for evangelism. Do it now. Look at all the people coming out of the town now to see me! What a harvest! Look what happens when one woman loves me! Do not wait! Use every opportunity! Get a sense of urgency. If you wait for a better time to evangelise you will never do it. Perhaps Paul was referring to this saying of Jesus when he coined the phrase,
Preach the word; be ready in season and out of season... 2 Tim 4:2a

Gospel ministry is teamwork
Already the one who reaps is receiving wages and gathering fruit for eternal life, so that sower and reaper may rejoice together.
For here the saying holds true, 'One sows and another reaps. I sent you to reap that for which you did not labor. Others have laboured, and you have entered into their labor." John 4:36-38

Jesus here taught his disciples about the perceived results of the ministry of God's servants. Some are called to sow and others to reap. But both are necessary so ministry is teamwork. In the widest context and that to which Jesus seems to be referring, the sowers are the Old Testament prophets, while the apostles have the role of reapers. So that Peter, John etc will not exalt themselves over those who faithfully sowed in previous ages he told them that they have been sent to reap the labour of others. So they must not take pride in the harvest they have reaped. Nor waste the work that has been done by those who have sown in previous ages by being unfaithful, timid, lazy or losing opportunities.

It seems that the One who reaps (v36) is Jesus himself and that

8. The Worshipping Witness - The Samaritan Woman

these wages are those who are saved, but the joy will be shared between sowers and (human) reapers.

The application for us is obvious. We are standing on giant's shoulders and any success in ministry is due to the faithful sowing by those who have gone before. Do we have a sound theology and practice? Are our hearers' hearts prepared? Is there basic bible knowledge in our churches? Are there structures in place that facilitate our work? Where did all that come from? The faithful labour, prayers and sacrifices of others.

Those who conduct a faithful ministry but see no visible results can assure themselves that they are preparing the ground for others to harvest later. Nothing done for Christ is wasted so be faithful and bold even when you and your message are rejected. Those who were faithful in the past are examples to us and we must reap what they have sown as well as sow that there may be a harvest in the future. Unfaithfulness shows in many ways. We are unfaithful when we fail to build on the work done before and we are unfaithful when we do not sow for the future.

It is intriguing to compare this story with Acts 8:5-17. Philip the Evangelist went to Samaria and proclaimed the gospel and the people of the city received the gospel 'with one accord'. This was only about 12 km from Sychar where so many had been convinced that Jesus was the Christ. Peter and John who came later and prayed for the new believers to receive the Holy Spirit no doubt remembered Jesus' visit to Sychar a few years earlier and the seed that had been sown then. So in Samaria, team work was in evidence. First Jesus, then the woman with her testimony, and then Philip, Peter and John form an excellent example of John 4:36-38.

In Japan where we work it has been estimated that it takes on average 15 years for someone to come to Christ from when they first hear the gospel. It is unlikely that one person will see them through the whole process. So we are all dependent on the ministry of others, as they are on us - one big team.

There is one more point to make. In v38 Jesus started to use the 2nd person and addressed the disciples personally. "I sent you to reap..." There is an accusation in these words. The disciples' priorities were wrong. Jesus sent them to reap, they went to buy bread. No doubt they shopped in Sychar with a sneer, despising the people there, thinking only of getting a good bargain and getting out as quickly as possible. By these words Jesus condemned their prejudice, lack of responsibility, and materialism. What about you? This week you will go shopping but Jesus sends you to reap. This week you will go to your workplace but Jesus sends you to reap. This week you will be admitted to hospital but Jesus sends you to reap. At work, at school, at the shops reap!

The crowd did not come because of the disciples. Jesus was obedient but the disciples were not. Let us be faithful in our generation and for that we need to be bold.

Your testimony is important
Many Samaritans from that town believed in him because of the woman's testimony, "He told me all that I ever did." So when the Samaritans came to him, they asked him to stay with them, and he stayed there two days. John 4:39-40

What changed Sychar? One woman's simple testimony to Jesus. The repetition of almost the same words in verses 29 and 39, implies that she did not say much more than that. But God wanted his truth incarnate in a Samaritan woman and he used her simple yet bold witness.

But we have this treasure in jars of clay, to show that the surpassing power belongs to God and not to us. 2 Cor 4:7

8. The Worshipping Witness - The Samaritan Woman

The same is true today. Don't neglect your responsibility because you despise yourself. That is what Saul did when as King of Israel he hid in the baggage (1 Sam 10:22). He was small in his own eyes and failed in his responsibility.

"...Though you are little in your own eyes, are you not the head of the tribes of Israel? The Lord anointed you king over Israel." 1Sam. 15:17

You may be weak and new to the faith but there are some people only you can reach.

The aim of ministry

And many more believed because of his word.
They said to the woman, "It is no longer because of what you said that we believe, for we have heard for ourselves, and we know that this is indeed the Saviour of the world." John 4:41-42

This is an interesting twist to the story. Some had believed in Jesus through the woman, many more believed when they met Jesus personally and both groups in effect said to the woman, "We have met Jesus personally now. Thanks for introducing us by your faithful witness. But we know this is the Saviour of the World and believe in him for ourselves". Thus her own faith was confirmed and she had the joy of being used by the Lord in the conversion of her town. There are different ways people believe but where faith is genuine they all progress to direct contact with Jesus through his Word.

Revival

Jesus apparently did no miracles in Sychar and only spent two days teaching and yet many Samaritans believed. We live in a day of small things but let us look to Jesus who gives his Spirit to make us witnesses. God can do what he did in Samaria to the immoral, multi-cultural faithless 'Samaritan' cities of our day. So let us pray that God will restore to us the joy of our salvation (Ps 51:12) and send us out.

9. Peter and Pentecost

Let all the house of Israel therefore know for certain that God has made him both Lord and Christ, this Jesus whom you crucified." Acts 2:36

The Day of Pentecost was the watershed for God's mission to the world and the true start of Gospel boldness. 49 days after the resurrection and 10 days after the ascension the Holy Spirit was poured out on the apostles and the disciples. His coming was accompanied by three signs, the sound of a mighty rushing wind, tongues as of fire distributed on each one and most remarkably all the disciples praising God in foreign languages. This attracted a great crowd of Jews from Jerusalem and at least 14 other countries who heard the gospel in their own languages.

And all were amazed and perplexed, saying to one another, "What does this mean?"
But others mocking said, "They are filled with new wine."
But Peter, standing with the eleven, lifted up his voice and addressed them: "Men of Judea and all who dwell in Jerusalem, let this be known to you, and give ear to my words. For these people are not drunk, as you suppose, since it is only the third hour of the day. Acts 2:12-15

All of them were amazed and some of them mocked and Peter stood up to preach.

His bold creativity

The coming of the Holy Spirit was sudden and unexpected. Everyone including the disciples were taken by surprise. Commentaries do not seem to draw attention to this, but have you ever considered that no one told Peter to preach? We take it for granted because he did. But it wasn't his 'turn', and he was not any preaching rota. But he saw the opportunity and took it. He saw the crowds gathering and asking questions and without hesitation he stood up to preach. He did not put it off until he was better prepared or leave it to later for some other reason because then the opportunity would have passed. This was creative open air evangelism. Gospel boldness is creative and opportunistic.

What a change! Peter had always been self-confident. He was also naturally brave. When Jesus prophesied his denial on the night of his arrest, how self confident he was!
And Jesus said to him, "Truly, I tell you, this very night, before the rooster crows twice, you will deny me three times." But he said emphatically, "If I must die with you, I will not deny you." And they all said the same. Mark 14:30-31

His self-confidence showed too in his inability to watch with Jesus and to pray not to fall into temptation.
And he came and found them sleeping, and he said to Peter, "Simon, are you asleep? Could you not watch one hour? Mark 14:37

Despite his confidence he denied Jesus three times when challenged by a servant girl in the courtyard of the high priest (Mark 14:66-72).

And yet Peter was not by nature a coward. He was prepared to lay down his life for Jesus (on his own terms). His chance to show his courage came when Jesus was arrested in the garden he drew his sword and attacked the nearest person.

Then Simon Peter, having a sword, drew it and struck the high priest's servant and cut off his right ear. (The servant's name was Malchus.) John 18:10

Peter was alone against an armed crowd. The odds were against him. He was risking his life. These are not the actions of a coward. In fact his experience seems to parallel Moses (Ch.2). He was by nature brave until thrown into confusion by God who allowed him to fail and then he appeared as a coward, and fled.

There is a basic difference between gospel boldness and natural bravery. Beneath gospel boldness is overflowing joy, assurance of salvation and glorying in God. Beneath natural bravery there can be various motives but perhaps fear, aggression, sense of duty and natural affection are the most common (as well as lots of adrenalin). But gritting your teeth and getting on with evangelism without gospel boldness is not enough. Would you like to have been evangelised by Peter in his state of mind in John 18:10 with his natural bravery? While gospel boldness and natural bravery may look superficially alike they are very different.

What we are seeing in Peter now is not natural courage. It is gospel boldness. He is not nervous or tense but relaxed and filled with conviction and joy. The first evidence of which is seizing the opportunity and standing up to preach. The next evidence of gospel boldness comes in the content of his sermon.

His sermon

Peter's sermon has been analysed in detail by others (eg John Stott) and I am only giving a brief overview and highlighting the points that relate to our topic.

Arresting introduction
The mockers were accusing them of being drunk. Notice first of all what Peter did not do.
He did not take offence. He did not say, 'How dare you say that about us!' Also he did not defend the disciples. This would have been easy because it was a stupid accusation that would

have failed the simplest of tests (Did they smell of drink? Were they speaking real languages?). And yet he did not try to prove the mockers wrong. That would have been pedantic and small-minded and the gospel opportunity would have been lost. Instead he disarmed the crowd with self-deprecating humour.

First he gave a mild inoffensive denial of their charge *"give ear to my words. For these people are not drunk, as you suppose",* followed by a witty non-sequitor about the time.
since it is only the third hour of the day...
It is as if he had said 'I know you fine people of Jerusalem don't think much of us Galileans. Maybe you think we like our wine a little too much. But *it is only the third hour of the day* which is too early even for us.'

This was hardly a defence (as JA Alexander[21]), because of course ancient Jerusalem had 24/7 drunks just like every modern city,

> *"When will I wake up so I can find another drink?"* Prov. 23:35.

Rather Peter creatively used self-deprecating wit to connect with a hostile audience. This disarmed them for a few moments and gave him a hearing.

Let us not treat this as of no importance. The Holy Spirit will make us less pompous. He will make us ready to smile and ready to laugh particularly at ourselves. Peter did not crack a prepared joke to make people laugh but he did manage to make their mockery look absurd in a humorous winsome way, and that drew their teeth long enough to get into the gospel message. Like Peter we should be well able to separate the

---

[21] Alexander, J.A. 1857 A Commentary on the Acts of the Apostles, The Banner of Truth Trust, Edinburgh & Carlisle pp 498

9. Peter and Pentecost

dignity of the gospel from our own and that takes humility. The new missionary, embarrassed and awkward, suffering from culture shock, or the new pastor anxious to look good will often be pompous and easily offended. Get over yourself ... quickly! A sense of humour is a robust view of the absurdities of life in a fallen world and one cannot minister to pagans without it nor last long on the mission field, or in any other ministry for that matter.

Using humour or not is an issue today is it not? Many modern preachers crack jokes, which are very often the only part of their sermons that are memorable. But Spurgeon used humour as a means to open his hearers' defences to the gospel.

I would sooner use a little of what some very proper preachers regard as a dreadful thing, that wicked thing called humour,— I would sooner wake the congregation up that way than have it said that I droned away at them until we all went to sleep together. Sometimes, it may be quite right to have it said of us as it was said of Rowland Hill, "What does that man mean? He actually made the people laugh while he was preaching." "Yes," was the wise answer, "but did you not see that he made them cry directly after?" That was good work, and it was well done. I sometimes tickle my oyster until he opens his shell, and then I slip the knife in. He would not have opened for my knife, but he did for something else; and that is the way to do with people. They must be made to open their eyes, and ears, and souls, somehow; and when you get them open, you must feel, "Now is my opportunity; in with the knife." [22]

His preparation

The Holy Spirit's coming was sudden and so Peter's sermon was extempory, meaning he did not preach a prepared talk using notes. What was thoroughly prepared however was his mind. His thinking was already running in the grooves of his

---

[22] Spurgeon, p47

sermon subject long before he preached it. So when he had to preach at short notice he could do so without extra preparation.

So what had happened before the Day of Pentecost? After 40 days of resurrection appearances in which the Lord opened their minds to understand the scriptures (Luke 24:45) and explained all the Old Testament in relation to Himself (Luke 24:27) He ascended into heaven. Then for the next 10 days the apostles and disciples were continually praising God in the temple with great joy (Luke 24:52-53), and they gave themselves to prayer for the promised power from on high (Acts 1:8, 14). We can imagine the excited bible discussions and the fresh insights as old little-understood texts were filled with meaning and the teaching of Jesus was brought to remembrance (John 14:26), remaining doubts (Matt. 28:17) removed as iron sharpened iron in the warm fellowship as their hearts burned with in them (Luke 24:32). Also they dealt with the problem of Judas (Acts 1:15-26). Having the example of Judas before them was a terrible warning that they too could fall away. So those 10 days were an intense retreat filled with praise, bible study, fellowship, self-examination and prayer. Peter's boldness is easier to understand in this context.

The coming of the Holy Spirit was a sovereign act of God but was also preceded by human activity inspired by the same God. The Methodists and older Pentecostal groups saw the connection between receiving the Spirit, and prayer and waiting on God. Reformed Christians too have always had a high view of the means of grace. God has linked being filled with the Spirit, and the purposeful use of these means.

His teaching
Peter was very bold but his content was reasoned and addressed to the mind of his hearers. There was no trace of emotionalism. He was not ranting or out of control. There were no unfinished sentences, flights of fancy or illogical statements. Peter displayed a 'sound mind' (2 Tim. 1:7). He

gave three appropriate Old Testament quotes logically explained and applied, but the core of his sermon was the life, death and resurrection of Christ. Peter started where his hearers were and so he was compelled to explain the visible signs of the coming of the Holy Spirit.

But this is what was uttered through the prophet Joel:
"'And in the last days it shall be, God declares, that I will pour out my Spirit on all flesh, and your sons and your daughters shall prophesy, and your young men shall see visions, and your old men shall dream dreams;
even on my male servants and female servants in those days I will pour out my Spirit, and they shall prophesy.
And I will show wonders in the heavens above and signs on the earth below, blood, and fire, and vapor of smoke;
the sun shall be turned to darkness and the moon to blood, before the day of the Lord comes, the great and magnificent day.
And it shall come to pass that everyone who calls upon the name of the Lord shall be saved.' Acts 2:16-21

'This is That'. FF Bruce has a book of that title on fulfilled prophecy. Peter quoted from Joel 2:28-32 to show that this phenomena that his hearers were witnessing was that which was prophesied. God promised to pour out His Spirit. The text says all God's people will receive the Spirit, men and women, young and old. Furthermore the filling of the Spirit will be intensive as well as extensive and will exceed all the experiences of the Old Testament prophets. The result is that they will prophesy. While the specific reference is to the events of Pentecost (this is that), we are all prophets in a sense. The Church has a prophetic role. We know so we speak.

The celestial wonders mentioned seem to be apocalyptic terminology equivalent to our expression 'turn the world upside down'. The purpose of the Holy Spirit's coming is salvation and when somebody is saved their world is turned upside down. Through the prophetic ministry of the Church, many will cry out to the Lord and those that do will be saved as 3000 will do by the end of the day. Truly the world was turned upside down and so it continues whenever people call on the Lord.

So much for the introduction: Peter has explained the scene to hearers, he next preached Christ.

"Men of Israel, hear these words: Jesus of Nazareth, a man attested to you by God with mighty works and wonders and signs that God did through him in your midst, as you yourselves know-- Acts 2:22

Peter showed that Jesus was indisputably sent by God and his ministry was continually validated by God who did miracles through him. And he told them his hearers that they all knew this!

this Jesus, delivered up according to the definite plan and foreknowledge of God, you crucified and killed by the hands of lawless men. Acts 2:23

And yet they crucified him and were guilty for his death! But behind their sin was the plan of God. Not only they but God delivered him up to crucifixion and death.

God raised him up, loosing the pangs of death, because it was not possible for him to be held by it.
For David says concerning him, "'I saw the Lord always before me, for he is at my right hand that I may not be shaken; therefore my heart was glad, and my tongue rejoiced; my flesh also will dwell in hope.
For you will not abandon my soul to Hades, or let your Holy One see corruption.
You have made known to me the paths of life; you will make me full of gladness with your presence.' Acts 2:24-28

9. Peter and Pentecost

Peter then declared the resurrection. Jesus' death was a massive contradiction. Death is the punishment for sin. Jesus was without sin. So how could He die? The only explanation was that He was dying for the sins of others, though Peter did not here explain the doctrine of substitution (or at least it is not recorded that he did). And after dying it was not possible for Him to be held by death. It was impossible for Him to stay dead. The resurrection was a moral necessity. God had to raise to Jesus. To prove this Peter quoted Ps 16 where Jesus is described the Holy One. And because Jesus is perfectly holy, death which is the penal consequence of sin had no hold on him.

"Brothers, I may say to you with confidence about the patriarch David that he both died and was buried, and his tomb is with us to this day.
Being therefore a prophet, and knowing that God had sworn with an oath to him that he would set one of his descendants on his throne,
he foresaw and spoke about the resurrection of the Christ, that he was not abandoned to Hades, nor did his flesh see corruption.
This Jesus God raised up, and of that we all are witnesses. Being therefore exalted at the right hand of God, and having received from the Father the promise of the Holy Spirit, he has poured out this that you yourselves are seeing and hearing.
Acts 2:29-33

Peter pressed home that David could not have been talking about himself in Ps 16. He says in effect 'You and me and David himself all know and agree that this is a Messianic psalm'. It refers to the resurrection of the Christ and the Christ is Jesus. But then he brought it close up and personal:
"We (ie I and the men standing around me) are witnesses of this resurrection". This would have come as thunderclap to his hearers. The rumour of the resurrection of Jesus had spread

through Jerusalem for the last 7 weeks. The Jewish rulers who by now must lost all credibility had spread the falsehood that the disciples had stolen the body (Matt. 28:13) - and who in his right mind would believe them!?

Additional proof that Jesus is the resurrected and ascended Christ is the outpouring of the Holy Spirit of which *they* are now the witnesses.
Peter's water-tight logical argument is impossible to escape. For any decent Jew who believed the scripture and had not been asleep for the past 2 months it was an argument they had to accept. To do less would be to throw away all integrity.

Next he concluded by pronouncing sentence on them and all Israel:
For David did not ascend into the heavens, but he himself says, "'The Lord said to my Lord, Sit at my right hand, until I make your enemies your footstool.'
Let all the house of Israel therefore know for certain that God has made him both Lord and Christ, this Jesus whom you crucified." Acts 2:34-36

The quote from Ps 110 is powerful: it is not just a proof text for the ascension and session of the Christ, it convicted them as enemies of God himself. And in order that they get the point he told them again their crime: they had crucified Jesus who was the Christ.

This is an awesome sermon. It is very simple, very clear and very logical. It is centred on Christ and him crucified, as Paul was later to summarise his own evangelism (1Cor. 2:2). While it is contextualised for the unique time (the day of Pentecost) and place (Jerusalem), its central message: the life, death, resurrection and lordship of Jesus Christ must be ours too. If our evangelism is different then it is not evangelism. But as yet his sermon is incomplete.

His appeal
Now when they heard this they were cut to the heart, and said to Peter and the rest of the apostles, "Brothers, what shall we do?"
And Peter said to them, "Repent and be baptized every one of you in the name of Jesus Christ for the forgiveness of your sins, and you will receive the gift of the Holy Spirit.
For the promise is for you and for your children and for all who are far off, everyone whom the Lord our God calls to himself."
And with many other words he bore witness and continued to exhort them, saying, "Save yourselves from this crooked generation." Acts 2:37-40

It appears these cries of anguish occurred during his sermon and that the crowd surged forward to address both him and the other apostles. Then he continued to preach and he pleaded with his hearers to repent and believe. The three-fold promise of forgiveness, the gift of the Holy Spirit, and the extension of these to their families must have been amazingly good news to such stricken consciences. And with many other unrecorded words he pleaded with them to save themselves.

In conclusion

There are three other points we should note in closing,

His Passion He shows his loving concern for the crowd, by using 'many other words' to persuade them to believe. He does not teach in a matter of fact disengaged way and close with 'take it or leave it'. He does not just sit down self-satisfied after preaching a good tightly-argued sermon and 'leave the results to the Holy Spirit'. He really wants his hearers to believe! He is the image of God who holds out his hands all day long (Rom 10:21 *see chapter 11*).

It is deeply interesting to me that many people who have not yet come to faith still enjoy being evangelised. I remember when I was a bus leader taking tsunami evacuees to hear Franklin Graham at an evangelistic event near Sendai on the anniversary of the tsunami. These evacuees were mostly elderly fisherfolk or farmers who had not heard the gospel before. For me it was good to hear a clear, biblical, bold and passionate declaration of core gospel truths. Not one of my busload had 'come forward' but when I questioned them they enjoyed not only the gospel singing but also Franklin's message. Even though they did not believe the gospel they enjoyed being spoken to by someone who did. For once in their life they were being spoken to with deep sincerity, love, passion and concern and they liked it. What does this mean for us? A passion that people would believe the gospel is part of our example. I am not arguing for emotionalism but I am arguing that we should be uninhibited in being passionate and showing it.

He fully used the time Peter spoke long enough to get his message across. To speak too briefly is also cowardice. To cut short one's message, to leave the battlefield early and be content with a truncated gospel is a sign of timidity. John Stott calls v14-38 a reliable summary of Peter's sermon[23] [24]. He is undoubtedly right that it is a summary but I am amazed nevertheless when I read the sermons in Acts at how long they are given the hostility of the situations. Consider also Stephen before the Sanhedrin whose summarised sermon runs to 52 verses (Acts 7:2-53). He would have gone on longer if he had not been killed. And also consider Paul before the crowd of Jerusalem (Acts 21-22). These men felt they had speak the full gospel before they were quite possibly murdered. The believer facing persecution who fully uses his time to preach the gospel is completely different from the verbose preacher in a comfortable church who waffles on endlessly. Let us not

---

[23] Stott, The Spirit, the Church and the World p69
[24] Stott, The Cross of Christ p41

confuse the two. One shows boldness, the other does not. Calvin has a great quote in this regard, "I love brevity...", which illustrates his point very well[25]. But when we have a chance to tell the gospel to unbelievers let us communicate the full gospel. We inevitably deceive if we give a truncated gospel. If we say only that "God is love", or "Just believe in Jesus" we are being deceptive. The message of the cross which Paul says was the central theme of his evangelism draws together all the big truths which the unsaved need to hear from the nature of God and human sin, through to salvation, faith and repentance. So let us above all preach the cross.

His carelessness He took no thought for whether he would live or die. He had no assurance he wouldn't be killed like our Lord. There was no hint of fear or timidity in Peter during the Day of Pentecost.

The old confident Peter relying on his natural bravery is dead and buried and the new Peter filled with the Holy Spirit and speaking with gospel boldness is alive and well. Do we ever pray that we will be bold? No, because we do not have a theology of gospel boldness and think a bit of courage is enough! But our own 'Cowboys Don't Cry' pseudo-toughness will let us down just like it did Peter.

---

[25] Calvin, The Golden Booklet p12

10. To Speak the Gospel with Boldness

When they were released, they went to their friends and reported what the chief priests and the elders had said to them.
And when they heard it, they lifted their voices together to God and said, "Sovereign Lord, who made the heaven and the earth and the sea and everything in them,
who through the mouth of our father David, your servant, said by the Holy Spirit,

"'Why did the Gentiles rage,
 and the peoples plot in vain?
The kings of the earth set themselves,
 and the rulers were gathered together,
  against the Lord and against his Anointed' —
for truly in this city there were gathered together against your holy servant Jesus, whom you anointed, both Herod and Pontius Pilate, along with the Gentiles and the peoples of Israel,
 to do whatever your hand and your plan had predestined to take place.
And now, Lord, look upon their threats and grant to your servants to continue to speak your word with all boldness, while you stretch out your hand to heal, and signs and wonders are performed through the name of your holy servant Jesus."
And when they had prayed, the place in which they were gathered together was shaken, and they were all filled with the Holy Spirit and continued to speak the word of God with boldness. Acts 4:23-31

It is always an immense privilege to be a Christian at any time in history or in any place. To be a child of God, forgiven, justified, united with Christ, heir of God and indwelt by the

10. To Speak the Gospel with Boldness

Holy Spirit are incomparable blessings which will keep us praising God for all eternity. But in relative terms the privilege of being a Christian varies according to time and place. To be a Christian in a place and at a time when there are only a few other Christians is the greatest privilege of all. To be a light in a dim place is one thing, but to be a light in one of earth's darkest places in the greatest of all. But with that comes responsibility. Perhaps no one has ever felt the weight of that responsibility more than Peter and John in Acts 4.

The apostles Peter and John had been arraigned before the Sanhedrin for preaching the gospel and blaming Jesus' death on the Jewish leaders. They had been strictly warned not to preach about Jesus and they boldly refuse. They were then threatened and released. So when they return, they gathered the church together and prayed for two things, boldness and miracles of grace.

They prayed for boldness

This prayer for boldness is notable for several reasons.

1. The apostles while harassed and threatened had not been severely persecuted or beaten. Persecution with violence and martyrdom would come but not yet. And the persecution they were experiencing was not yet universal. That too would come under Saul of Tarsus (Acts 9). And yet even though they had been only verbally harassed they prayed for boldness.

2. They had been bold up to this point. From the day of Pentecost they had spoken boldly and there was no hint of timidity, slackening of zeal or compromise. In fact in this very story their enemies judge them to be bold (Acts 4:13). Even in the apostles' own judgement they had been bold, because they actually prayed *"to continue to speak your word with all boldness"*. The tense is present continuous (ESV). So they prayed for something they already have.

3. They prayed with great intensity. They marshalled impressive biblical arguments. They reminded themselves that God was the omnipotent Creator who predestined all that comes to pass including the events of the crucifixion, that this persecution was prophesied in Ps 2 and was the same as experienced by the Lord himself when the world powers of the day united against him to crucify him. They identified themselves as servants along with the 'Holy Servant Jesus'. In other words they recognised afresh their call to the work and that God had sent them, in a parallel mission to Jesus himself. The intensity and urgency of their prayer is remarkable.

So why did they pray for boldness when they already had it and when they had not yet been severely persecuted and why did they pray with such intensity? The answer is that they knew their own weakness and the effectiveness of threats. So they prayed for continuing grace to be bold. They asked God to look down from heaven and consider their enemies' threats.

"Look upon their threats. And consider <u>my own weakness</u>. Consider how I, Peter, was taken by surprise and threatened by a servant girl. And now we being threatened by the whole Sanhedrin, the same body of men who condemned our Lord. I am too weak to continue to be bold. I feel in grave danger of cooling off and giving in."

"Look upon their threats. And consider <u>your own honour</u>. If we should fail then the name of Jesus will be mocked and the gospel treated as empty words and the new church will weakened."

"Look upon their threats. And consider <u>your mission</u>, in which you have made co-workers. We are the weakest link. If we give in to these threats then your mission will fizzle out."

Threats come in various guises and are often unexpected, and can throw us off balance. Moses was threatened by Pharaoh and escaped to Midian. Elijah was threatened by Jezebel and although he was so bold until then, his boldness quickly melted away and he fled into the desert. Never underestimate the power of threats, or overestimate your power to deal with them.

Another reason why threats are so dangerous is that they are dressed as kindness. We can be sure that the Sanhedrin did not say "we are really itching to punish you but are afraid of the crowd". That would have been the truth. But no, they probably said, "we could punish you but we will just give you a warning", or "this time we will let you off but don't get into trouble again", or "we have killed the ringleader Jesus but you are just common uneducated men so we are going to be kinder to you". Then the temptation is to respond to this 'kindness' by compromising and by softening one's evangelism. Perhaps this happens to us more than we perceive. Living in a modern secular (or an Islamic, or Buddhist, or Hindu) state which 'tolerates' us can produce in us the wrong kind of gratitude and subservience. Let us remember that those who threaten us are slaves to their own fears and are not acting out of kindness at all but self-interest. The Sanhedrin were not being kind but feared the crowd (v21) and the apostles saw that clearly.

They ask God to do miracles

while you stretch out your hand to heal, and signs and wonders are performed through the name of your holy servant Jesus."Acts 4:30

They asked for healing miracles, signs and wonders through Jesus. Signs and wonders authenticate the message by showing divine authority. Our authority is the written Word of God so perhaps we do not ask for wide-spread healings to authenticate its message. But we do ask for miracles in every prayer meeting. We ask God to do miracles when we ask for people to be saved. These are miracles of saving grace greater than any healing. And in a sense they are also signs which bear witness to the truth and power of the gospel. When the drunk, the proud atheist, the religious fanatic, the TV-show-addicted elderly person, the empty-headed youth, or the bribe-taking politician become serious, joyful, hardworking Christians they become signs pointing to the glory of Jesus and his power to save.

The apostles saw the connection however: they must be bold witnesses. They must tell the gospel boldly, '_while_' God will do the miracles in the world around them. He will work in the hearers and do miracles according to his own timing, will and pleasure. They do not just pray in a pietistic way for God send revival and change the world and make it much more comfortable for Christians. They do not ask God just to save people without also praying for grace to tell the gospel. It is unbiblical to pray for revival without also praying for boldness for his church.

They saw the connection in those two prayers. Do we?

God answers both prayers

And when they had prayed, the place in which they were gathered together was shaken, and they were all filled with the Holy Spirit and continued to speak the word of God with boldness. Acts 4:31

There were two miracles here. The first was an earthquake. It was a small tremor confined apparently to the house they were in. It was a sign of God being with his people, that their prayer had been heard, that it pleased Him and that He would answer them. Though this earthquake was not a disaster God sends earthquakes that are disastrous and allow me to digress into the subject of earthquakes. It is commonly said that earthquakes are signs of the end of the world and so they generate a lot of religious excitement. Jesus spoke of earthquakes.

10. To Speak the Gospel with Boldness

For nation will rise against nation, and kingdom against kingdom. There will be earthquakes in various places; there will be famines. These are but the beginning of the birth pains. "But be on your guard. For they will deliver you over to councils, and you will be beaten in synagogues, and you will stand before governors and kings for my sake, to bear witness before them.
And the gospel must first be proclaimed to all nations.
And when they bring you to trial and deliver you over, do not be anxious beforehand what you are to say, but say whatever is given you in that hour, for it is not you who speak, but the Holy Spirit. Mark 13:8 -11

But earthquakes and disasters are not signs of the end but birth-pangs of the kingdom. Jesus says they must happen. Birth-pangs are painful but the start of something wonderful, a new life. Our appropriate response to a disaster is not to speculate about the end times or to hunker down in a little Christian ghetto but to tell the gospel boldly to the lost. Now our text was not a disastrous earthquake but a small well-timed tremor for the apostles' encouragement. But God sends both and both are in fact signs that God is with his church and opening the door for evangelism. So what must we do? Preach the gospel to all nations (v10) - and then the end will come. God brings not only great disasters but the small personal tragedies all around us. We must be awake and with love and gentleness but with also boldness be alert for all opportunities.

Believers became bold

The second miracle in v31 is that God gave them boldness.
" and they were all filled with the Holy Spirit and continued to speak the word of God with boldness"

First of all this earthquake produced in them the assurance that God was with them. They did not know how things would work out for them but it did not matter because God would be with them. That gave them peace and assurance. But this was more than just a natural state of mind caused by knowing that the tremor was a miracle. They were miraculously filled with the Holy Spirit. And the fruit of the Spirit was to speak the word of God with boldness. The boldness that God gave in answer to this prayer was an unstoppable wave and boldness is subsequently a major theme in the rest of the Acts of the Apostles. Speaking boldly and being filled with the Spirit are almost interchangeable phrases. For example in this very chapter compare v8 and v13. In v8 Peter speaks 'filled with the Holy Spirit' and in v 13 we read 'they saw the boldness of Peter and John'. So the outward expression of being filled with the Holy Spirit while speaking God's word was boldness. Similar examples are Acts 6:10, 13:9. Almost every story in the book shows their boldness but here is just a sample:

So he went in and out among them at Jerusalem, preaching boldly in the name of the Lord. Acts 9:28
And Paul and Barnabas spoke out boldly, saying, "It was necessary that the word of God be spoken first to you. Since you thrust it aside and judge yourselves unworthy of eternal life, behold, we are turning to the Gentiles. Acts 13:46
So they remained for a long time, speaking boldly for the Lord, who bore witness to the word of his grace, granting signs and wonders to be done by their hands. Acts 14:3
And he entered the synagogue and for three months spoke boldly, reasoning and persuading them about the kingdom of God. Acts 19:8

It is significant that the last words in the book speak of the same subject.
proclaiming the kingdom of God and teaching about the Lord Jesus Christ with all boldness and without hindrance. Acts 28:31
It is a great theme in Acts. I repeat, the boldness of the early church was miraculous, and whenever today you see a bold Christian you are seeing a walking miracle.

10. To Speak the Gospel with Boldness

Was Peter always bold after this event in Acts 4? No, not at all. Paul recounts Peter's timidity in front of the 'circumcision party' in Gal 2:11-14. Until these nationalistic Jews arrived at the Antioch church, Peter had enjoyed fellowship meals with Gentile believers. But criticism by his own countrymen was too strong for him and so he separated from his non-Jewish brothers. What a failure!

To me this fall of Peter shows,

1. That he was sincere in his prayer for boldness in Acts 4. He was not imagining his weakness when confronted by threats,

2. He needed to keep the danger of threats before him all his life,

3. That threats to our boldness may arise from within our Christian fellowships, not just from the world. Perhaps the more theologically uniform our denomination, the stronger the pressure to conform, not from theological conviction but from the fear of our fellows. The Pharisees were prime examples of this 'intra-fellowship fear'.

4. That Peter who was filled with boldness on the Day of Pentecost and here too in Acts 4 could lose it. It was not a once and for all baptism of the Holy Spirit.

5. That today our lack of prayer for boldness is astonishingly guilty and wilfully ignorant.

Miraculous signs
God answered their second prayer request too. What are some of the signs and wonders that followed? In the next chapter of we read of numerous miracles (v12), numerous conversions (v14) and such extraordinary healings that Peter's shadow had the power to heal (v15). Peter was miraculously delivered

from prison (5:19) to the surprise of a praying church. Later we are told of more conversions and a growing church (6:1). And even large numbers of priests were converted (6:7). Stephen was converted and filled with boldness (6:8) and the gospel spread to Samaria which received it wholesale (8:6-8). Then Paul was converted (9:4-5) and the mission to the Gentiles started in earnest with all the marvellous growth in the kingdom which has resulted in the gospel spreading around the entire world. One might even say that your conversion 2000 years later is the result of the apostles' prayer in Acts 4 for God to *"stretch out his hand"*...

Is it conceivable that God would have acted alongside the church in this way if they had been too timid to tell the gospel clearly? In parallel with the apostles speaking boldly God does miracles of grace. This was the same cycle we saw in Daniel (Ch.5). The believers stand for God and boldly declare his truth and God works in the surrounding world.

What must we do?

1. We must now pray for boldness too
We are so far behind the apostles. They intensely prayed for boldness when they already had it. We do not pray for it even though we do not have it. Something is wrong. Most of us have never been seriously threatened. We must pray for this individually and corporately as a church as the apostles did. It is the crying need. We have dropped the baton. To pray for revival without praying for boldness is unbiblical and a little presumptuous. For those of us who still have doubts and objections, we will need to pray to be able to pray for boldness.

2. Worship Jesus and be joyful
In reading Acts one cannot be fail to be impressed by the apostles' boldness. But underlying this was their irrepressible and overflowing joy. They gloried in the Cross. They had the

highest view possible of Jesus' person, work and authority. In short they worshipped him. Many of our problems with our timid approach to evangelism would dissolve if we continually worshipped Him. In Christ we have been rescued. And those who have been rescued will be worshipful and be joyful. These are not automatic responses. We have to obey and cooperate and purposefully worship Him and rejoice in Him. To maintain your joy is a Christian duty, as much as loving your neighbour or reading your bible.

3. Be proud of the good news
The apostles were convinced that the gospel was a message from God and that they had been sent on the highest authority and had received an absolute command to deliver it as Peter emphasised to the Sanhedrin (Acts 4:10-12).

The apostles were convinced of the effectiveness of the gospel. They knew it could save the worst of sinners. The gospel fits all conditions and all people everywhere universally. As Paul was later to state the gospel is 100% effective and has a zero failure rate.

For I am not ashamed of the gospel, for it is the power of God for salvation to everyone who believes, to the Jew first and also to the Greek. Rom 1:16

4. Know that God is with us
We do not need an earth tremor in our prayer meetings to know that God is with us. His promise is enough. He will be with his church as He was with Moses, Daniel, the prophets, Jesus and the apostles. He will be with his church dynamically, feeding it grace and power to witness, and he will be with his church for all time and in all places until the end of the age (Matt 28:20).

5. Know your responsibility
While the privilege of being a Christian is enormous the

responsibility of being a light in a dark place is enormous too. Peter and John expressed this responsibility to the Sanhedrin.

"...for we cannot but speak of what we have seen and heard."
Acts 4:20

We also cannot be lazy, casual, or let down our guard. Rev Takata was surveying the destruction left by the tsunami of 11th March 2011 at Shichigahama, NE Japan and said, 'This is our last chance'. I said 'What do you mean?' And he replied, 'If the Japanese church doesn't use this opportunity God will give up on us'. He was right. I have been impressed by the relief effort mounted by the small Christian community but appalled by the unwillingness of many evangelicals to tell the gospel to the victims.

After the serious earthquake we were warned 40 mins before the tsunami that it was coming. Someone was faithfully reading from a text into a microphone that was then broadcast along the coast, "There is a huge tsunami coming, escape to high ground". In some places municipal workers faithfully read out that warning until the wave went over their heads. Without that persistent, clear warning the casualties would have been much higher. Indeed some, like me, thought it was probably another false alarm. We had been warned before of tsunamis that never came. But the warning and means of escape that the church has been given to pass on is no false alarm. Let us know our responsibility and be faithful.

God sends disasters so that the church will be bold (Mark 13:8,10). If God sent this earthquake to us in Japan in 2011, should not we tell the gospel boldly? Does God have to send another one so we get it right? God will send earthquakes. God also brings the many small-scale but equally devastating tragedies into the personal lives of those around us. God will also do miracles of salvation. God is in heaven and does these things but we and his Spirit are on the earth and we have to be

10. To Speak the Gospel with Boldness

bold witnesses. Paul calls us co-workers (cooperators, 2 Cor. 6:1) with God. But if when we have opportunity instead we sit on our hands and say nothing, or when we do speak are so timid that no one knows what we mean then we are being very un-cooperative co-workers!

11. The outstretched Hands of God

But concerning Israel he says, "All day long I have held out my hands to a disobedient and obstinate people." Rom 10:21
Please read Romans 10

It is a popular opinion that the gospel is caught not taught, that somehow just friendship with Christians and receiving their loving help, enjoying the fellowship of the church and being attracted by its life and events is enough to bring someone to faith. This is the main point of books like '*The Celtic Way of Evangelism, How Christianity Can Reach the West . . .Again*' by George Hunter. This is a half truth which seems plausible, and yet it conveys a dangerous error. It is plausible because I have also noticed over years of ministry in Japan that most people who get converted have spent a long time attending meetings, receiving meals and participating in evangelistic events before eventually they come to faith. But while warm fellowship and loving friendship are a necessary part of our witness, they are not a substitute for gospel preaching. The essential precursor to faith is the verbal preaching of the gospel, as Paul says in this passage.

God's attitude - compassion

You see them in shops, parks and other public places: mothers with their hands stretched out to their children. The remarkable thing is that God's hands are outstretched too. Of course, God does not have physical hands because he does not have a body. But this speaks of his attitude. It is one of great kindness, concern, appeal and invitation.

Furthermore this "all day long" refers to the entire Old Testament age. God is long-suffering.

And this is especially "concerning Israel": Even in the time when the gospel was not fully revealed, with the sacrificial and temple system, God still was holding out his hands. How much more today! God even held out his hands to those who continued to be disobedient and obstinate (v21) and who did not believe (v16).

How does God hold out his hands?

It would be easy to draw unwarranted conclusions from this verse. For example, "if God is appealing to me then he is obviously needy so I will come when I'm good and ready", or "if God is so kind he will bless me even if I do not accept Christ", but let us answer this question from the context.

Firstly he offered the Jews a righteousness that they had not earned.

Since they did not know the righteousness that comes from God and sought to establish their own, they did not submit to God's righteousness. Rom 10:3

This righteousness of God is an outright gift. And because it is the righteousness of God it is as righteous as righteous can be. It is the greatest gift that God in his love can offer sinners. It includes forgiveness and all the other gospel blessings, a right relationship with God, eternal life, adoption, the Holy Spirit etc follow from this great gift.

Secondly he offered this righteousness freely by faith. Is this righteousness so far away that it is impossible to receive? Do we have climb up to heaven to receive it (v6) or go through the pains of hell (v7)? No. This salvation is as far off as the tip of your tongue (v8). You are saved by calling on the Lord. The method God has chosen for us to receive this gift shows his willingness and sincerity to save: his outstretched hands.

Thirdly he stretches out his hands by gospel preaching. This is not the gift offered (which is righteousness), nor the manner of receiving it (which is faith) but rather the method by which it is offered. When the preacher or the missionary or the Christian takes the gospel to the lost, God is holding out this hands. When the lost hear gospel preaching it is the word of Christ - Christ is speaking and God is appealing.

The gospel is freely offered to all Rom 10:11-13
Paul is emphatic and absolute about the free offer of the gospel. God is not discriminatory about who he saves. ALL who believe will be saved. He blesses ALL who call on him. EVERYONE who calls on the name of the Lord will be saved. Neither is God stingey about dispensing what he has promised. They will NEVER put to shame. He RICHLY blesses all who call on him. So the gospel is not a half-baked offer from an insincere God. It is Good News. Those who reject this wonderful offer are disobedient and obstinate. And yet God continues to hold out his hands to them also (v21).

There are 5 simple steps in gospel preaching Rom 10:14-17
All are essential. Failure at one point breaks the chain and no one will be saved. God has promised emphatically, unreservedly and universally to save those who call on him.
You need to call, to do that...
You need to believe, to do that...
You need to hear, to do that...
You need a preacher, to do that...
God must send a preacher.
So let us look at these in turn.

To call on the Lord you must believe
How, then, can they call on the one they have not believed in? Rom 10:14 a
The first essential is to call on The Lord. No one is saved without this and no one who calls is left unsaved. But to do this

they must first believe. There must be conviction. You must be convinced that you desperately need to be saved, that Jesus is a sufficient Saviour, and that his promises are true. How can you say you believe but cannot pray? No. All who believe will call on the Lord. But no one who does not believe will truly call.

To believe you must hear the clear message
And how can they believe in the one of whom they have not heard? Rom 10:14 b
The Word of God comes in through the ears, down into the heart before it comes up out of the mouth as a prayer. Faith comes by hearing, not by deduction, or research. It is not just 'felt' and imbibed from the worship atmosphere, but is doctrine given in words received by faith. God tells us what to believe. And true faith swops one's belief system for God's. No longer does one stand in judgement over scripture. One humbly accepts it all. This true faith is what Paul calls 'obedience from the heart' (Rom. 6:17) and 'the obedience of faith' (Rom. 1:5, 16:26).

So what does this mean for those who evangelise? We must explain the Gospel clearly. It is absolutely necessary that we teach the message of the cross and resurrection and second coming.

To hear clearly there must be a preacher
And how can they hear without someone preaching to them? Rom 10:14 c
One who preaches is first of all a human being. Not an angel. Not a book. Not a DVD. But a person, like yourself. Secondly 'one who preaches' is one who is real in faith, who understands the gospel personally. He/she is a sinner, who has been forgiven and a failure who has been restored. Thirdly 'one who preaches' is one who makes it personal to you, and speaks to your heart, stands in your shoes, answers your heart's questions, challenges your wrong thinking and exposes your motives and has a pastoral conversation with you convincing

you to believe. I have heard it said that a true sermon is not a monologue but a dialogue where the preacher enters into conversation with you. It seems that Paul actually welcomed interaction, even heckling, so he could have this dialogue (suggested in Rom. 2:1, 17, 3:1, 5, 8, 6:1).

So 'one who preaches' is not necessarily an ordained minister standing behind a pulpit. Nor is it only formal bible teaching. But it is one who engages the hearts of the lost with such gospel penetration that they 'hear'.

To preach clearly someone must be sent
And how can they preach unless they are sent? As it is written, "How beautiful are the feet of those who bring good news!" Rom 10:15

Someone who is 'sent' receives a message and faithfully passes it on. The apostles were sent. That is what the word means. The apostolic church does the same and passes on the apostles' gospel. So the true preacher faithfully delivers the glorious gospel, not his own worldly wisdom, or clever speech. It is the good news of the gospel. The gospel always has to be brought from one place to another. The Gospel is such good news that even the method of locomotion is beautiful. That is why the feet of those who bring it are beautiful. So this phrase emphasises the goodness of the good news.

Calvin says *"St. Paul desires the Christians to pray for him. Wherefore let us learn that to step up into the pulpit and to expound some passage of Scripture is not all that is to be done, but there must be a higher skill which does not grow in the gardens of men, but proceeds from the extraordinary goodness of God. And here he shows what he says in another place, that no man can perform the duty of a good and faithful teacher, unless he is sent. [Rom. 10:15] Now this sending means that God gives men that which is requisite for the execution of their charge, because they lack it in themselves."*[26]

11. The outstretched Hands of God

So have a high view of evangelism
When Isaiah preached on a street corner to unbelieving Jews, or when Paul argued in the market place with Greeks or when you tell the gospel to your friends, it is not a mere human activity, God is holding out his hands. So do it. Often. Take it seriously. Pray about it. Do it as a church body.

So have a high view of mission
When we go to Japan or some other country where people have not heard of Christ before and sincerely and faithfully tell the gospel, God is visiting those people. Christ is standing among them, holding out his hands. So make sure your church sends missionaries. And make sure your missionaries, know and love and tell the gospel.

So have a high view of the gospel
God is only holding out his hands when we are faithful. If we change the gospel message then we are false teachers who have run without being sent. There will always be pressure to do this because people reject the message, like the Israelites in Isaiah's day. Isaiah was not believed by his contemporaries. Beautiful feet are rejected. It is terrible to not believe. They are rejecting God! People today are disobedient and stubborn: they have heard, they understand but do not want to believe.

Let us be sincere, like God.
If God is holding out his hands, we should too. If God is doing so 'all day long' we should be persistent and loving. What greater love did Jesus show than to stretch out his hands on the cross for the salvation of the 'disobedient and obstinate'.

So feel our need of boldness!
If God doesn't give up when people are disobedient and stubborn neither should we!

---

[26] Calvin, Sermons on Ephesians p696

Boldness is consistent with the gospel message. It is the announcement of an opposing worldview. It is humbles the pride of man. It brings the sinner face to face with God. Now to bring that message requires boldness.

Bold preaching is consistent with the exercise of faith. Hearers are required to repent from sin and trust in the promises of God. They cannot negotiate the terms of their surrender, amend the conditions God lays down or widen the narrow gate. To issue these requirements requires boldness.

Boldness is also consistent with the nature of unbelievers. They are rebels and need to be commanded to repent. They prefer to hide from God and retreat into the darkness rather than turn and be converted.

Boldness is consistent with our role as God's ambassadors, who are sent to deliver an unpopular message uninvited and usually unwelcomed.

Let us have a high view of our responsibility
We say, "I cannot tell the gospel" because "I'm shy", or "I'm not very close to God", or "I don't have the gift of the gab" etc. But God gave this responsibility to the whole church, of which you are a part. There are some people only you can reach. Perhaps God is sending you to those who would be put off by a more confident 'powerful' person. So overcome your objections by faith and obey God.

Let us have confidence in the sovereign God
And Isaiah boldly says, "I was found by those who did not seek me; I revealed myself to those who did not ask for me." Rom 10:20

While God does stretch out his hands all day long he is not helpless. He reveals himself in sovereign grace to some of those who are disobedient and obstinate who do not call on him. They are his elect whom he has chosen from the foundation of the world (Eph 1:4, Rom. 8:29). If he did not none of us would be saved. Praise him for his infinite love!

And if you are not yet a believer...
God's hands are now outstretched in mercy to you but for how long? Do not delay until the Day of Judgement overtakes you.

It is a dreadful thing to fall into the hands of the living God. (Heb 10:31).

Throw yourself in surrender into his loving arms now rather than wait for that terrible day!

12. Prayer Request from Prison

'praying at all times in the Spirit, with all prayer and supplication. To that end keep alert with all perseverance, making supplication for all the saints,
and also for me, that words may be given to me in opening my mouth boldly to proclaim the mystery of the gospel,
for which I am an ambassador in chains, that I may declare it boldly, as I ought to speak.' Eph 6:18-20

In 1995 I visited Hebron School in Ooty, India with a view to sending our children there. The kind Christian gentleman who showed me round was Graham Staines. Later when we took our children there in August 1998 for their first term we met the whole family and saw them praying together. Graham Staines was on the Hebron Council and was a special friend to us. He was always gentle, concerned for the welfare of all the children and anxious that biblical standards were maintained at the school. His son Philip was very kind to our son Andrew especially when he was homesick. Andrew said he was one of the strongest Christians in their dorm and class. His bed was next to Andrew's. Esther Staines was our daughter Amy's best friend. They were inseparable at Hebron, in the same class and dormitory. Five months later when Graham and his two sons were attending a Christian camp in Orissa the car in which they were sleeping was surrounded by an extremist Hindu mob and they were beaten and burned to death[27]. There had been many previous attacks on Christians in that Indian state and Graham knew of the danger. But the Staines murder seemed to unleash a wave of intense persecution against Christians especially in the central Indian states. Hundreds were killed and thousands beaten and driven from their villages. This tragedy is continuing and yet what is so impressive for me is the boldness and joy of many ordinary Indian pastors. Men who

---

[27] Martis & Desai

12. Prayer Request from Prison

I frankly admit I would never have gone to hear or who would never have been invited to speak at conferences etc were strengthened and empowered to be bold witnesses.

Do you pray for your minister? How should you pray for the missionaries you support or the Christian workers you know? How do pray for the persecuted church (assuming you do)? This text tells us that the top priority and their greatest need is for gospel boldness and yet it is astonishing that this clear teaching is largely ignored by most of us so we never intercede for those in ministry that they will speak with boldness. Paul wrote to the Ephesians during his first Roman imprisonment around AD 60. He was in chains, perhaps chained to a guard. As a result the whole Praetorian guard knew that his imprisonment was for Christ (Phil. 1:13). He was waiting to defend himself before Nero, and to Paul that meant an opportunity to preach the gospel as we see from his prior example before the Roman tribune and Jerusalem mob (Acts 22:1-21), Governor Felix (Acts 24:10-21), his successor Festus and King Agrippa (Acts 26:1-23). Let us see how he arrives at this prayer request, what he asks for and what we can learn from this text.

Paul tells the Ephesians that they are in a war (Eph. 6:10-12). Not a war against their human enemies at Ephesus who persecute them, tempt them, slander them or try to mislead them but against numerous, powerful and invisible demons. These demons who control so much of the thinking of the world are attempting to destroy them. The attacks of demons are in form of lies, because the Devil is a liar. Paul tells the Ephesians, and us, that we must put on the full armour of God, the belt of truth, the breastplate of righteousness, the shoes of the gospel of peace, the shield of faith, the helmet of salvation, and the sword of the Spirit to be able to stand against these attacks (Eph. 6:13-17). The different parts of armour Paul describes are different applications of the one gospel to the devil's assorted lies, because the gospel is the only defence against these lies. These lies of the Devil will be against the entire body of God's truth but especially against the gospel itself. A daily practical rejoicing in God and Jesus Christ from a sincere heart convinced of the objective apostolic gospel is the only defence against the daily temptations (fiery darts) as well as the surprise all-out attack 'on the evil day' (Eph. 6:13).

From v 18 Paul then asks them to pray,
And pray in the Spirit on all occasions with all kinds of prayers and requests. With this in mind, be alert and always keep on praying for all the saints.

Paul speaks very intensely (*all occasions... all kinds of prayers... always... all the saints*). It is not hard to follow his train of thought. If our enemies are spiritual beings whose primary attacks are against our faith then we need to pray to God for spiritual help.
All Christians pray when in serious trouble. But Paul says 'on all occasions', for example, when you are happy and rejoicing or sad and discouraged and after many years of disappointments, whether you are alone or gathered. All Christians pray sometimes and soon give up. But Paul here says 'always'. All Christians pray in a desultory way. Paul says 'in the Spirit' and 'be alert'. We all pray for some of the saints. But Paul says 'for all the saints'. Why such intensity? Because the Devil's spiritual attacks are of many kinds and from many angles, against all Christians (the leaders, the new in the faith, the strong, and the weak), day and night and yet with varied strength.

Now he narrows down to one specific prayer request, a Spirit-led prayer. This is a request for prayer from the Ephesians and of course is one which he prayed himself. It must be of great significance. And for me, this was a surprise.

12. Prayer Request from Prison

Before we study this let us look at an incomplete list of prayers that Paul is known to have prayed,

1. For King Agrippa's conversion (*Paul replied, "Short time or long—I pray God that not only you but all who are listening to me today may become what I am, except for these chains." Acts 26:29*)
2. The safety of his shipmates (*God has granted you all those who sail with you.' Acts 27:24*)
3. To be able to visit Rome (*always in my prayers, asking that somehow by God's will I may now at last succeed in coming to you. Rom. 1:10*)
4. For the conversion of the Jews (*For I could wish that I myself were accursed and cut off from Christ for the sake of my brothers, my kinsmen according to the flesh. Rom. 9:3*)
5. For the growth of the Corinthians (*For we are glad when we are weak and you are strong. Your restoration is what we pray for. 2Cor. 13:9*)
6. For the enlightenment of the Ephesians, earlier in this epistle (1:16-23) and Colossians (Col. 1:9-12).
7. For the Philippians' growth in grace (Phil. 1:9-11)
8. For the sanctification of the Thessalonians (1Th. 5:23)
9. For the spread of the gospel (*Finally, brothers, pray for us, that the word of the Lord may speed ahead and be honored, as happened among you, 2Th. 3:1*)

With the above list for reference, think of all the Spirit-filled prayers he could have asked prayer for as he lies in chains in a Roman prison. Such as,

1. "For revival in Rome such as you have experienced in Ephesus and that swept many of you into the kingdom"
2. "For you to be evangelistic and to take the gospel to the rest of Asia Minor".
3. "For the poor and persecuted believers in Jerusalem. Shouldn't we remember those in prison as if in prison with them and weep with those that weep?"
4. For the church in Rome.
5. For the conversion of the Emperor.

All these and many more prayers would have been in agreement with the Lord's Prayer and led by the Spirit. But what does he ask prayer for?

He asks for prayer for himself, but not that he would be released from prison or for his protection but that he would speak the gospel with boldness.

His priority, as an apostle was to speak the gospel (*Woe to me if I do not preach the gospel! 1Cor. 9:16b*). He was probably thinking of his defense before Nero. Even though he was an apostle, he was wise enough to know he needed prayer and humble enough to ask for it as he did on many occasions (eg *Brothers, pray for us. 1Th. 5:25*).

Calvin says on this verse, *"You see here that St. Paul who is held closely, as a poor offender, looks daily for nothing but death, and yet for all that, he cares not so much for his life as for the advancement and preferment of God's Word, insomuch that he would rather die than be slothful in doing what was enjoined him. That is in sum what we have to remember from this passage."*[28]

It is a mistake to think that Paul's teaching on spiritual warfare ends with v17 or 18. It ends at verse 20. The Puritan, William Gurnall, who wrote a 2 volume treatise on Ephesians 6:10-20 called The Christian in Complete Armour totalling 1189 pages, also took this view. He concluded his study at verse 20, under the heading "Direction Twelfth: The Duty of every Christian in Complete Armour to aid by Prayer the Public Ministers of Christ". [29] So clearly, he also considered praying for gospel boldness as part of spiritual warfare and not as an after-thought tagged on at the end of

---

[28] Calvin, p692
[29] Gurnall, part 2, p540

the epistle.

Pray for me

and also for me, that words may be given to me in opening my mouth boldly to proclaim the mystery of the gospel, for which I am an ambassador in chains, that I may declare it boldly, as I ought to speak. Eph. 6:19-20

What did Paul mean exactly? He seems to be asking for two things, firstly the words to speak (*that words may be given to me*) and then the boldness to say them (*I may declare it boldly*). Closer examination shows however that boldness is the result of being given the right words. He is implying that if only God put His words in his mouth then he would be bold.

The Greek word used throughout the New Testament (parrhesia) is usually translated boldness and when used with speech means to speak frankly, cheerfully and plainly. In the parallel passage in Col 4:4 Paul used a different word which means 'clearly' or 'to make manifest'. But the two words (boldly and clearly) converge in meaning. The bold gospel speaker is clear and his meaning is unmistakeable. The timid speaker is vague, foggy and difficult to understand. Paul asks to be given the right words so that he will bold and therefore clear.

Let us correct our priorities
A prayer for boldness doesn't even come at the bottom of our list of the prayers of most of us, while it should be near the top. According to the apostle's priorities revealed in this text boldness should be one of the most urgent desires for all speakers of God's word and those who pray for them. No wonder the work of gospel in many parts of the world is up to the axles in the sand. We do not even know how to pray!

We should pray for ministers

Many people complain about their ministers. They should rather recycle those complaints into prayers. God would richly bless Japan and many other countries if the churches prayed for their pastor's sermons and evangelistic efforts. Some ministers you can't understand. They never arrive at the point. Why? Because they are not bold. They are gospel cowards. Conversely bold ministers are usually easy to understand. It is a common thing over here to complain if your minister is straight-talking. Maybe you do that too. Rather you should pray for him if he is not. Therefore commit yourself to pray for your minister, pastor and other Christian workers, that they will be given the words to boldly speak the mystery of Christ.

Paul asks to be able to make known the mystery of the gospel.

He means that the gospel itself is the mystery. A mystery in the New Testament is something we only know by revelation, and cannot know by human knowledge, research or deduction. The fact that the Son of God died for the sins of the whole world could never have been figured out: it had to be revealed.

Now a mystery is the New Testament is not a secret to be kept but revelation from God to be declared clearly and plainly. But because it is a mystery, unearthly and inexplicable by human reason it has to be declared so clearly that there is no ground for misunderstanding. Unconverted hearers cannot put 2 and 2 together or 'connect the dots'. They will inevitably misunderstand an unclear or partial message. And so because the gospel is a mystery it must be declared clearly, boldly, passionately, repetitively, and not submerged in a sea of distractions. And yet while the Holy Spirit may use the most inadequate evangelism we cannot expect Him to bless our timidity.

So what is the gospel which Paul preached? There are some very brief summaries in his letters which show us the content of Paul's evangelistic preaching.

The briefest is 2 Cor. 4:5a *For what we proclaim is not ourselves, but Jesus Christ as Lord.*

In writing to the Corinthians he slightly expands on this summary of his preaching content. *For I decided to know nothing among you except Jesus Christ and him crucified.* 1Cor. 2:2. Even allowing for some hyperbole, the fact and meaning of the crucifixion were central in Paul's proclamation of the gospel.

Then again, when he describes his initial evangelism of the Galatians he says,

It was before your eyes that Jesus Christ was publicly portrayed as crucified. Gal. 3:1b

Again the fact and meaning of the crucifixion are emphasised. But further there was personal application of the death of Christ. As Paul preached the Galatians saw clearly with the eye of faith that Jesus was a suitable, sufficient and glorious Saviour and as Paul applied the gospel to them personally they reached out by faith, received Christ and were born again. In short the Galatians had Christ presented to them in such a manner that they received him in the very opposite way to which they were now rejecting him (as he complains frequently in that epistle, for example Gal 4:14-15).

So I understand from these texts that the proclamation of mystery of the gospel for which Paul prays for boldness has as its core the crucifixion and Lordship of Christ, clearly explained and passionately and personally applied. This is what Paul lived and breathed for, worked and suffered for.

But today Christians get intense about almost everything else. The list is long and tedious: abortion, anti-gay marriage, trade justice, nuclear disarmament, poverty, pacifism, recycling, environmental issues etc. No matter how important these issues are to your group, they are peripheral. Paul was bold about the mystery of the gospel: let us keep in step with the Spirit and be the same. Many need to repent for being more zealous about such secondary issues. But perhaps the cause is deeper than just a mistake about priorities. In most of the issues above, some group in the world or in another religion will support us. These are not specifically Christian issues. Only preaching Christ puts us completely outside the pale as far as the world is concerned. So timidity makes us zealous about these secondary issues. Now let us make Christ and him crucified our sole passion and proclamation, repent for our timidity concerning the gospel, and let us make Paul's prayer our own.

Ambassador in chains

for which I am an ambassador in chains, that I may declare it boldly, as I ought to speak. 6:20

What a great irony! All ambassadors are treated with respect even by enemy states and nations at war but Paul the apostle and therefore ambassador of Christ was treated with contempt and abuse.
This is the third time he mentions he was a prisoner in this letter.

For this reason I, Paul, the prisoner of Christ Jesus for the sake of you Gentiles-- 3:1

As a prisoner for the Lord, then, I urge you to live a life worthy of the calling you have received. 4:1

He was a prisoner for the Lord, for the gospel, and for the salvation of Gentiles. He was threatened with death many times and constantly abused. So why does Paul send out a call for prayer for boldness?

Why indeed when you consider,

12. Prayer Request from Prison

<u>His moral courage</u> There is no doubt that Paul had spade loads of moral courage. For example, after his conversion he wanted to stay in Jerusalem and minister there. He felt the fact that he was well-known as a converted persecutor of the church would carry great weight in his evangelism of the Jews. His life expectancy would have been very short but that did not bother him. The Lord however had other ideas and sent him to the Gentiles (Acts 22:17-21). So Paul was courageous. But he did not trust in his natural moral courage. He knew he needed gospel boldness.

<u>His previous experiences</u> He had continual experiences of the Lord strengthening him against persecution and giving him boldness to speak the Word. For example,

He talked and debated with the Grecian Jews, but they tried to kill him. Acts 9:29

When the Jews saw the crowds, they were filled with jealousy and talked abusively against what Paul was saying. Then Paul and Barnabas answered them boldly: "We had to speak the word of God to you first. Since you reject it and do not consider yourselves worthy of eternal life, we now turn to the Gentiles. Acts 13:45-46

One night the Lord spoke to Paul in a vision: "Do not be afraid; keep on speaking, do not be silent.
For I am with you, and no one is going to attack and harm you, because I have many people in this city."
So Paul stayed for a year and a half, teaching them the word of God. Acts 18:9-11

Paul entered the synagogue and spoke boldly there for three months, arguing persuasively about the kingdom of God. Acts 19:8

Paul lay in prison singing praises (Acts 16:25), withstood

rioting mobs in Jerusalem (Acts 21:40), witnessed to kings (Acts 26) etc. And yet he did not trust in his past experience of the Lord's help.

And this great apostle of such moral courage with such experience of divine help still feels his need of boldness to the extent that he makes it his top priority prayer request. Perhaps these three reasons stand out,
1. He did not trust himself and he felt his own weakness when confronted by threats. At present where our church is active in the disaster area in Japan there are no threats and God is protecting our work. We can preach the gospel anywhere and anytime. If you are in a free country you can probably do the same. But we are weak! What would happen if there was even a little threat? If somebody said to us "Give up preaching, stop talking, stop preaching the cross, don't come here..", we would inevitably falter and fail. And so we need to pray for boldness. How about you in *your* situation?

2. He took seriously the bad examples he had witnessed. I believe all the apostles even Paul were deeply affected by the apostasy of Judas. Paul also had numerous examples of fellow workers deserting him in Rome (whether these were happening at the time of writing or were still future).

For Demas, in love with this present world, has deserted me and gone to Thessalonica. Crescens has gone to Galatia, Titus to Dalmatia. 2 Tim 4:10

Better men than us have given into cowardice. We only stand by grace. But if we do not pray for boldness our over-confidence may be our downfall.

3. His standards of boldness were much higher than ours (*that I may declare it boldly, as I ought to speak.*). We pat ourselves on the back if we say anything for God. Paul felt a divine imperative as Christ's ambassador to speak as he

'ought', and would have rigorously criticised himself if he left anything out. He declared the whole counsel of God so that he would be clear from the blood of all (Acts 20:26, 27).

Calvin says, *"Now then, let such as are called to the office of teaching God's church understand their own weakness, and put themselves wholly into God's hand so that they may be made able to perform the work, well knowing that they will never accomplish it, no, nor one hundredth part of it, unless it is given them from above. And therefore let all men pray for those who are thus ordained to be teachers and ministers of the Word, for it is a singular gift of God when-we have such shepherds of our souls as are able to guide us well. Wherefore let it be known both to small and great, that to maintain the church in her estate and in her soundness, God must give strength to those whose duty it is to teach, and men must pray for them, for in so doing every man procures his own good and his welfare. And if we are negligent in this, it is a sign that we set no value either on our spiritual life, or all the common welfare of the whole church."*[30]

So how did it work out for Paul? Did God answer his prayers and the Ephesians' intercessory prayers for him? Let us fast forward a few years:

At my first defense no one came to stand by me, but all deserted me. May it not be charged against them! But the Lord stood by me and strengthened me, so that through me the message might be fully proclaimed and all the Gentiles might hear it. So I was rescued from the lion's mouth. 2 Tim. 4:16-17

He was alone. None of his companions stood by him. It is not good for a Christian to be alone. It is harder to be bold by yourself. When Christians gather for evangelism they

---

[30] Calvin, p694

encourage each other. Paul did not have that advantage.

And yet the Lord answered those prayers and stood by him, strengthened him and gave him the words he asked for. So Paul did speak the gospel with boldness to Nero. He spoke plainly and freely so that the Emperor and all the others heard the gospel. He would have spoken of the cross, Christ as Lord and perhaps his testimony, clearly and fully, and winsomely appealed for Nero's conversion. And so he was rescued *'from the lion's mouth'*. Not that Nero was the lion. The lion he refers to is the Devil. Paul by the grace of God did not give into his threats and so withstood in the *'evil day'*.

Nothing else can soundly defeat the powers of darkness in heavenly places (Eph. 6:12) so much as the bold declaration of the gospel well watered by the prayers of God's people (Eph. 6:18-20). So let us pray for boldness for ourselves and other believers, for spiritual warfare is not just conducted by prayer but also by preaching.

13. A Spirit of Power and Love and a Sound Mind

For this reason I remind you to fan into flame the gift of God, which is in you through the laying on of my hands,
for God gave us a spirit not of fear but of power and love and self-control.
Therefore do not be ashamed of the testimony about our Lord, nor of me his prisoner, but share in suffering for the gospel by the power of God,
2 Tim 1:6 -8

You have the Holy Spirit

The gift Paul refers to in v 6 is the Holy Spirit as v7 makes clear. In the apostolic age the Holy Spirit was often given by the laying on of the apostles' hands but today the Holy Spirit is given when someone believes on Christ. This is the spiritual baptism in which the believer becomes an member of Christ and the start of the application of all the benefits of redemption.

Maybe you doubt that you have the Holy Spirit! After all you do not look different from what you were before! The difference is internal. You love Jesus. You have a deep sense that without him you would be lost forever. You glory in the cross because your sins were paid for there. Jesus Christ to you is now the most valuable, beautiful and essential person ever. This is the sure work of the Holy Spirit.

Paul was sure that Timothy was such a person because of his sincere faith. It was 'For this reason' that Paul then told Timothy to fan this gift into flame. It is as if he says, "the Holy Spirit is pretty dormant in you isn't he? Use the bellows and let Him burn within you." In Timothy's case and certainly in ours the problem was cowardice which had encroached on his faith and was hindering his ministry.

Let's learn about this work of the Holy Spirit.

for God gave us a spirit not of fear but of power and love and self-control. 2 Tim 1:7

Cowardice

This is in all of us. We cannot tell the gospel. We are afraid of people and ashamed of the gospel. What is this cowardice? It is the fear of man. We are afraid of others by nature. Brave men who are unafraid of dangerous adventure sports or even modern warfare often do not have the moral courage to stand up to wrongdoing and criminal behaviour. And those who do have moral courage and stand up for some good cause in the world, entirely lack gospel boldness. In short, we cannot tell the gospel. Why? Because we are afraid of people.

Now Paul tells us that God did not give us this fear of man. It is emphatically not from God. Yet how often we excuse our fear of man by calling it spiritual names, like wisdom or tact or love. Paul tells us that this fear is induced by shame.

Therefore do not be ashamed of the testimony about our Lord, nor of me his prisoner, but share in suffering for the gospel by the power of God, 2 Tim 1:8

What is shame? We read of it first in the Garden of Eden (Genesis 2:25, 3:7). Adam and Eve felt shame because they were naked and because they had sinned. Shame is a feeling of intense discomfort at being ugly, or sinful or lacking in something important. If someone causes a scandal and their wrongdoing is exposed they feel shame. If someone's secret sin is exposed they feel shame. I feel a mild sense of shame at having been in Japan for 30 years and not being better at the

13. A Spirit of power and love and a sound mind

language! And such shame in the case of ugliness, sin or failure is entirely appropriate.

Now Paul warns Timothy not to be "ashamed of the testimony about our Lord". In other words, not to be ashamed of preaching Jesus as Saviour and Lord. To be ashamed of Jesus Christ is shockingly inappropriate. It is the same as saying that the most valuable, beautiful and essential person ever is ugly, sinful and a failure. It is to call good evil and white black and night day. No wonder the Lord so absolutely condemns it (Luke 9:26). Rather the Holy Spirit teaches us to glory in the gospel and to boast in the cross (Gal 6:14).

Paul also warns Timothy not to be ashamed of him in prison and in general to share in 'the suffering for the gospel'. Why would Timothy be ashamed of Paul in prison? Simply, because prison is for bad people and so in most people's judgement Paul must be bad (2 Tim. 2:9 *for which I am suffering, bound with chains as a criminal*). An extension of this is shame at suffering in general. It is human nature to despise those who suffer as bad people suffering the judgement of God. Job experienced this from his three friends and eloquently expressed it (eg Job 12:5, 16:20, 30:11). The disciples assumed the man born blind must have had sinful parents or sinned himself (John 9:2). And crowd assumed that disasters strike those who are more sinful than others (Luke 13:2, 4).

And so there is a connection in worldly people's thinking between an easy life, avoiding persecution and pride. Make sure you think biblically; that you glory in your calling, your Saviour and your future as Paul goes on to tell Timothy in the verses that follow (2 Tim. 1:9-12).

Now shame is usually more strongly felt among those with whom we have close relationships. This is why it is easier to be a Christian in the big city where you work than in the village where you grew up. Jesus referred to this in Luke 4:23-24 (*Ch.*

6). It is why those in close relationships or peer groups which they value (eg the Pharisees) feel more shame and show more fear of man than those who have nothing to lose (the tax-collectors and sinners). And it perhaps explains why so many of those who get converted in Japan are not the high-flyers with a lot to lose but those who have slipped to the bottom of society.

Paul's power, love and self control

To illustrate this text we will look at an incident in the life of Paul himself, which had taken place a few years earlier.

Paul during his third missionary journey had been taking up a collection for the poor in Jerusalem. When he returned went to Jerusalem to deliver this collection to the church, on the advice of James he went to the temple to fast and pray. But he was seen by some who knew him who raised the alarm and we join the story in Acts 21:30. Let us specifically look for his power, love and self-control. It is not hard to find.

Then all the city was stirred up, and the people ran together. They seized Paul and dragged him out of the temple, and at once the gates were shut.
And as they were seeking to kill him, word came to the tribune of the cohort that all Jerusalem was in confusion.
He at once took soldiers and centurions and ran down to them. And when they saw the tribune and the soldiers, they stopped beating Paul.
Then the tribune came up and arrested him and ordered him to be bound with two chains. He inquired who he was and what he had done.
Some in the crowd were shouting one thing, some another. And as he could not learn the facts because of the uproar, he ordered him to be brought into the barracks.
And when he came to the steps, he was actually carried by the soldiers because of the violence of the crowd,

13. A Spirit of power and love and a sound mind

for the mob of the people followed, crying out, "Away with him!" Acts 21:30-36

A huge crowd (which took a cohort to suppress so it probably numbered thousands) were stirred to a high pitch of religious fanaticism and intense hatred. They surged upon Paul, beat him and tried to kill him. Just in time the Roman soldiers arrived and managed to rescue him, but the violence and the hatred that inspired it were so great that the heavily-armed Roman soldiers had to carry Paul to protect him. Why such hatred? Because Paul had been telling the gospel to the Gentiles.

Paul was now doubtless winded, bleeding and badly injured. How would you feel if you had just had his experience? What terror! What a sense of injustice! What a victim! What indignation! What injured pride! What longing for revenge! But there was no hint of these things in Paul at all. So how did he respond? With power, love and a sound mind!

Paul insisted on being allowed to speak to the crowd. He returned to the steps up which he had just been carried and faced the crowd who so vehemently hate him and gave a long speech. He had no assurance that he would not be killed. And he spoke at length. That is POWER!

How did Paul speak to the crowd? He was now under the watchful protection of Roman soldiers but there was no bitterness or blame or rancor in his voice, even though he could speak from a position of relative safety. Instead he was polite and courteous. *"Brothers and fathers, hear the defense that I now make before you."* Acts 22:1 He spoke with sympathy as a fellow Jew and appealed to their reason. He was seeking to win them to the Truth. In short he LOVES them.

Next see his self control. There was no panic, anxiety or intemperance in his speech. Instead you have the impression of an excellent mind going into top-gear using all its resources to speak as clearly and effectively as possible. His talk was a well-thought-out appeal to the reason of Jewish people (22:12ff). He described how he was a zealous Jew (22:3), and even a persecutor of the church (22:4). He explained his conversion in a detailed, personal and sympathetic way (22:5-16). Next he showed that as a Christian he continued to respect the temple (22:17). He also told of his concern to preach the gospel to the Jews in Jerusalem, only to be counter-manded by the Lord to go to the Gentiles (22:18-22). And only when he finally mentions that word does the crowd go wild. So though Paul was ultimately unsuccessful in breaking down their violent prejudice, he wisely and carefully presented his case so that anyone who was not entirely blinded by Jewish nationalism might see that his mission to the Gentiles was indeed from the Lord. So see his SOUND MIND.

Without Paul's boldness and indefatigable fight to take the gospel to the Gentiles you would not be a Christian today. But this boldness was not Paul's natural character but the Holy Spirit's which he had received from God.

"for God gave us a spirit not of fear but of power and love and self-control." 2 Tim 1:7

Now you too, along with Paul and Timothy, have the same Holy Spirit.

Power

The power given to a believer by the Holy Spirit is the strength to be bold and clear, to do and say what is right, and to endure opposition. In these days of the prosperity gospel it is worth making crystal clear what this power is not.

Not worldly strength
This power of God is not to make us powerful people by the standards of this world. For example it does not make us rich,

13. A Spirit of power and love and a sound mind

respected, influential, or to put us into a high social position. In the context of this letter when Paul exhorts Timothy to be strong by the grace that is in Christ Jesus,
You then, my child, be strengthened by the grace that is in Christ Jesus 2 Tim. 2:1

The following context shows what he has in mind: strength to speak boldly as he himself did (2 Tim. 1:13), to guard the faith (2 Tim. 1:14), to entrust this faith to faithful men (2 Tim. 2:22) etc.

Not just being nice

How often we congratulate ourselves that we have been a 'good witness' if we have been nice to someone. Christians should be 'nice'! Nasty Christians are a terrible witness. But this is not enough. Before he ascended in Heaven, Jesus said that the apostles would receive power when the Holy Spirit came upon them. This power enabled them to become his witnesses.

But you will receive power when the Holy Spirit has come upon you, and you will be my witnesses in Jerusalem and in all Judea and Samaria, and to the end of the earth." Acts 1:8

The apostles were all eye-witnesses to Christ's resurrection. But also they were Christ's witnesses who told his message to the world. Further they were God's witnesses <u>against</u> the world because Christ's message told the world to repent. Because they were against the world in this way they were often killed, so that the Greek word for *witness* became the English word *martyr*. Now a faithful biblical church is an apostolic church in that it carries on the work of the apostles under their authority. And the work of being a witness is a verbal witness. A silent witness is no witness at all. This why the Holy Spirit's power is necessary to give the church boldness and endurance in suffering. So you see that being a 'good witness' requires bold speech and is so much more than just being a nice person.

Good works and blameless conduct play their part (Matt. 5:16, 1Pet. 2:12, 3:1) but in themselves do not constitute being a 'good witness'.

Not a matter of feeling strong
This power of God may not make us feel spiritually strong. Paul brings these two elements together in an amazing passage describing his evangelism in Corinth,

And I was with you in weakness and in fear and much trembling, and my speech and my message were not in plausible words of wisdom, but in demonstration of the Spirit and of power, 1 Cor 2:3 -4

He tells us that his speech and his message demonstrated the power of the Holy Spirit, exactly what in 2 Tim 1:7 he inculcates on Timothy and yet his internal feelings were weakness, fear and trembling. How often we let our feelings dictate our obedience. We feel weak and so we do not obey. We feel afraid and so we speak timidly or not at all. Whereas Paul obeyed no matter how he felt. He trusted in the Word of God and the Spirit's power. May we do so too.

Love

The Holy Spirit doesn't just give power but love. Jesus was full of love, so was Stephen etc. Paul too. On trial for his life before King Agrippa and Festus, he gives a detailed account of his conversion and the Lord's commissioning of him to take the gospel to the Gentiles. When Festus in alarm calls him mad, Paul dramatically and persuasively appeals for their conversion (Acts 26:24 -29).

Paul in speaking of his time in Thessalonica says,

But we were gentle among you, like a nursing mother taking care of her own children.

13. A Spirit of power and love and a sound mind

So, being affectionately desirous of you, we were ready to share with you not only the gospel of God but also our own selves, because you had become very dear to us. 1 Thess 2:7-8

"Affectionately desirous"! What a beautiful attitude for any evangelist! If we love people we will be "affectionately desirous" for their salvation. If we love people we will not be afraid of them, for to be a coward is self-centred. If we love people let us pray for people. The richest and proudest person without Christ is needy, weak and short-lived. We should pity them all. Alfie Silas, a gospel singer who performed at evangelistic events after the tsunami in Sendai had this line in one of her songs, 'You think I'm crazy but you are the one I pray for when I get on my knees and pray'. Love will make us bold, passionate, not rude but polite and prayerful. So love is an essential constituent of gospel boldness.

Sound mind

"for God gave us a spirit not of fear but of power and love and self-control." 2 Tim 1:7.

This is translated self-control (ESV), self-discipline (NIV), sound mind (KJV, RSV), discipline (NASB). In the context where it is the opposite of the fear of man induced by shame, its meaning is to <u>think</u> clearly and biblically. It is a determination to be ruled by the mind instead of the feelings and is the opposite of cowardice where a person is ruled by their feelings. A sound mind is disciplined by faith. And so we conclude that gospel boldness starts in the mind. It is to think clearly and biblically with right priorities, to be steady despite the danger. It is to be governed by sanctified reason rather than by the irrational fear of man. In many respects it is similar to that other fruit of the Spirit, meekness.

Paul repeats the importance of a sober mind to Timothy at the end of his letter.

As for you, always be sober-minded, endure suffering, do the work of an evangelist, fulfill your ministry. 2 Tim 4: 5

The opposite of a sound mind is panic. How we should take this to heart! So whenever you feel rising fear, quell it and remember God's promises. Confront feelings of shame with conscious thoughts about the greatness of God and the gospel. This is the first step to a sound mind. Let us pray not be like Peter in the courtyard of the high priest on the night of Jesus' betrayal. He panicked. And in his flustered panic-stricken state he lost control of his speech.

After a little while the bystanders came up and said to Peter, "Certainly you too are one of them, for your accent betrays you."
Then he began to invoke a curse on himself and to swear, "I do not know the man." And immediately the rooster crowed. Matt 26:73-74

All four gospels mention this failure of Peter. Why is it so important? It is important for you to know that Peter was weak, in fact just like you, and that only the power of the Holy Spirit made him different.

Interestingly when Peter wrote to wives he also cautioned them against 'fearing anything that is frightening'.

For this is how the holy women who hoped in God used to adorn themselves, by submitting to their own husbands, as Sarah obeyed Abraham, calling him lord. And you are her children, if you do good and do not fear anything that is frightening. 1Pet. 3:5-6

Perhaps Peter understood the position and feelings of Christian wives married to non-Christian men more than most pastors and ministers today!

13. A Spirit of power and love and a sound mind

In Paul's letter to fellow-minister Timothy there are practical points for all believers as we grapple to be bold today. It seems that the passage we have analysed (2 Tim 1:6-8) is the burden of the letter. It is the first command he gives Timothy and appears to be his main concern. Thus we would expect what Paul says next to buttress this command with motives and application. So finally I will give five brief practical points mostly drawn from this letter, but before you read them please pray that God will make you want to change.

1. Remember grace...
Paul's encouraging letter to Timothy is filled with references to the love of God, the grace of Christ and the greatness of the salvation we have received. Only a believer filled with joy because of GRACE will be bold and persevering.

You then, my child, be strengthened by the grace that is in Christ Jesus. 2 Tim. 2:1

So use this grace to strengthen yourself. Meditate on it. And sing it.
This grace is found in God's word. So dig for it and mine it for grace:

But as for you, continue in what you have learned and have firmly believed, knowing from whom you learned it and how from childhood you have been acquainted with the sacred writings, which are able to make you wise for salvation through faith in Christ Jesus. 2Tim. 3:14 -15

2. Remember your high calling...
While we rejoice that we have received salvation can we ignore those who are in darkness under the wrath of God? What an honour, responsibility and duty to tell the gospel to others
who saved us and called us to a holy calling 2Tim. 1:9
We have a great salvation by a great God who has shown us

great grace and entrusted this ministry to us!

Remember Jesus Christ, risen from the dead, the offspring of David, as preached in my gospel,
for which I am suffering, bound with chains as a criminal. But the word of God is not bound! 2Tim. 2:8 -9
I charge you in the presence of God and of Christ Jesus, who is to judge the living and the dead, and by his appearing and his kingdom:
preach the word; be ready in season and out of season; reprove, rebuke, and exhort, with complete patience and teaching. 2Tim. 4:1-2

3. Trust in God's power to enable you to be faithful

It is so easy to sink under the responsibility and weight of this duty and get discouraged with our daily failure to be bold. Let us remember this is the Holy Spirit's work! He will keep us faithful and bold.

which is why I suffer as I do. But I am not ashamed, for I know whom I have believed, and I am convinced that he is able to guard until that Day what has been entrusted to me. 2 Tim. 1:12
By the Holy Spirit who dwells within us, guard the good deposit entrusted to you. 2 Tim. 1:14

Let us pray for this power everyday in spite of our great weakness.

4. Say what needs to be said and do not be pressured by people

There is almost nothing in the ministry of the Word that does not require boldness. Whether it is training up other believers to be faithful (and correcting them when they are not),

and what you have heard from me in the presence of many witnesses entrust to faithful men who will be able to teach

13. A Spirit of power and love and a sound mind

others also. 2Tim. 2:2

Or whether it is putting a stop to an arcane destructive quarrel in the church,

Remind them of these things, and charge them before God not to quarrel about words, which does no good, but only ruins the hearers.

Or whether it is the steady ministry of faithful exposition which will inevitably be criticised and despised from all sides,

Do your best to present yourself to God as one approved, a worker who has no need to be ashamed, rightly handling the word of truth. 2Tim. 2:14-15

you will need boldness. So do it depending on his grace!

5. Do not be surprised at suffering
Are you ready for persecution from the world? Paul told Timothy to prepare for it.

Share in suffering as a good soldier of Christ Jesus. 2 Tim. 2:3

While persecution comes to all who live for Christ,

Indeed, all who desire to live a godly life in Christ Jesus will be persecuted, 2 Tim. 3:12

it will especially come to those who are bold and evangelistic.

Therefore I endure everything for the sake of the elect, that they also may obtain the salvation that is in Christ Jesus with eternal glory. 2 Tim. 2:10
Remember Jesus Christ, risen from the dead, the offspring of David, as preached in my gospel,
for which I am suffering, bound with chains as a criminal. 2

Tim. 2:8-9

The easiest way to live a quiet life is to give up evangelism. Persecution is extremely unpleasant, embarrassing to the extent that we feel shame, and may not be understood even by fellow Christians (as was Paul's experience). But forewarned is forearmed and Jesus told us to jump for joy when we are persecuted (Luke 6:23).

But Paul warned Timothy (and us) to prepare himself for fierce opposition within the church as well as from the world outside.

But understand this, that in the last days there will come times of difficulty. 2 Tim. 3:1
while evil people and impostors will go on from bad to worse, deceiving and being deceived. 2Tim. 3:13

Impostors are false Christians who have got into churches and gained a following from which they oppose true teaching and faithful ministers. Preaching and teaching in this kind of church is hard. The more faithful, true, Christ-like, passionate and loving you are the more criticism you will receive.

The instigator of persecution from outside and of opposition from within is the same. It is Satan. Small wonder then if there is some coordination between these attacks. For example, just when you are reeling from a vicious attack from the world, some disgruntled 'impostor' within will try to split the church. Few of us have any inkling of what a full-scale Satanic attack is like.

14. Boldness in History

And you, O son of man, behold, cords will be placed upon you, and you shall be bound with them, so that you cannot go out among the people.
And I will make your tongue cling to the roof of your mouth, so that you shall be mute and unable to reprove them, for they are a rebellious house. Ezek. 3:25-26

God told Ezekiel that he will be bound so that he cannot go out and struck dumb so that he cannot speak. Why? It is an object lesson to the wicked of his day that God will no longer send prophets with warnings to repent. The reason? For they are a rebellious house. They had advanced so far down the road of rebellion that God would soon give up and let them perish. That this formed part of his prophecy shows that God had not yet entirely given up. They could hear of this warning object lesson, take heed and repent. Yet when God does remove his Word it is the final sign of abandonment to the wrath of God. From then on all is hopeless. Those two elements 'Go' and 'Teach' are also the main verbs in the Great Commission. And yet today there are whole families, neighbourhoods, towns, cities and nations where there is no gospel witness. No one goes to them. And no one teaches them. They are spiritual wastelands of gospel silence. In some cases this is because of oppressive regimes which forbid gospel preaching, but in most places it is because the church and Christians were long ago bound with the 'cords' of worldly cares and wrong priorities and 'struck dumb' through cowardice.

The purpose of this chapter is to compare the past with the present and see how far we have fallen. But I hope you too like me will be encouraged and fed by those giants in church history who are so different from today's believers and teachers.

So firstly we will see how gospel boldness is correlated with times of revival. And secondly we will see what great teachers of the past taught about gospel boldness, how they admired it and sought it for themselves. And if I can un-earth these authors so that many today will read them then it will do the church great benefit.

Gospel Boldness is correlated with times of revival

In times of remarkable revival invariably God made his people bold. Both the revival and the boldness were the work of the same Spirit. This is the same relationship we saw in Acts 4 where the apostles prayed for boldness and miracles of grace. It is very edifying to read of these great times because they make us hungry for God to do the same in our day, but unfortunately we can only look at a few examples.

Hugh Latimer
Hugh Latimer was one of the reformers of the Church in England in the 16th century. England at that time was in the darkness of Roman Catholic superstition and complete ignorance of the gospel. Latimer went throughout England preaching salvation by faith in Jesus Christ.

Bishop Ryle writes,
"I might supply many proofs of his courage and faithfulness as a minister. He did not shrink from attacking anybody's sins, even if they were the sins of a King. When Henry VIII. checked the diffusion of the Bible, Latimer wrote him a plain-spoken letter, long before he was a Bishop, remonstrating with him on his conduct, He feared God, and nothing else did he fear. "Latimer, Latimer," he exclaimed at the beginning of one of his sermons, "thou art going to speak before the high and mighty King Henry VIII., who is able, if he think fit, to take thy life away. Be careful what thou sayest. But Latimer, Latimer,

remember also thou art about to speak before the King of kings', and Lord of lords, Take heed that thou dost not displease Him." [31]

Ryle writes how Latimer was martyred,

"Then they brought a faggot kindled with fire, and laid it down at Ridley's feet, to whom Latimer then spake in this manner: 'Be of good comfort, brother Ridley, and play the man; We shall this day light such a candle, by God's grace, in England, as I trust never shall be put out.'
"And so the fire being kindled, when Ridley saw the fire flaming up towards him, he cried with a loud voice, 'Lord, into Thy hands I commend my Spirit: Lord, receive my spirit l' and repeated the latter part often. Latimer, crying as vehemently on the other aide of the stake, 'Father of heaven, receive my soul!' received the flame as if embracing it. After he had stroked his face with his hands, and as it were bathed them a little in the fire, he soon died, as it appeared, with very little pain"
"And thus much," says Fox, "concerning the end of this old blessed servant of God, Bishop Latimer, for whose laborious services, fruitful life, and constant death, the whole realm has cause to give great thanks to Almighty God."

George Whitefield

George Whitefield was converted when a student at Oxford University in 1735 and he soon committed himself to mission work in Georgia in the American colonies.

These are all quotes from Arnold Dallimore's excellent biography. The first quote shows George Whitefield on board a small sailing ship as he crossed the Atlantic for the first time. On board were a large number of soldiers and of course sailors and it is fascinating how he gradually began to win the crew for Christ.

---

[31] Ryle, p163 and 165

He started a
"catechism class for the soldiers. Only six or seven were present on this first occasion, but the numbers steadily increased, until in a week's time the class had an attendance of twenty, and the study had been enlarged to include an exposition of the Lord's Prayer. Finding this acceptance he began to preach whenever he read Prayers.

To these public efforts Whitefield added personal associations. These were principally with the officers and his Journals contain such reports as: 'Breakfasted with some of the gentlemen in the great cabin, who were very civil and let me put in a word for God.' 'Had an hour's conversation with a gentleman on board, on our fall in Adam and the necessity of our new birth in Christ Jesus, and hope it was not unpleasant to him.' 'Had some religious talk with the surgeon, who seems very well disposed.' 'Had near an hour's conversation with one who, I hope, will become an altogether Christian.' 'Gained an opportunity, by walking at night on the deck, to talk closely to the chief mate and one of the sergeants, and hope my words were not spoken in vain.' Yet he also established friendship with the crew and we find him writing, 'About eleven at night, I went and sat down with the sailors in the steerage, and reasoned with them about righteousness, temperance and a judgment to come.'

Steadily gaining the good will of all aboard, Whitefield quickly began other activities. He held a daily catechism class for the women and soon added a Bible study. He had Habersham give daily instruction in elementary education for the children, and also invited any soldiers and sailors who wished to learn to read and write to attend.

Then the ship's Master, Captain Whiting, began to show favour. Noticing that Whitefield had no place of privacy for study and prayer, he offered him the use of his cabin....[32]

---

[32] Dallimore, p153

14. Boldness in History

He did not mince words when he preached on board. Here is an extract from one of his sermons on board entitled the Heinous Sin of Drunkeness.

Believe me, ye unhappy men of Belial (for such, alas! this sin has made you), it is not without the strongest reasons, as well as utmost concern for your precious and immortal souls, that I now conjure you, in the Apostle's words, 'Not to be drunk with wine, or any other liquor, wherein is excess ...
But think you, O ye drunkards, that you shall ever be partakers of the inheritance of the saints in light? Do you flatter yourselves, that you, who have made them often the subject of your drunken songs, shall be exalted to sing with them the Heavenly songs of Zion? No, as by drunkenness you have made your hearts cages of unclean birds, with impure and unclean spirits must you dwell ...
Let not a servile fear of being despised by a man that shall die, hinder thy turning unto the living God. For what is a little contempt? It is but a vapour which vanisheth away. Better be derided by a few companions here than be made ashamed before men and angels hereafter. Better be the song of a few drunkards on earth, than dwell with them, where they shall be eternally reproaching and cursing each other in hell! ... But turn ye, turn ye from your evil ways. Come to Jesus Christ, with the repenting prodigal saying, 'Father, we have sinned! We beseech Thee, let not this sin of drunkenness have any longer dominion over us!' Lay hold on Christ by faith, and lo! it shall happen to you even as you will! ...
Behold I have told you before! Remember, you were this day informed what the end of drunkenness would be! And I summon you, in the name of that God Whom I serve, to meet me at the judgment seat of Christ, that you may acquit both my Master and me, and confess with your own mouths that your damnation was of your own selves."
Such was the preaching heard aboard the Whitaker, the Ann and the Lightfoot. At the close of this sermon Captain Mackay arose and 'made a useful speech, exhorting the men to give

Gospel Boldness

heed to the things spoken', [33]

George Whitefield on returning to England found that many churches closed their doors to him and he began to preach in the fields.

"The burning desire to reach the hosts of mankind with the message of saving grace overruled all trials that came in the way, and he testified to the Divine assistance he experienced in learning the task, and the joy that was his as he performed it, saying:
As the scene was new and I had just begun to be an extempore preacher, it often occasioned many inward conflicts. Sometimes, when twenty thousand people were before me, I had not, in my own apprehension, a word to say either to God or them. But I never was totally deserted, and frequently ... so assisted, that I knew by happy experience what our Lord meant by saying, 'Out of his belly shall flow rivers of living water", The open firmament above me, the prospect of the adjacent fields, with the sight of thousands and thousands, some in coaches, some on horseback, and some in the trees, and at times all affected and drenched in tears together, to which sometimes was added the solemnity of the approaching evening, was almost too much for, and quite overcame me.'
Any doubts about the open-air ministry that Whitefield may have had when he came to Bristol, had now vanished. The unmistakable evidence of the Divine approval, manifest in the conversion of the colliers and others, had overruled the seemingly contradictory commands of the Church, and had given him a mighty boldness in the face of whatever opposition his extraordinary proceedings might provoke. 'My preaching in the fields', he exclaimed, 'may displease some timorous, bigoted men, but I am thoroughly persuaded it pleases God, and why should I fear anything else!'"[34]

---

[33] Dallimore, p159
[34] Dallimore, p268-269

14. Boldness in History

Charles Wesley

Charles and John Wesley were also students at Oxford and soon after Whitefield's conversion also found salvation in Christ alone. They started immediately to preach. In one of the most moving passages in his journal, Charles relates how he ministered to the condemned convicts in Newgate Prison who were hanged at Tyburn.

1738 Sun. July 16th. Metcalf and Savage came: the latter received faith on Friday night, in prayer, and is now filled with comfort, peace, and joy. I took coach with Metcalf; preached the threefold state with boldness; gave the sacrament....

Mon., July 17th... At Newgate I preached on death (which they must suffer the day after to-morrow)... At one I was with the Black in his cell; James Hutton assisting. Two more of the malefactors came. I had great help and power in prayer. One rose, and said, he felt his heart all on fire, so as he never found himself before; he was all in a sweat; believed Christ died for him. I found myself overwhelmed with the love of Christ to sinners. The Black was quite happy. The other criminal was in an excellent temper; believing, or on the point of it. I talked with another, concerning faith in Christ: he was greatly moved. The Lord, I trust, will help his unbelief also.

...At six I carried Bray and Fish to Newgate again, and talked chiefly with Hudson and Newington. He declared he had felt, some time ago in prayer, inexpressible joy and love; but was much troubled at its being so soon withdrawn. The Lord gave power to pray. They were deeply affected. We have great hopes of both.

Tues., July 18th. At night I was locked in with Bray in one of the cells. We wrestled in mighty prayer. All the criminals were present; and all delightfully cheerful. The soldier, in particular, found his comfort and joy increase every moment. Another, from the time he communicated, has been in perfect peace. Joy was visible in all their faces. We sang, "Behold the

Saviour of mankind, Nail'd to the shameful tree! How vast the love that him inclined To bleed and die for thee," &e.

It was one of the most triumphant hours I have ever known. Yet on

Wed., July 19th, I rose very heavy, and backward to visit them for the last time. At six I prayed and sang with them all together.

At half-hour past nine their irons were knocked off, and their hands tied.... By half-hour past ten we came to Tyburn, waited till eleven: then were brought the children appointed to die. I got upon the cart with Sparks and Broughten: the Ordinary endeavoured to follow, when the poor prisoners begged he might not come; and the mob kept him down.

I prayed first, then Sparks and Broughton. We had prayed before that our Lord would show there was a power superior to the fear of death. Newington had quite forgot his pain. They were all cheerful; full of comfort, peace, and triumph; assuredly persuaded Christ had died for them, and wanted to receive them into paradise. Greenaway was impatient to be with Christ..

The Black had spied me coming out of the coach, and saluted me with his looks. As often as his eyes met mine, he smiled with the most composed, delightful countenance I ever saw. Read caught hold of my hand in a transport of joy. Newington seemed perfectly pleased. Hudson declared he was never better, or more at ease, in mind and body. None showed any natural terror of death: no fear, or crying, or tears. All expressed their desire of our following them to paradise. I never saw such calm triumph, such incredible indifference to dying. We sang several hymns; particularly, "Behold the Saviour of mankind, Nail'd to the shameful tree ;" and the hymn entitled, "Faith in Christ," which concludes, "A guilty, weak, and helpless worm, Into thy hands I fall: Be thou my life, my righteousness, My Jesus, and my all."

We prayed Him, in earnest faith, to receive their spirits. I could do nothing but rejoice: kissed Newington and Hudson; took leave of each in particular. Mr. Broughton bade them not be

14. Boldness in History

surprised when the cart should draw away. They cheerfully replied, they should not; expressed some concern how we should get back to our coach. We left them going to meet their Lord, ready for the Bridegroom. When the cart drew off, not one stirred, or struggled for life, but meekly gave up their spirits. Exactly at twelve they were turned off. I spoke a few suitable words to the crowd; and returned, full of peace and confidence in our friends' happiness. That hour under the gallows was the most blessed hour of my life.[35]

What a wonderful example of gospel boldness! And Charles had been converted only 2 months.

He then followed Whitefield in preaching in the fields and lanes of England. Arnold Dallimore tells us,

Charles became an open-air preacher of great power. He was more oratorical and dramatic than his brother, and apparently was second only to Whitefield, Rowland and perhaps Cennick in these gifts. A report by one of his hearers has come down to us:
I found him, standing on a table-board in an erect posture, with his hands and eyes lifted up to heaven in prayer; he prayed with uncommon fervency, fluency, and variety of proper expressions. He then preached about an hour in such a manner as I scarce ever heard any man preach. Though I have heard many a finer sermon, according to the common taste ... I never heard any man discover such evident signs of a vehement desire, or labour so earnestly to convince his hearers that they were all by nature in a sinful, lost, undone state ... He showed how great a change a faith in Christ would produce in the whole man ...
With uncommon fervour he acquitted himself as an ambassador of Christ, beseeching them in His name. and praying them in His stead to be reconciled to God. And

---

[35] Wesley

although he used no notes nor had anything in his hand but a Bible, yet he delivered his thoughts in a rich, copious variety of expression, and with so much propriety, that I could not observe anything incoherent or inanimate through the whole performance.[36]

Howell Harris

Howell Harris was Whitefield's contemporary and friend and preached throughout Wales.

Harris often found himself the centre of violent conflicts. Wherever he went he was bitterly hated by many, but loved with equal intensity by many more. He was passionately devoted to the Church of England, yet even among her evangelical clergy some encouraged and others opposed his unordained evangelizing. He made warm friends of a number of the Nonconformist ministers, but these friendships were not without their frictions because of his refusal to leave the Church and join with them. He was not a man of deep Biblical learning, but during these early post-conversion years he gradually grew in knowledge, and has left written testimony regarding the manner in which he came to clear Calvinistic convictions. He gave away his possessions to help the poor and often went without food and without sufficient sleep, until his health began to suffer. His zeal sometimes overran his discretion; for instance, there was an occasion when, as he returned from a very late meeting, trudging in the darkness across the Black Mountains adjacent to his home, he fell exhausted when trying to cross a stile in a farmer's field and was found there asleep at dawn.
But despite his opposers and his excesses, Harris's triumph abounded. When Joseph wrote, reporting complaints which had been made against him, he replied:
I am no more concerned to hear their threats than to hear a fly. I should tremble to hear a holy man reprimand me, but

---

[36] Dallimore p376-377

Drunkards, etc., have not ye keeping of ye door to Christ's vineyard ... Though I should leave all to follow such a work, I know my enemies shall have no room to insult, for those that honour Him He'll honour.

He estimated that he walked more than 2,500 miles in going to and from his meetings in two years, and said that as he travelled, 'I devoted myself to exhorting everyone I met to flee from the wrath to come'.[37]

Mary Slessor

In Chapters 4 & 8 we saw two women of the Bible who displayed gospel boldness. Not just male preachers but lay women too who gave themselves to the work of gospel and displayed boldness. So lest anyone think that in church history boldness is limited to men, let me quote a passage from Mary Slessor's biography.

Mary evangelised the Okoyong tribe, a 'tribe of terrorists' in West Africa, now Nigeria. Some were deeply affected by the gospel. One of the chiefs "Edem acted nobly. He not only arranged for the housing of the two men, but gave them a piece of ground and seed for food plants. When she went to tell him all had been done, he simply said, "Thank you, Ma." But in the evening he came alone to her, knelt and held her feet, and thanked her again and again for her wonderful love and courage, for her action, in forbidding them to take life at his son's death, and for all the peaceful ways which she was introducing. "We are all weary of the old customs," he said, "but no single person or House among us has power to break them off, because they are part of the Egbo system." And one by one, secretly and unknown to each other, the free people came to her and thanked her gratefully for the state of safety she was bringing about, and charged her to keep a stout heart and to go forward and do away with all the old fashions, the end of which was always death."[38]

---

[37] p 244 Dallimore

Gospel Boldness was taught in the past

Christians in earlier ages were far more concerned about this than we are. I have included many lengthy quotes from these authors which I hope the reader will not find tedious but rather edifying. So here is a brief look at the famous teachers from the past and what they taught about boldness.

John Calvin
Firstly Calvin greatly admired boldness in Bible characters.
While doing this study I have been surprised, by the lyrical praise Calvin heaps on the prophets and apostles for their boldness. Calvin was not given to excitement and hyperbole especially in his lectures, yet the things he says in his commentaries come close. (A matter of semantics: I trust the reader will understand that his commentaries were translated from French or Latin notes of his lectures and that words like 'courage', 'bravery' and 'heroism' often come close in meaning to the 'gospel boldness' which I have been using in this book.).

Jeremiah has before shewn that he possessed an heroic courage in despising all the splendor of the world, and in regarding as nothing those proud men who boasted that they were the rulers of the Church: Here we may notice the boldness of the Prophet; he had not been broken down by all the evils he had met with, but ever faithfully performed the office committed to him. (About the Prophet Jeremiah. Commentary on Jer 15:18)

... Though the Prophet dreaded the sufferings of the prison, though he also feared death, he yet overcame all these feelings, and presented his life as a sacrifice, when he openly and boldly answered the king, that the Chaldeans would shortly be conquerors, and make him a captive. (About the Prophet Jeremiah. Commentary on Jer

[38] Livingstone, p74

37:17)

We hence perceive how invincible was his courage, for he marched through certain deaths, and was yet terrified by no dangers, but performed the office entrusted to him by God. (About the Prophet Jeremiah. Commentary on Jer 43:8-10)

When therefore he dared to prophesy against the king, the whole people, and the land, we hence see how great must have been his firmness and his courage, still boldly to discharge his office; for he was not terrified by danger, but promulgated whatever God had committed to him. We then have here a singular example of magnanimity; for the Prophet hesitated not to risk his own life while obeying God. (About the Prophet Jeremiah. Commentary on Jer 44:29)

We then see that he was endued with the spirit of invincible courage, so as to discharge his office freely and intrepidly.
(About the Prophet Jeremiah. Commentary on 51:60-64)

...we have here an example of most manly prudence and of singular consistency, united with a magnanimity truly heroic. (From the Preface of Commentary on Daniel)

It hence appears with how great and with how invincible courage and perseverance he was endued by the Holy Spirit. (About the Prophet Hosea. Commentary on Hosea 1:1)

Thus anciently the Prophets and Apostles had invincible courage and magnanimity, which stood firm against the dreadful attacks of the whole world, because they knew by whom they were sent. (Commentary on John 8:54)

... the apostles, (with a stout stomach,) with a lively courage and invincible violentness [force] of mind, did, notwithstanding, execute the office which they knew was enjoined them by God; and also, what innumerable troubles they suffered with great perseverance, what wearisomeness they passed over, how patiently they sustained most cruel persecution; and, lastly, how meekly they suffered reproach, sorrow, and calamity of all sorts. (From the Argument of

the Commentary on Acts)

...the readers may weigh with themselves the invincible and heroic fortitude which was in Paul... (Commentary on Acts 21:1-6)

For a virtue so heroic is, as it were, a heavenly seal, by which the Lord marks out his Apostles. (Commentary on 2 Corinthians 12:12)

O heroic breast, which drew from a prison, and from death itself, comfort to those who were not in danger! (About Paul in prison in Rome. Commentary on Eph 3:13)

Calvin then greatly admired the prophets, apostles and others who displayed boldness. They were his heroes. He sought to emulate them and prayed for grace to be bold himself. I believe it is impossible to understand Calvin's character and ministry without this element. Small wonder then that in Geneva which was surrounded by powerful enemies and that after so many trials he continued to boldly preach the gospel. In continuing to do this for many years and with such great consistency he provided a vital ministry to exiles from persecution from other European countries as far afield as Scotland, England, France and Italy, many of whom returned to their home countries to continue the Reformation at the cost of their lives. What was the secret of his great strength? He prayed for gospel boldness.

Secondly Calvin, saw that boldness was indispensible.
The prophets and apostles could not have conducted their ministry without boldness. And ministers today need the same, argues Calvin.
As to the word Cry, I have no objection to view it as denoting both boldness and clearness; because prophets ought not to mutter in an obscure manner, but to pronounce their message with a distinct voice, and to utter boldly and with open mouth whatever they have been commanded to declare. Let every one, therefore, who is called to this office constantly remember and believe, that he ought to meet difficulties of every sort with unshaken boldness, such as was always manifested both by prophets and by apostles. (Commentary on Is 40:6)

Here Micah, in a courageous spirit, stands up alone against all the false teachers even when he saw that they were a large number, and that they appealed to their number, according to their usual practice, as their shield. Hence he says, I am filled with power by the Spirit of Jehovah. This confidence is what all God's servants should possess, that they may not succumb to the empty and vain boastings of those who subvert the whole order of the Church.
He then adds courage. These two things are especially necessary for all ministers of the word, — that is, to excel in wisdom, to understand what is true and right, and to be also endued with inflexible firmness, by which they may overcome both Satan and the whole world, and never turn aside from their course, though the devil may in all ways assail them. (Commentary on Micah 3:8)

And the more bold the reprobate are to oppress the truth, the more courage ought we to take to ourselves. For the servants of God must be armed with invincible constancy of the Spirit, that they may never give place to the devil, nor to his ministers; as the Lord commandeth Jeremiah to encounter with the reprobate with a face of iron. (About Paul and Barnabas. Commentary on Acts 13:46)

Thirdly, Calvin taught that boldness is a gift of the Holy Spirit.

All the fortitude, courage, strength and boldness shown the prophets and apostles was solely due to the Holy Spirit.
This passage contains a useful doctrine, from which we learn that strength shall never be wanting to God's servants, while they derive courage from the conviction that God himself is the author of their calling and become thus magnanimous; for God will then supply them with strength and courage invincible, so as to render them formidable to the whole world: but if they be unhinged and timid, and turn here and there, and be influenced by the fear of men, God will render them base and contemptible, and make them to tremble at the least breath of air, and they shall be wholly broken down; — and why? because they are unworthy that God should help them, that he should stretch forth his hand and fortify them by his power, and supply them, as it has been already said, with that fortitude, by which they might terrify both the Devil and the whole world.
Jer. 1:17

"Take heed to thyself; for if thou be timid, I will cause thee really to fear, or, I will break thee down before them."

It is indeed a godly truth, that God would give courage to his Prophet so as to render him invincible against his enemies; and doubtless he would exhort us in vain, were he not to supply us with fortitude by his Spirit.

GOD supplies here his servant with confidence; for courage was necessary in that state of trembling which we have observed. Jeremiah thought himself unfit to undertake a work so onerous; he had also to do and to contend with refractory men, and not a few in number; for the whole people had already, through their ungodly and wicked obstinacy, hardened themselves in the contempt of God. As, then, there was no more any care for religion, and no regard manifested by the people for heavenly truth, Jeremiah could not, diffident as he was, undertake so heavy a burden, without being supported by the hand of God. (Commentary on Jeremiah 1:18)

God in this verse briefly reminds his servant, that though he would be supplied with invincible power, yet he would have great trials, so that his office would not be, according to a common saying, a mere play. He then shews for what purpose he would be made like a fortified city, an iron pillar, and a brazen wall, even that he might manfully fight, and not for the purpose of keeping away all dangers, and all fightings, and everything hard and grievous to the flesh. We, in short, see that the promise was given for this end, — that Jeremiah, relying on God's aid, might not hesitate to set himself against all the Jews, and that whatever might be their fury, he might still be courageous. (Commentary on Jeremiah 1:19)

Would that all who are called upon to make a confession of their faith would rely on that assurance; for the power and majesty of the Spirit would be displayed in a different manner for overthrowing the ministers of Satan. Now that we are partly carried away by our own feelings, and, swelled with pride, rush on heedlessly, or advance farther than is proper, and partly confine ourselves within the limits of improper timidity, sad experience shows that we are deprived of the grace of God and the assistance of the Spirit. As Christ affirms, according to Matthew and Mark, that it is the Spirit of the Father that speaketh in us, (Matthew 10:10; Mark 13:11,) and here declares that he will give a mouth, we infer that it is His prerogative to fortify us by the Spirit. (Commentary on Mark 13:11)

But this heroical courage and nobleness of heart was a work of the Holy Ghost; because God doth mightily show forth his power in those whom he appointeth unto great matters, that they may be able to fulfill their function. (Commentary on Acts 7:24)

Fourthly, Calvin distinguishes human courage from divine.

... how courageous he was to keep the course of his calling, and how bold he was ever now and then to enter into new dangers. This so invincible fortitude of mind, and such patient enduring of the cross, do sufficiently declare, that Paul labored not after the manner of men, but that he was furnished with the heavenly power of the Spirit. (About Paul in Commentary on Acts 17:1)

Hence we are taught, first, that not one of us possesses that firmness and unshaken constancy of the Spirit, which is requisite for fulfilling our ministry, until we are endued from heaven with a new power. And indeed the obstructions are so many and so great, that no courage of man will be able to overcome them. It is God, therefore, who endues us with "the spirit of power;" for they who, in other respects, give tokens of much strength, fall down in a moment, when they are not upheld by the power of the Divine Spirit. (Commentary on 2 Tim 1:7)

Fifthly, Calvin sees boldness as fruit of the Spirit that must be cultivated.

Let us, however, remember, that in these words the Holy Ghost dictates to us a form of prayer; and that, therefore, we are enjoined to cultivate a spirit of invincible fortitude and courage, which may serve to sustain us under the weight of all the calamities we may be called to endure, so that we may be able to testify of a truth, that even when reduced to the extremity of despair, we have never ceased to trust in God; that no temptations, however unexpected, could expel his fear from our hearts; and, in fine, that we were never so overwhelmed by the burden of our afflictions, however great, as not to have our eyes always directed to him. (Commentary on Ps 44:19)

Sixthly, Calvin sees that the root of boldness is a strong faith and conviction of the truth.

....wherever there is firm faith, there to speech will flow ultroneously (=spontaneously)... "Lord, support not only my heart by faith, lest I be overwhelmed with temptation, but grant me also freedom of speech, that I may fearlessly sound forth thy praises among men." We observe, when he asks to be endued with boldness of speech, that he begins with the heart.... Conscious of this weakness, which is perceptible in all mankind, he accommodates his prayer in the following manner: "Though I am not always prepared with that boldness of speech which is desirable, suffer me not to continue long silent." By this language the prophet tacitly admits, that he had not been so steadfast and bold as was requisite, but that he was, as it were, struck speechless by reason of fear. Whence we may learn, that the faculty of speaking freely is no more in our power than are the affections. of the heart. As far, then, as God directs our tongues, they are prepared for ready utterance; but no sooner does he withdraw the spirit of magnanimity, than not only our hearts faint, or rather fail, but also our tongues become mute. (Commentary on Ps 119:43)

We then see that there can be no courage in men, unless God supports them by his word, so that they may recover their lost strength and regain their alacrity. Had the Prophet only bidden them to take courage, they might have replied, that there was nothing in their circumstances to encourage them; but when the word of God was set before them, every excuse was taken away; and they were now to gird up the loins, and boldly to fight, inasmuch as God supplied them with weapons. (Commentary on Zech 8:9)

With good reason does he add this; for there is nothing that tends so much to produce liberty as a good conscience and a life free from crime and reproach; as, on the contrary, timidity must be the lot of those who have a bad conscience. (Commentary on 1 Tim 3:10)

Seventhly, Calvin taught that God may give fear and timidity as a punishment.

Let us however learn, that it is in God's power to bend men's hearts either way, so as both to cast down the courageous with terror, as well as to animate the timid. (Commentary on Ex 23:27)

Hence we gather that the bravery of men is in God's power, so that He can make cowards of the boldest whenever He so pleases. And we must bear in mind what we shall see elsewhere, "How should one chase a thousand, and two put ten thousand to flight, except God had sold them and had shut them up" under their hand? (Deuteronomy 32:30.) And for this reason God calls Himself the God of hosts, in order that believers may live securely under His guardianship; whilst the wicked, and the despisers of the Law, should dread the slightest motion when He is wroth with them. (Commentary on Deut 28:25)

Hence it is, that the hearts of the brave become cowardly, and also, that the most timid become sometimes bolder than lions, even when it pleases God either to weaken or to strengthen the hearts of men. (Commentary on Jer 49:22)

He then adds, that their valor had failed or languished, even because terror stupefied them when they heard that the city was taken. So also true became what is added, that they became women, that they were like women as to courage, for no one dared to oppose the conquerors. (Commentary on Jer 51:30)

We hence learn, that there is in men no courage, except as far as God supplies them with vigor. As soon then as He withdraws his Spirit, those who were before the most valiant become faint-hearted, and those who breathed great ferocity are made soft and effeminate: for by the word heart is meant inward boldness or courage; and by the knees and loins the strength of body is to be understood. (Commentary on Nahum 2:10)

Calvin then sees both natural courage and gospel boldness as gifts of God, given according to his own sovereign will.

Eighthly and finally Calvin prayed for boldness.

This was the secret to Calvin's perseverance throughout his long and arduous ministry in Geneva.

This example shows us how earnestly God should be entreated constantly to support us with new supplies of His grace, since otherwise the boldest of us all would fail at every moment. (Commentary on Numb 20:6)

Grant, Almighty God, that as we are assailed on every side by enemies, and as not only the wicked according to the flesh are incensed against us, but Satan also musters his forces and contrives in various ways to ruin us, — O grant, that we being furnished with the courage thy Spirit bestows, may fight to the end under thy guidance and never be wearied under any evils. And may we, at the same time, be humbled under thy mighty hand when it pleases thee to afflict us and so sustain all our troubles that with a courageous mind we may strive for that victory which thou promises to us, and that having completed all our struggles we may at length attain that blessed rest which is reserved for us in heaven through Jesus Christ our Lord. Amen. (Calvin's Prayer after Commentary on Joel 3:9-10)

The apostles had showed a token of heroic fortitude; now again they pray that they may be furnished with boldness. So Paul desireth the faithful to pray unto the Lord that his mouth may be opened, whereas, notwithstanding, his voice did sound everywhere (Ephesians 6:19) Therefore, the more we perceive ourselves to be holpen by the Lord, let us learn to crave at the hands of God that we may go forward hereafter; and especially seeing the free confession of the gospel is a singular gift of God, we must continually beseech him to keep us in the same. (Commentary on Acts 4:30-31)

And forasmuch as Christ hath promised the same Spirit to all his servants, let us only defend the truth faithfully, and let us crave a mouth and wisdom of him, and we shall be sufficiently furnished to speak, so that neither the wit, neither yet the babbling of our adversaries, shall be able to make us ashamed. (About Stephen. Commentary on Acts 6:9)

Thus we see from these quotes that Calvin has a very high view of gospel boldness. He sees that boldness is indispensible to gospel ministers and all believers, that it is a gift of God and fruit of the Holy Spirit, and should be prayed for constantly.

John Bunyan
John Bunyan lived in England in the mid-17th century and as a Baptist was imprisoned under the Act of Uniformity for preaching without a licence. Who can read his most famous

book, Pilgrim's Progress without crying out for power, perservance and boldness? Let's consider a few of John Bunyan's characters Despondency, Much-Afraid, Giant Despair and his wife Diffidence, and two places, Hill of Caution and Doubting Castle.

Giant Despair, lives in Doubting Castle. He is not alone. He lives with his wife Diffidence. And together they trap pilgrims of their way to the Celestial City. What is diffidence? It is an unwillingness to assert an opinion because of uncertainty. Today many Christians would see diffidence as a 'grace'. Why would Bunyan include diffidence as one of three formidable enemies of the Christian (along with doubt and despair)? Because Bunyan with his unerring instinct for spiritual reality in Christian experience sees that doubt, despair and diffidence are inseparably connected. Addressing people's doubts with apologetics and reasoned argument is very necessary. But the reason why droves have apostasized in recent decades is that they are too timid and ashamed to confess Christ. This timidity finds a useful excuse because the person has doubts which are welcomed as reasons not to confess Christ in public. In short, the same cycle of which Bunyan warned against: cowardice leading to doubts being welcomed and a despair leading away from faith in Christ, is repeated again and again.

Later the shepherds point out to Christian a mountain called Caution upon which many blind people were stumbling among the tombs. The shepherds explain, *"from there is a path that leads directly to Doubting Castle, which is kept by Giant Despair; and these men (pointing to them among the tombs) came once on pilgrimage, as you do now, even until they came to that same stile. And because the right way was rough in that place, they chose to go out of it into that meadow, and there were taken by Giant Despair, and cast into Doubting Castle; where after they had a while been kept in the dungeon, he at last did put out their eyes, and led them among those tombs, where he has left them to wander to this very day, that the saying of the wise man might be fulfilled, "He that wandereth out of the way of understanding shall remain in the congregation of the dead." Prov. 21:16.*[39]

Thus to Bunyan, timidity, diffidence and caution are not minor faults but are dangerous spiritual enemies that lead not just to the loss of our witness and sap our strength for evangelism but threaten the eternal well-being of our souls.

Other prisoners released from Doubting Castle were Master Despondency and Much-afraid, his daughter. In Bunyan's story they turn out to be true pilgrims for all their weakness but Despondency's final words carry a ringing message for all today's Christians. *"You know what we have been, and how troublesomely we have behaved ourselves in every company. My will and my daughter's is, that our desponds and slavish fears be by no man ever received, from the day of our departure, forever; for I know that after my death they will offer themselves to others. For, to be plain with you, they are ghosts which we entertained when we first began to be pilgrims, and could never shake them off after; and they will walk about, and seek entertainment of the pilgrims: but for our sakes, shut the doors upon them."*[40]

Note that Bunyan did not think that only ministers needed to be bold. To give in to cowardice, timidity and caution are as dangerous for laymen as much as ministers, and women as much as men.

George Whitefield

We have seen Whitefield's Spirit-filled boldness. Did he think it was for only for exceptional evangelists like himself or did he actually teach it and inculcate it upon others who were not as gifted?

He had preached to ministerial students and after he left he

---

[39] Bunyan, p112
[40] Bunyan, p280

14. Boldness in History

wrote to them these words;

"I heartily pray God that you may be burning and shining lights in the midst of a crooked and perverse generation... Indeed, my dear brethren, it rejoiced me much to see such dawnings of grace in your souls, Only I thought that most of you were bowed down too much with a servile fear of man ... Unless your hearts are free from worldly hopes and worldly fears you will never speak boldly as you ought to speak ... Study, therefore, brethren, your hearts as well as books. Ask yourselves again and again, whether you would preach for Christ if you were sure to lay down your lives for so doing." [41]

And when anticipating his ministry in America, he wrote;

"I love those that thunder out the Word. The Christian world is in a deep sleep. Nothing but a loud voice can awaken them out of it."

A Rev Henry Piers of Bexley had proved timid about declaring the Gospel as opposed to a works-righteousness, and Whitefield entreated him:

"Let me exhort you, by the mercies of God, to continue unwearied in well-doing. You have seen the afflictions of God's spiritual Israel. 'Do and live' is the most they hear, and what is this but requiring them to make bricks without straw? Arise, arise then, my dear Mr Piers and proclaim the Lord to be their righteousness ... Fear not the face of man ... I hope my dear friend ere now hath prevented my exhortations. Methinks I see him, with all boldness, declaring the whole counsel of God and the attentive people joyfully receiving the gracious words which proceed out of his mouth." [42]

---

[41] Dallimore, p399-400
[42] Dallimore, p397-398

To Whitefield then, gospel boldness was indispensible for those who aspired to teach others. For him it was the crying need of the 18th Century. What would he say to us today?

Jonathan Edwards

Jonathan Edwards was a central figure to the Great Awakening in North America. He had seen revival break out in his own church at Northampton, New England, and later welcomed George Whitefield who had crossed the Atlantic and ministered as an itinerant evangelist in N America. He greatly admired Whitefield for his boldness, which he saw as an absolute necessity in those called to preach.

In his classic "*Some Thoughts Concerning the Present Revival of Religion in New England*," he praises boldness in this fashion.

"And the great things that Mr. Whitefield has done, every where, as he has run through the British dominions, (so far as they are owing to means,) are very much owing to the appearance of these things (ie zeal and resolution) which he is eminently possessed of. When the people see these in a person, to a great degree, it awes them, and has a commanding influence upon their minds. It seems to them that they must yield; they naturally fall before them, without standing to contest or dispute the matter; they are conquered as it were by surprise. But while we are cold and heartless, and only go on in a dull manner, in an old formal round, we shall never do any great matters. Our attempts, with the appearance of such coldness and irresolution, will not so much as make persons think of yielding. They will hardly be sufficient to put it into their minds; and if it be put into their minds, the appearance of such indifference and cowardice does as it were call for and provoke opposition.—Our misery is want of zeal and courage; for not only through want of them does all fail that we seem to attempt, but it prevents our attempting any thing very remarkable for the kingdom of Christ. Hence oftentimes, when

14. Boldness in History

any thing very considerable is proposed to be done for the advancement of religion or the public good, many difficulties are in the way, and a great many objections are started, and it may be it is put off from one to another; but nobody does any thing. And after this manner good designs or proposals have often failed, and have sunk as soon as proposed. Whereas, if we had but Mr. Whitefield's zeal and courage, what could not we do, with such a blessing as we might expect!

Zeal and courage will do much in persons of but an ordinary capacity; but especially would they do great things, if joined with great abilities. If some great men who have appeared in our nation, had been as eminent in divinity as they were in philosophy, and had engaged in the christian cause with as much zeal and fervour as some others have done, and with a proportional blessing of heaven, they would have conquered all Christendom, and turned the world upside down. We have many ministers in the land that do not want abilities, they are persons of bright parts and learning; they should consider how much is expected and will be required of them by their Lord and Master, how much they might do for Christ, and what great honour and glorious a reward they might receive, if they had in their hearts a heavenly warmth, and divine heat proportionable to their light."[43]

In his sermon "CHRIST THE EXAMPLE OF MINISTERS", he says this.

"They should imitate him (Christ) in the manner of his preaching; who taught not as the scribes, but with authority, boldly, zealously, and fervently; insisting chiefly on the most important things in religion, being much in warning men of the danger of damnation, setting forth the greatness of the future misery of the ungodly; insisting not only on the outward, but also the inward and spiritual, duties of religion; being much in declaring the great provocation and danger of spiritual pride,

---

[43] Edwards Vol 1, p 424

and a self-righteous disposition; yet much insisting on the necessity and importance of inherent holiness, and the practice of piety."[44]

And yet Jonathan Edwards was concerned also about the various abuses of the revival. One of those was false boldness caused by spiritual pride. Spiritual pride causes those who have not been converted or those who are immature in the faith to harshly criticise and censor others. This he says is not following the example of Christ who was always meek and rebuked out of a love for men's souls and for the glory of God. If ever God in his mercy revives his Church in our day, there will undoubtedly be many who will need to heed his warnings so I have quoted him at length in Appendix II.

Robert Haldane

Haldane was a Scottish nobleman who sold his castle to plant churches in Scotland. Later he lectured in Geneva where he had a remarkable number of conversions. I quoted Haldane in the Introduction to show that gospel boldness is dependent on the quality of the believer's hope. The quote came from his famous commentary on Romans and he is commenting on Romans 5:5. The text does not speak about boldness at all, yet Haldane felt sufficiently strongly about boldness to draw that application for his readers from it.

Charles Bridges

Charles Bridges was an influential minister in the Church in England in the first half of the 19th Century. In his book *'The Christian Ministry; WITH AN INQUIRY INTO THE CAUSES OF ITS INEFFICIENCY."*, after confessing that the fear of man is one of his own greatest difficulties, hear what he says to us all,

"Indeed the subterfuges of cowardice and self-deception are

---

[44] Edwards Vol 2, p 392

14. Boldness in History

endless, when "the wisdom of this world" has begun to prevail against the simplicity of faith. How seldom do the rich and poor share alike in the faithfulness of Ministerial reproof! How hard it is, instead of "receiving honour one from another," to seek the honour that comes from God only! How ready are we to listen to cautions from influential quarters against excessive zeal! How much more afraid we are of others going too far, than of coming short ourselves of the full requirements of the Scriptural standard!—sometimes preferring intercourse with our brethren of a lower standard, or even with the world, rather than with those whose Ministry most distinctly bears the mark of the cross! In how many cases of conviction is the "light hidden under a bushel," or exhibited only to the friends of the Gospel! How many shrink from "witnessing a good confession," except under the shelter of some great name! How often are opportunities of usefulness neglected! and the "endurance of afflictions "in "making full proof of our Ministry" avoided from the fear of the cross! 'We cannot' (we say) 'do everything at once. We hope to gain our point little by little. We dare not, therefore, by taking a bold step upon the impulse of the moment close the avenues of distant and important advantage.' But does our conscience clear us of a desire to follow our Master, without "taking up <u>the daily cross</u>?" Are we not afraid of "being fools for Christ's sake?" Do we not sometimes "become all things to all men," when we ought to remember that, "if we still please men, we cannot be the servants of Christ?" Christian prudence indeed is most valuable in its own place, connexion, and measure; and the lack of it brings with it great inconvenience. But except it be the exercise of faith, combined with boldness, and encircled with a warm atmosphere of Christian love, it will degenerate, and become the time-serving spirit of the world. "The fear of man" often assumes the name of prudence, while a worldly spirit of unbelief is the actual dominant, though disguised, principle. "[45]

---

[45] Bridges, p124-125

When we read of these concerns from an age when Christians were far bolder than we are today, one can not help comparing their attitude, prayers and concerns with our own. I am sure if men like Bridges came back and spoke to us today, it would be about our lack of boldness.

Charles Haddon Spurgeon in *The Soul Winner*
Spurgeon wrote much about boldness in his voluminous writings as well as exemplifying it in his long and successful ministry in London in the late Victorian times, but perhaps his most concentrated and explicit teaching on boldness is in his book, '*The Soul Winner*', which was written not just for ministers but laymen as well. I have quoted him extensively though it is worth reading the whole book.

Here is what he says about zeal and earnestness;

If any gentleman here would present me with a cannon-ball, say one weighing fifty or a hundred pounds, and let me roll it across the room; and another would entrust me with a rifle-ball, and a rifle out of which I could fire it, I know which would be the more effective of the two. Let no man despise the little bullet, for very often that is the one that kills the sin, and kills the sinner, too. So, brethren, it is not the bigness of the words you utter; it is the force with which you deliver them that decides what is to come of the utterance. I have heard of a ship that was fired at by the cannon in a fort, but no impression was made upon it until the general in command gave the order for the balls to be made red-hot, and then the vessel was sent to the bottom of the sea in three minutes. That is what you must do with your sermons, make them red-hot; never mind if men do say you are too enthusiastic, or even too fanatical, give them red-hot shot, there is nothing else half as good for the purpose you have in view. We do not go out snow-balling on Sundays, we go fire-balling; we ought to hurl grenades into the enemy's ranks.

14. Boldness in History

What earnestness our theme deserves! We have to tell of an earnest Saviour, an earnest heaven, and an earnest hell. How earnest we ought to be when we remember that in our work we have to deal with souls that are immortal, with sin that is eternal in its effects, with pardon that is infinite, and with terrors and joys that are to last for ever and ever! [46]

And again,

We are not half as earnest as we ought to be. Do you not remember the young man, who, when he was dying, said to his brother, "My brother, how could you have been so indifferent to my soul as you have been?" He answered, "I have not been indifferent to your soul, for I have frequently spoken to you about it." "Oh, yes!" he said, "you spoke; but somehow, I think, if you had remembered that I was going down to hell, you would have been more earnest with me; you would have wept over me, and, as my brother, you would not have allowed me to be lost." Let no one say this of you. [47]

Without doubt one of Spurgeon's motivations was <u>hell</u>, the second death. The wrath of God on his hearers was always uppermost his mind. Read these long quotes.

A dying man is needed to raise dying men. I cannot believe that you will ever pluck a brand from the burning without putting your hand near enough to feel the heat of the fire. You must have, more or less, a distinct sense of the dreadful wrath of God and of the terrors of the judgment to come, or you will lack energy in your work, and so lack one of the essentials of success. I do not think the preacher ever speaks well upon such topics until he feels them pressing upon him as a personal burden from the Lord. "I did preach in chains," said John Bunyan, "to men in chains." Depend upon it, when the death

---

[46] Spurgeon, p36
[47] Spurgeon, p97

that is in your children alarms, depresses, and overwhelms you, then it is that God is about to bless you. [48]

Again, dear friends, the Christian has other reasons for seeking to save some; and chiefly because of the terrible future of impenitent souls. That veil which hangs before me is not penetrated by every glance but he who has his eye touched with heavenly eye-salve sees through it, and what does he see? Myriads upon myriads of spirits in dread procession passing from their bodies, and passing—whither? Unsaved, unregenerate, unwashed in precious blood, we see them go up to the solemn bar whence in silence the sentence comes forth, and they are banished from the presence of God, banished to horrors which are not to be described nor even to be imagined. This alone is enough to cause us distress day and night. This decision of destiny has about it a terrible solemnity. But the resurrection trumpet sounds. Those spirits come forth from their prison-house. I see them returning to earth, rising from the pit to the bodies in which they lived: and now I see them stand—multitudes, multitudes, multitudes, multitudes—in the Valley of Decision. And He comes, sitting on a great white throne, with the crown upon His head, and the books before Him; and there they stand as prisoners at the bar. My vision now perceives them— how they tremble! How they quiver, like aspen leaves in the gale! Whither can they flee? Rocks cannot hide them, mountains will not open their bowels to conceal them! What shall become of them? The dread angel takes the sickle, reaps them as the reaper cuts up the tares for the oven; and as he gathers them, he casts them down where despair shall be their everlasting torment. Woe is me, my heart sinks as I see their doom, and hear the terrible cries of their too-late awaking. Save some, O Christians! By all means, save some. By yonder flames, and outer darkness, and the weeping, and the wailing, and the gnashing of teeth, seek to save some! Let this, as in the case of the apostle, be your great, your ruling

---

[48] Spurgeon, p81

14. Boldness in History

object in life, that by all means you may save some. [49]

Others are wickedly prudent, and judge that certain truths which are evidently God's Word, had better be kept back. You must not be rough, but must prophesy smooth things. To talk about the punishment of sin, to speak of eternal punishment, why, these are unfashionable doctrines. It may be that they are taught in the Word of God, but they do not suit the genius of the age; we must pare them down! Brothers in Christ, I will have no share in this. Will you? O my soul, come not thou into their secret! Certain things not taught in the Bible our enlightened age has discovered. Evolution may be clean contrary to the teaching of Genesis, but that does not matter. We are not going to be believers of Scripture, but original thinkers. This is the vainglorious ambition of the period. Mark you, in proportion as the modern theology is preached, the vice of this generation increases. To a great degree, I attribute the looseness of the age to the laxity of the doctrine preached by its teachers. From the pulpit they have taught the people that sin is a trifle. From the pulpit these traitors to God and to His Christ have taught the people that there is no hell to be feared. A little, little hell, perhaps, there may be; but just punishment for sin is made nothing of. The precious atoning sacrifice of Christ has been derided and misrepresented by those who were pledged to preach it. They have given the people the name of the gospel, but the gospel itself has evaporated in their hands. From hundreds of pulpits the gospel is as clean gone as the dodo from its old haunts; and still the preachers take the position and name of Christ's ministers. [50]

But the saving of a soul from death is a far greater matter. Let us think what that death is. It is not non-existence; I do not know that I would lift a finger to save my fellow-creature from mere nonexistence. I see no great hurt in annihilation;

---

[49] Spurgeon, p138-139
[50] Spurgeon, p151

certainly nothing that would alarm me as a punishment for sin. Just as I see no great joy in mere eternal existence if that is all that is meant by eternal life, so I discern no terror in ceasing to be; I would as soon not be as be, so far as mere colourless being or not being is concerned. But "eternal life" means in Scripture a very different thing from eternal existence; it means existing with all the faculties developed in fulness of joy; existing not as the dried herb in the hay, but as the flower in all its beauty. "To die," in Scripture, and indeed in common language, is not to cease to exist. Very wide is the difference between the two words to die and to be annihilated. To die, as to the first death, is the separation of the body from the soul; it is the resolution of our nature into its component elements; and to die the second death, is to separate the man, soul and body, from his God, who is the life and joy of our manhood. This is eternal destruction from the presence of the Lord and from the glory of His power; this is to have the palace of manhood destroyed, and turned into a desolate ruin, for the howling dragon of remorse, and the hooting owl of despair, to inherit for ever.

The descriptions which Holy Scripture gives of the second death are terrible to the last degree. It speaks of a "worm that never dies," and a "fire that never can be quenched," of "the terror of the Lord," and "tearing in pieces", of "the smoke of their torment which goeth up for ever and ever," and of "the pit which hath no bottom." I am not about to bring all these terrible things together, but there are words in Scripture which, if pondered, might make the flesh to creep, and the hair to stand on end, at the very thought of the judgment to come. Our joy is, that if any of us are made, in God's hands, the means of converting a man from the error of his way, we shall have saved a soul from this eternal death. That dreadful hell the saved one will not know, that wrath he will not feel, that being banished from the presence of God will never happen to him. Is there not a joy worth worlds in all this? Remember the addition to the picture.

If you have saved a soul from death, you have introduced it

into eternal life; by God's good grace, there will be another chorister amongst the white-robed host to sing Jehovah's praise, another hand to smite eternally the harpstrings of adoring gratitude, another sinner saved to reward the Redeemer for His passion. Oh, the happiness of having saved a soul from death.[51]

To Spurgeon then hell was real, horrible and very close. He felt its danger and this motivated him to be evangelistic and bold.

Spurgeon was a minister but longed for all believers to be soul-winners, not just fellow preachers. It is more difficult to speak to one in the street than 200 from behind a pulpit. And it is always easier to give a tract than use our own words. Here Spurgeon charges us all to get out and do **personal evangelism**.

Further, let me commend to you, dear friends, the art of button-holing acquaintances and relatives. If you cannot preach to a hundred, preach to one. Get a hold of the man alone, and in love, quietly and prayerfully, talk to him. "One!" say you. Well, is not one enough? I know your ambition, young man; you want to preach here, to these thousands; be content, and begin with the ones. Your Master was not ashamed to sit on the well, and preach to one; and when He had finished His sermon, He had really done good to the whole city of Sychar, for that one woman became a missionary to her friends. Timidity often prevents our being useful in this direction, but we must not give way to it; it must not be tolerated that Christ should be unknown through our silence, and sinners unwarned through our negligence. We must school and train ourselves to deal personally with the unconverted. We must not excuse ourselves, but force ourselves to the irksome task till it becomes easy. This is one of the most honourable modes of soul-winning; and if it requires more than ordinary zeal and courage, so much the more reason for our resolving to master

---

[51] Spurgeon p164

it. Beloved, we must win souls, we cannot live and see men damned; we must have them brought to Jesus. Oh! then, be up and doing, and let none around you die unwarned, unwept, uncared-for. A tract is a useful thing, but a living word is better. Your eye, and face, and voice will all help. Do not be so cowardly as to give a piece of paper where your own speech would be so much better. I charge you, attend to this, for Jesus' sake. [52]

Amy Carmichael
There are many others who deserve to be quoted here, but let us close with part of Amy Carmichael's famous poem, "If". [53]

If I am afraid to speak the truth lest I lose affection, or lest the one concerned should say, "You do not understand", or because I fear to lose my reputation for kindness; if I put my own good name before the other's highest good, then I know nothing of Calvary love.

---

[52] Spurgeon, p129
[53] Carmichael

15. Boldness Today

In this book we have seen that God is present with his people. He enables them with his Spirit, working in the world in which they witness and protecting them from evil. The Holy Spirit will make Christ known and loved to the believer and enable the Christian to speak the gospel with boldness. Boldness is different from courage and is a fruit of the Holy Spirit with an organic connection to faith, hope, love, meekness and self-discipline. It is essential to the mission of the church worldwide and should be prayed for by all. Furthermore, we have seen that timidity can have deep complex roots in our hearts. It may arise from failure to understand God's purposes, lack of faith, confusion concerning evangelism, concerns about being unloving or unwise, etc. In this chapter we will look at the present situation. It is necessarily critical but I hope constructive if it leads to prayer and seeking God for the revival we need.

Timidity: the result of unbelief or its cause?

Is the rise of liberalism and postmodernism and the 'hollowed-out' churches in the West the result of genuine doubt, or just timidity? It is common to blame Charles Darwin with his theory of evolution and the German higher critics for the huge apostasy from the faith throughout the 20th century. Certainly these men have done great harm by sowing doubt concerning the reliability of the Bible. But is this where the blame really lies? When strange ideas and teachings sweep through the world they do not necessarily have to cause the church to decline. But where there is already a propensity to be timid, to avoid direct evangelism, to bow to the outside culture, to be acceptable to the academic and political world etc then doubts will be welcomed as a ready excuse to retreat from bold proclamation of the gospel. The blame lies with the fear of man.

I have before me a book entitled *Evangelism: Its Shame and Glory* written in 1932 by a Methodist preacher, J Rattenbury. It is a sad book because he seems to sense the nuclear winter which was descending on the Church. He writes,

"The cultured mind reacts from the sensationalism of the Cross. The Church influenced as it is by humanistic culture seeks out the quieter ways of developing the spiritual life of its children; it listens to the voice of the child psychologist, who often has had no serious combat with the devil, and talks of the spiritual battle in the vocabulary of Mr Worldly Wiseman. The consequence in Methodism already is, for instance, a generation of people with no evangelical experience, wistfully wondering at times why they miss the radiant joy and triumphs of their fathers. Evangelical religion is from above: it is not drawn out of the spiritual resources of an individual by a process of culture. That teaching is merely Humanism however much etherealized. The saving grace of our crucified Saviour must be received: it is a gift, and no humanistic theory is big enough to account for it. Evangelism can only be effective as this conviction is primary. We hold the conviction to-day with a trembling hand. It can only be dominant again when we have the courage to affirm that culture will not save; that the gospel is more important than education; and that good manners, good temper and good taste are trifles compared with the experience of salvation which lifts men into the heavenly places in Christ Jesus.
If I were asked what is the greatest objection to Evangelism in the mind of the modern cultured minister of religion, or for that matter cultured layman, I should have no hesitation in affirming that it is the fear of the humanistic mentality of the modern Church."[54]

There you have it. It is the fear of man. Not so much fear of the

---

[54] Rattenbury, p58-59

outside world but fear of the modern Church which has already has already succumbed to the spirit of the age.

For example a concern with academic respectability can quickly morph into timidity. In the same way when laziness, weariness in well-doing and loss of passion get a hold of an individual, a church or a denomination, gospel boldness will be an early casualty. So, there are many ways in which declension can set in and boldness can give way to timidity. This is a big subject but the point I want to make here is that outside influences are not the first cause of apostasy. The blame for that is uncrucified timidity.
Rattenbury is surely right when he continues, *"The greatest problem is not intellectual, nor is it to be found in the atmosphere of the age. It is whether a man will make a fool of himself for Christ's sake."*[55]

In addition, the few converts there are will rarely be bolder than those who preached to them. If no one risked scorn or embarrassment to tell them the gospel is it probable that they will take risks to pass the torch onto others? And so the downward spiral continues.

Social embarrassment: English Timidity

I have in front of me a blog post written by a leader of a group of independent evangelical churches in England who expresses his embarrassment at being in a train carriage when an unknown Christian brother preached the gospel. He admits that the preacher was polite, faithful ("gave a clear presentation of the good news of the death and resurrection of Jesus to save sinners"), warm and personal ("told his personal story of salvation, which was moving"), and was brief (5 minutes). He says he admired the preacher's boldness but prickled with embarrassment and was tempted to apologise to fellow-

---

[55] Rattenbury, p64

passengers. He admits to a mix of emotions but comes firmly down on the side of concluding the preacher was wrong. He argues that it was wrong to preach in a public space such as train where he did not have 'permission' to speak. He concludes that we should all pray for boldness and opportunities to tell the gospel (but presumably never in a train). Fatally for evangelism he urges caution while at the same time encourages prayer for boldness.[56] His analysis cannot be sustained by an appeal to biblical teaching or by the example of Jesus or his apostles. This is not a liberal theologian or an ecumenical minister but someone who would consider himself a direct spiritual descendant of the Puritans.

Christian leaders should judge by the Word of God rather than their feelings. He felt the train preacher was wrong. But on what biblical basis?. It would be more honest to say 'I'm a coward and could not do what he did' rather than justifying timidity. The fact that people who the church could not reach heard the gospel clearly and passionately was wonderful. It was the time of God's visitation for them and could well have been the most important day of their lives. Instead of supporting him and standing up and saying, 'I am an ordained pastor and would ask you to give heed to what you heard' he sits silently squirming with embarrassment and afterward writes an article criticising him. Who was filled with the Spirit? Who was obedient to "preach the word; be ready in season and out of season" (2 Tim. 4:2)? To me the answer is clear.

As my brother Rev Chris Thomas says, "We don't need permission when we have Christ's Commission.". So true!

As English Christians we acutely feel the embarrassment of our fellow Englishmen. We do not want to make others feel uncomfortable in any way and we do not want to be accused of

---

[56] Stevens

wasting their time. We do not want to be accused even unjustly of being offensive or intrusive. This is timidity. But please let us confess it as sin and not excuse it as wisdom or love. Again this is not a plea to be crass or rude or loud but for prayerful, loving gospel boldness.

Timidity as culture in Japan

In the Burma campaign of World War II the Japanese 15th Army launched an attack against the British and Indian 14th Army defending Imphal and Kohima at the eastern border of India. After a terrible siege the Japanese offensive ran out of steam. It became imperative for them to retreat to save thousands of soldiers' lives. Fergal Keane in *Road of Bones - the Epic Siege of Kohima 1944* describes a 'conversation' between Lt Gen Mutaguchi of 15th Army and his superior Lt Gen Kawabe of the Burma Area Army.

Then came one of those moments upon which destiny turns. The two men looked at each other in silence for a few moments. After the war, Mutaguchi would claim that he almost asked Kawabe to cancel the Imphal operation. 'I guessed Kawabe's real purpose in coming was to sound out of my views on the possibility - or otherwise - of continuing the Imphal operation. The sentence, "The time has come to give up the operation as soon as possible" got as far as my throat; but I could not force it out in words. But I wanted him to get it from my expression: According to the historian and Japanophile Louis Allen, Mutaguchi may have tried to use hara-gei, *Japanese 'belly art', in which meanings are conveyed by subtle changes of facial expression. The intelligence officer Lieutenant Colonel Fujiwara believed that 'face' prevented either man from admitting defeat. This may be a generous interpretation. Certainly the unwillingness to confront failure was an important cultural trait; both had gambled their prestige on the success of the invasion and Kawabe had promised imperial headquarters that he could control Mutaguchi.*

But equally relevant here is Mutaguchi's self-serving nature. He never lost an opportunity to divert blame for what happened on to both his subordinates and his superiors. It was Kawabe's fault, he implied, that he did not guess Mutaguchi's real wishes. As a result of the meeting, Kawabe told imperial headquarters and Southern Area Army about some of the problems facing 15th Army, but he did not seek permission to cancel the operation. 'Belly art' or no, both Kawabe and Mutaguchi showed themselves to be moral cowards. The Imphal operation was allowed to run for another disastrous month. [57]

Here we have two high-ranking Japanese generals who had physical courage in abundance unable to speak plainly to each other about a matter of great importance. The reason? Moral cowardice disguised as culture. In fact one blamed the other for not guessing his wishes even though he had not expressed them verbally. As a result thousands of their men died. What drove this moral cowardice? Shame before man. It is frequently said that in Japan and some other Asian countries there is a shame culture rather than a guilt culture as in the West. Shame is concerned with 'face', image before men, not being embarrassed, keeping one's pride and status at all costs. A 'guilt culture' is concerned with right and wrong, truth and falsehood, maintaining one's integrity at all costs. However the difference between East and West can be exaggerated. Japanese feel guilt too. And Westerners feel shame. Perhaps too shame culture is increasing in the West as image becomes more important and relative values rather than absolute ones take hold.

Why should this be? There are various causes in Japan. Japanese are taught from a young age that group harmony is a value to be sought and maintained at all costs. So argument, disagreement, going against the prevailing opinion are

---

[57] Keane, p393-394

15. Boldness Today

regarded as evils. From nursery school and kindergarten, children are not taught that right and wrong are absolutes, rather they are told not to cause trouble by being different, and they are disciplined by the disapproval of the group, "Look, you are causing trouble for the others!". Although this is slowly changing, children are not reared to regard truth as an absolute value nor truth-telling as a virtue. A well-known proverb says "The nail that sticks up will be hammered down'. And of course there is no Christian legacy in Japan, rather there is the history of centuries of tight social control of feudal and military governments which made your reputation among your neighbours a matter of life or death. So moral cowardice is built into Japanese culture.

The church, its pastors and missionaries have in general not coped well in this society. Many have never overcome their timidity and are ashamed to confess Christ in public. There are Christians who have never told their families that they have been baptized... for years. I heard of two Christians who worked in the same office for 20 years but never knew the other was a Christian. Evangelism when it happens is usually weak. The great truths of the nature of God, human sin and the day of judgement, rarely receive a mention. There is no urgency and unbelievers are not pressed to decide for Christ. Instead the evangelistic 'sermons' are sweet talks about how God loves everybody or psychology dressed up in Christian language, even though the evangelists involved are good evangelical men who sincerely believe the gospel but somehow they fear to express it. In short there is no gospel boldness.

Furthermore this timidity is not recognised or repented of. Rather the church is in denial. Institutional timidity is called 'wisely fitting in with the culture' and the 'Japanese need soft and slow evangelism'. This denial is reinforced when someone is offended by the gospel or complains about the activities of a zealous Christian. Then the default assumption is that the Christian has overstepped the mark and needs to retreat.

What is more when new missionaries receive orientation they are often inculcated into this mindset. One is told never to confront others, or to put them 'on the spot' by embarrassing them with anything uncomfortable. And so there is steady pressure on evangelical missionaries not to clearly tell the gospel.

This resolves into various non-biblical solutions. We are told some events are pre-evangelism. These are events specially put on just to attract people without telling them the gospel. Or there is the emphasis on friendship evangelism. Of course it is good to be friendly and make friends and evangelise them. But proponents of friendship evangelism would say that you do not have the right to tell the gospel until you have earned people's trust and 'built bridges'. They would frown on 'cold evangelism', that is telling the gospel to those you do not know, despite the New Testament's support for it.

Timidity in face of need

A subset of Japanese timidity, which is probably replicated in other cultures is the unwillingness of Christians to evangelise those who are suffering. In the Introduction I mentioned the pastor who advised us not to do evangelism in the aftermath of the 2011 tsunami. He had experienced the Great Hanshin earthquake of 1995 and was regarded as an expert so he was invited to speak to us in NE Japan. He and his church had decided that evangelism was "taking advantage of people's weakness" so they decided to only do relief work. This was falsely considered wise and loving but is a very great error. Let us consider why. God is sovereign in all the events of this world. Disasters are no exception. God sends them.

"I overthrew some of you, as when God overthrew Sodom and Gomorrah, and you were as a brand plucked out of the burning; yet you did not return to me," declares the LORD.

15. Boldness Today

Amos 4:11

According to Amos, God sends disasters so that the survivors may repent. Jesus when questioned by a self-righteous hearer about those who died horribly in disasters says that their purpose is that the survivors may repent (Luke 13:1-5). If this is God's purpose in disasters then should not the church preach the gospel of repentance and forgiveness of sin in the aftermath of a disaster? Of course it should!

This is true not just in national disasters but in cases of personal need. For example when your friend whom you have been praying for suffers a setback or a tragedy it is time to see that God is giving you an opportunity to show evangelistic love and passionately and prayerfully and tenderly yet boldly tell them the gospel clearly and fully. You will not be taking advantage of their weakness by doing so but rather cooperating with the Holy Spirit.

Political power is useless for evangelism

In the early days of the British in India, merchants and administrators of the East India Company were careful to observe Indian customs and were sensitive to the culture. This was a pragmatic policy for the sake of their business. Missionaries and evangelicals were few and found difficulties thrown in their way not just by the native Hindus and Moslems but by the Company employees whose only aim was to make money. William Carey in Calcutta, Bengal and Serampore from 1793 to 1834 found opposition rather than assistance from his compatriots. Later, Victorian evangelicals pressed for and succeeded in large-scale social reforms in industrial Britain and then they looked with genuine social concern to the darkness of India. There was indignation and horror at practices like *suti* (widow-burning) and child prostitution. As British power grew evangelicals found they had the means and political clout to force through these social reforms. However the conversion of Indians to the gospel did not keep pace with the new legislation. In addition to seeing the forced change of their culture by foreigners, Indians saw the arrogance and racism of many of the British.[58] This resentment exploded in the Indian Mutiny in 1857 which was ruthlessly crushed but resulted in a slightly more enlightened rule. The lesson of India is that it is difficult to evangelise from a position of political power, or racial superiority. And certainly political power is useless for evangelism and often a hindrance.

Another more recent example is apartheid South Africa. For 10 years I was involved in planting two churches on the Cape Flats in South Africa. Large townships had been built to house the Cape Coloured (mixed race) people. Many spoke Afrikaans and had Afrikaans names but there was universal hurt that they had been rejected by the government and classed as second-class citizens. The welcome I received was always mixed: they were friendly and grateful that I had come but cautious in case I was a 'superior' white. In particular any show of zeal was difficult. Was my desire to do evangelism because I thought they were especially bad? Did my concern to deal with sin in the church have a racist motive? I was young and immature but gradually built trust with the congregations. But new people always needed assurance that I was not a racist white. To me apartheid was a curse because it made evangelism so difficult. After we had left for Japan apartheid was abolished and the churches in South Africa saw a time of growth.

Why these historical examples? Today the greatest military, political and economic force in world is the USA. It has also the largest and richest population of evangelicals who are highly motivated to be influential. They are often politicised and aligned with various causes, usually Right and Republican. They would argue that these causes are biblical eg family, morality, pro-life etc. Is it wrong to value these? No of course

---

[58] Dalrymple

not. But it is wrong to put them first. When they replace Christ they become idols. When fighting for some righteous cause becomes more important than making Christ known as the Saviour of sinners then we inevitably put people off the gospel. How careful we need to be not to bully others or be arrogant or get intense about minor issues. Far better to be a fool for Christ and then we will always be in a position of weakness and despised by all in the world (1 Cor 2:3, 3:18).

As I write the great cause occupying US evangelicals is the threat from militant Islam. Is Islam a man-made religion and Mohammed a false prophet? Of course, but so what? Moslems are made in the image of God and the Son of God died for them too. And how wonderful when one of them believes in Jesus. So fear and hate must give way in our hearts to evangelistic love and we must renounce racial and political superiority so we can boldly tell the gospel as equals to equals. Rather than seeking political power and then forcefully using it, Christians need to realise that political power is useless for evangelism. Somehow the opposite is true. When Christians are politically weak and persecuted yet filled with gospel boldness then the Word of God spreads powerfully. Christians are usually far more attractive when they are the underdogs.

A controversy and a way forward

Dr Martin Lloyd-Jones was a formidable and very influential evangelical preacher in London for nearly 30 years in the mid-20th century. His bold evangelical preaching became famous throughout the world. He is one of the few preachers from that era whose audio sermons are widely available today so we can still listen to him. He spoke of the Holy Spirit's assistance in preaching as the 'sacred anointing' or 'unction'. He intensely sought this throughout his ministry and taught others to seek it too. As a result there are today two views of preaching. There is the 'Welsh' view held by the spiritual descendants of Lloyd-Jones (espoused by Olyott and others), that the Spirit is not inseparably present when the Word of God is preached. So the preacher and prayer meetings 'will strive and agonize in prayer for God to accompany the Word'. Secondly there is the 'Moore College' view (advanced by Woodhouse) that rejects Lloyd-Jones' teaching on 'unction' and holds that the Spirit is always present in preaching and so the preacher can be confident that if he is faithful to God's Word then the Holy Spirit will inevitably be present.

Cunnington tries to solve this controversy by turning to the Reformers' view of the sacraments. He claims that Calvin taught that the sacraments and the Spirit are distinct and not separate, in the same way that the two natures of Christ are 'distinct but not separate' . He uses the model of the hypostatic union and argues in an analagous way that the Spirit is to be distinguished from the Word but never separate. So Cunnington would come down on the side of the Moore College view.[59]

However these two positions are not as wide as apart as they seem. I doubt those who hold the 'Welsh' view would disagree with Cunnington's argument that the Word and Spirit are never separate. But they would still argue that the degree of his influence is a matter of prayer, but that after they have prayed they would go into the pulpit with the quiet confidence that the Spirit would use the faithfully preached Word.

I believe that Ward expresses it best when he describes the Holy Spirit as being in every part of the speaking operation: the speaker's preparation, his character, his verbal and even non-verbal conformity to the Holy Spirit's message. And the degree of his influence will finally depend on the will of God[60].

I think this confusion could have been avoided if Lloyd-Jones

---

[59] Cunnington
[60] Ward p165-171

had not used the terms 'sacred anointing' or 'unction' or 'divine afflatus' at all. These are highly subjective and mystical terms. Also they are extra-biblical and cannot be defined or tested by scripture. (It is true that these words may appear in scripture but are used in different senses. For example, unction does occur in the KJV of 1 John 2:20 but the apostle here is speaking of the enlightenment of the new birth, not assistance in speaking.) Tony Sargent says that Lloyd-Jones 'believed that unction prompts greater boldness, clarity and power in preaching'[61]. But how much better if he used an objective term like boldness and taught others to seek that!

In Ch 10 we noted from Acts that to speak boldly and to speak with the Holy Spirit are almost interchangeable terms. The Holy Spirit is not boldness, of course. But perhaps we can say that while boldness and the Holy Spirit are distinct they are never separate in the speech of a believer. Boldness is an objective term. I know when I have been bold and when I have held back through fear of man, diffidence or doubt. Also I know when you have been speaking boldly to me. We can also pretty much distinguish between Holy-Spirit inspired gospel boldness and man-made courage. It can be observed by both the preacher and the hearers and it can be tested by scripture. So let us pray for boldness. For then we are standing on the same solid ground as the apostles.

But perhaps we should ask ourselves how we even got into this state and why there should even be a controversy at all. I would contend that the aversion to boldness goes deep into all of us, even the best Christian workers and we need to repent of this.

Leaving Evangelism to the Holy Spirit

It is interesting to compare Acts 8 and 10. Of course Luke's

---

[61] Sargent, p50-52

main theme in the stories of the Ethiopian eunuch and Cornelius is the calling of the Gentiles. Yet there is a subsidiary theme which is also important. It is that God uses men to evangelise other men. He does not use angels and he does not do evangelism directly himself.

An angel tells Philip to go the desert road (8:26) and then the Spirit tells him to go up to the chariot (8:29) but Philip must tell the gospel. Similarly, Cornelius sees an angel who tells him to send for Peter in Joppa who has an important message for him (10:4-6, 22). But the angel himself does not tell the message to Cornelius. The doctrine is plain: the gospel must be told by men. God will not do it directly either by his Spirit or by angels. By implication unless we are obedient to the Holy Spirit to fully teach the truths of the gospel so that our hearers may be saved then they will not be saved. While no one can be saved without the new birth generated by the Holy Spirit, we are not permitted to leave the evangelism to him!

I have before me an article on John 1:43-51 by a well-known evangelical speaker and writer, Gordon Keddie. In it he comments on Philip's words to Nathanael. "Now we might have been tempted to try to persuade Nathanael, but Philip is content to let the Lord speak for himself. All he says is "Come and see". From this Keddie argues, "Could it be a lack of confidence in the Lord is for the kind of hyper-evangelism that tries to 'seal the deal' on the spot before allowing the target to go away and think before making people a commitment… and sometimes the simplest and even sparest answer is the best"[62]. I am not sure what hyper-evangelism is. As I have said previously putting pressure on people is not gospel boldness. But I know of no passage of Scripture, including the one quoted, where we are taught to hold back with gospel truths and 'leave it to the Holy Spirit'. (I am truly sorry to attack the opinions of respected evangelical brothers but unless we deal

---

[62] Keddie p5

with misunderstandings concerning boldness at the top of the evangelical church we have no chance of changing direction).

Finally,

Yet even our timidity is not the ultimate cause for the church's decline. We are all timid sinners by nature, Christ came to save his church by dying for her sins and giving her the Holy Spirit. Timidity is just one more sin. So, the ultimate cause is that we do not pray for grace to be bold according to the biblical pattern. And why do we not do that? Because we are terrified that God might actually answer our prayer and make us bold. <u>And that is too scarey to contemplate!</u>

Appendix I Why did John Mark leave the mission?

One favourite subject for missionary conferences is the failure of John Mark to continue on Paul and Silas' first missionary journey.

Now Paul and his companions set sail from Paphos and came to Perga in Pamphylia. And John left them and returned to Jerusalem, Acts 13:13

After the mission to Cyprus and they crossed to Pamphylia and then we are often told, he chickened out of missionary work when he realised such a hard life was not for him. Perhaps he was afraid of persecution, or he missed home. Later his failure has repercussions for the missionary team.

Now Barnabas wanted to take with them John called Mark. But Paul thought best not to take with them one who had withdrawn from them in Pamphylia and had not gone with them to the work.
And there arose a sharp disagreement, so that they separated from each other. Barnabas took Mark with him and sailed away to Cyprus.
Acts 15:37-39

And so we are often told that the 'good guy' in this story is Barnabas and that Paul is too harsh and unforgiving. So we should be like Barnabas and encourage and help younger missionaries who are fearful. Later Paul relents and welcomes John Mark after he has become a fully fledged missionary.

.... Mark the cousin of Barnabas (concerning whom you have received instructions—if he comes to you, welcome him), Col. 4:10

Appendix I   Why did John Mark leave the mission?

And eventually Mark becomes Paul's right-hand man.

Luke alone is with me. Get Mark and bring him with you, for he is very useful to me for ministry. 2Tim. 4:11

So we are told that Barnabas took the right approach with young John Mark. Through his encouragement of a young missionary whom Paul initially rejected John Mark's missionary career is saved and he is reconciled to the Apostle Paul.

So be like Barnabas and not like Paul, we are told.

There are serious problems with this interpretation.

1. Acts 13:13 does not say anything about the missionary team facing persecution or of John Mark being fearful of persecution or missionary work.

2. What happened on Cyprus prior to John Mark giving up the mission? There were two things of significance for a Jewish believer like John Mark. The Roman proconsul, Sergius Paulus, 'was amazed at the teaching of the Lord', and believed. And we know Paul would not have circumcised him or instructed him to keep the law of Moses. Secondly the Jewish magician who withstood the gospel was struck blind. These two stories are clear and shocking proof that God (and Paul) did not intend for the Gentile converts to follow the Jewish law, and that being a Jew according to the flesh counted for nothing.

3. The word for 'left' carries the negative sense of 'deserted'. [63]

4. We know from the Acts and Paul's letters that his chief

---

[63] Witherington, p396

anxiety was that there should be no schism between Jews and Gentiles in the Church. For this reason he so opposed the Judaizers who hindered his ministry and who insisted that Gentile converts should keep the law of Moses. Barnabas on the other hand, though a good man and full of the Holy Spirit, was easily carried away by this deception and hypocrisy (Gal. 2:13).

5. John Mark's failure and the consequent clash between Paul and Barnabas was a serious issue to Luke the author of Acts otherwise it would not have received a mention in a book of limited space.

6. John Mark was an early disciple and a thorough Jew and his mother had a house in Jerusalem (Acts 12:12).

With these considerations it is easy to see what probably happened on Cyprus. John Mark was shocked that Gentiles should be accepted as equals in the kingdom of God. He could not take accept it. And so he left the mission at Perga. Did the fear of man play a role? Undoubtedly. But it was not the fear of the Gentiles or future persecution from them. It was the fear of the Jewish church in Jerusalem. What would they say to him when he returned?!

Because of this Paul refused to take him until he had thoroughly revised his attitude which he apparently did by the time of writing of Colossians. Hence 'instructions' concerning him were necessary (Col. 4:10).

Paul could not risk one of the missionary team being ambivalent about the conversion of the Gentiles. So that is why he had a 'sharp contention' with Barnabas. Not because he was irritable with younger missionaries but because the future of the church was at stake.

I submit that this interpretation is better than the usual one which I outlined at the beginning of this appendix. The text does not give the reason for Mark's failure explicitly but the New Testament context makes it very likely correct.

John Mark was not the last missionary whose behaviour has been strange and inconsistent on the mission field because of fear of their church at home.

Appendix II Jonathan Edwards on False Boldness

Edwards wrote an account for the revival in New ENGLAND and he was concerned for the abuses that sometimes attended it. He wrote that one cause of errors attending a great revival of religion, is undiscerned spiritual pride. ...

Another effect of spiritual pride is a certain unsuitable and self-confident boldness before God and men. Thus some, in their great rejoicings before God, have not paid a sufficient regard to that rule in Psal. ii. 11. They have not rejoiced with a reverential trembling, in a proper sense of the awful majesty of God, and the awful distance between him and them. And there has also been an improper boldness before men that has been encouraged and defended by a misapplication of that scripture. Prov. xxix. 25. "The fear of man bringeth a snare." As though it became all persons, high and low, men, women, and children, in all religious conversation, wholly to divest themselves of all manner of shamefacedness, modesty, or reverence towards man; which is a great error, and quite contrary to Scripture. There is a fear of reverence that is due to some men, Rom. xiii. 7. "Fear to whom fear, honour to whom honour." And there is a fear of modesty and shamefacedness in inferiors towards superiors, which is amiable, and required by Christian rules, 1 Pet. iii. 2. "While they behold your chaste conversation coupled with fear;" and 1 Tim. ii. 9. "In like manner also, that women adorn themselves in modest apparel, with shamefacedness and sobriety." The apostle means that this virtue shall have place, not only in civil communication, but also in spiritual communication, and in our religious concerns and behaviour, as is evident by what follows, 1 Tim. ii. 11, 12. "Let the women learn in silence, with all subjection. But I suffer not a woman to teach, nor to usurp authority over the man, but to be in silence." Not that I would hence infer that women's mouths should be shut up from Christian conversation; but all that I mean from it at this time is, that modesty, or shamefacedness, and reverence towards men, ought to have some place, even in our religious communication one with another. The same is also evident by 1 Pet. iii. 15. "Be ready always to give an answer to every man that asketh you a reason of the hope that is in you, with meekness and fear." It is well if that very fear and shamefacedness, which the apostle recommends, have not sometimes been condemned, under the name of a cursed fear of man.

Edwards continues,

And it is beautiful for a minister, when he speaks in the name of the Lord of hosts, to be bold, and to put off all fear of men. And it is beautiful in private Christians, though they are women and even children, to be bold in professing the faith of Christ, in the practice of all religion, and in owning God's in the work of his power and grace, without any fear of men; though they should be reproached as fools and madmen, frowned upon by great men, and cast off by parents and all the world. But for private Christians, women and others, to instruct, rebuke, and exhort, with a like sort of boldness as becomes a minister when preaching, is not beautiful. [64]

Edwards is saying something very practical and important. All Christians must be bold but it must be appropriate to their gender, age, and station in life. In other words we must not copy those we admire but be led by the Holy Spirit to be bold. Learn from all but copy none.

In his famous work, *A TREATISE CONCERNING RELIGIOUS AFFECTIONS IN THREE PARTS* Edwards shows that gospel boldness is not inconsistent with the grace of meekness, but

---

[64] Edwards, Vol 1, p402

that false boldness comes from pride.

But here some may be ready to say, Is there no such thing as Christian fortitude, and boldness for Christ, being good soldiers in the Christian warfare, and coming out bold against the enemies of Christ and his people?

To which I answer, there doubtless is such a thing. The whole Christian life is fitly compared to a warfare. The most eminent Christians are the best soldiers, endued with the greatest degrees of Christian fortitude. And it is the duty of God's people to be stedfast, and vigorous in their opposition to the designs and ways of such as are endeavouring to overthrow the kingdom of Christ, and the interest of religion. But yet many persons seem to be quite mistaken concerning the nature of Christian fortitude. It is an exceeding diverse thing from a brutal fierceness, or the boldness of beasts of prey. True Christian fortitude consists in strength of mind, through grace, exerted in two things; in ruling and suppressing the evil passions and affections of the mind; and in stedfastly and freely exerting and following good affections and dispositions, without being hindered by sinful fear, or the opposition of enemies. But the passions restrained, and kept under in the exercise of this Christian strength and fortitude, are those very passions that are vigorously and violently exerted in a false boldness for Christ. And those affections which are vigorously exerted in true fortitude, are those Christian holy affections, that are directly contrary to the others. Though Christian fortitude appears in withstanding and counteracting enemies without us; yet it much more appears in resisting and suppressing the enemies that are within us; because they are our worst and strongest enemies, and have greatest advantage against us. The strength of the good soldier of Jesus Christ appears in nothing more, than in stedfastly maintaining the holy, calm meekness, sweetness, and benevolence of his mind, amidst all the storms, injuries, strange behaviour, and surprising acts and events, of this evil and unreasonable world. The Scripture seems to intimate that true fortitude consists chiefly in this, Prov. xvi. 32. "He that is slow to anger, is better than the mighty; and he that ruleth his spirit, than he that taketh a city."

The surest way to make a right judgment of what is a holy fortitude in fighting with God's enemies, is to look to the Captain of all God's hosts, our great leader and example, and see wherein his fortitude and valour appeared, in his chief conflict. View him in the greatest battle that ever was or ever will be fought with these enemies, when he fought with them all alone, and of the people there was none with him. See how he exercised his fortitude in the highest degree, and got that glorious victory which will be celebrated in the praises and triumphs of all the hosts of heaven, through all eternity. Behold Jesus Christ in his last sufferings, when his enemies in earth and hell made their most violent attack upon him, compassing him round on every side, like roaring lions. Doubtless here we shall see the fortitude of a holy warrior and champion in the cause of God, in its highest perfection and greatest lustre, and an example fit for the soldiers to follow, that fight under this Captain. But how did he show his holy boldness and valour at that time? Not in the exercise of any fiery passions; not in fierce and violent speeches, vehemently declaiming against the intolerable wickedness of opposers, giving them their own in plain terms; but in not opening his mouth when afflicted and oppressed, in going as a lamb to the slaughter, and, as a sheep before his shearers is dumb, not opening his mouth; praying that the Father would forgive his cruel enemies, because they knew not what they did; nor shedding others' blood, but with all-conquering patience and love shedding his own. Indeed one of his disciples, who made a forward pretence to boldness for Christ, and confidently declared he would sooner die with Christ than deny him, began to lay about him with a sword: but Christ meekly rebukes him, and heals the wound he gives. And never was the patience, meekness, love, and forgiveness of Christ, in so glorious a manifestation, as at that time. Never did he appear so much a Lamb, and never did he show so much of the dove-like spirit, as at that time. If therefore we see any of the followers of Christ, in the midst of the most violent, unreasonable, and wicked opposition, maintaining the humility, quietness, and gentleness of a lamb, and the harmlessness, love, and sweetness of a dove, we may well judge that here is a good soldier of Jesus Christ.

When persons are fierce and violent, and exert their sharp and bitter passions, it shows weakness, instead of strength and fortitude. 1 Cor. iii. at the beginning, "And I, brethren, could not speak unto you as unto spiritual, but as unto carnal, even as unto babes in Christ.—For ye are yet carnal; for whereas there is among you envying, and strife, and divisions, are ye not carnal, and walk as men?"

There is a pretended boldness for Christ that arises from no better principle than pride. A man may be forward to expose himself to the dislike of the world, and even to provoke their displeasure, out of pride. For it is the nature of spiritual pride to cause men to seek distinction and singularity; and so oftentimes to set themselves at war with those whom they call carnal, that they may be more highly exalted among their party. True boldness for Christ is universal, and carries men above the displeasure of friends and foes; so that they will forsake all rather than Christ; and will rather offend all parties, and be thought meanly of by all, than offend Christ. And that duty which tries whether a man is willing to be despised by those of his own party, and thought the least worthy to be regarded by them, is a more proper trial of his boldness for Christ, than his being forward to expose himself to the reproach of opposers. The apostle declined to seek glory, not only of heathens and Jews, but of Christians; as he declares, 1 Thess. ii. 26 (sic)[65]. He is bold for Christ, who has Christian fortitude enough to confess his fault openly, when he has committed one that requires it, and as it were to come down upon his knees before opposers. Such things as these are much greater evidence of holy boldness, than resolutely and fiercely confronting opposers. As some are much mistaken

---

[65] Edwards means 1 Thess. ii. 6

Appendix II Jonathan Edwards on False Boldness

concerning the nature of true boldness for Christ, so they are concerning christian zeal. It is indeed a flame, but a sweet one; or rather it is the heat and fervour of a sweet flame. For the flame of which it is the heat, is no other than that of divine love, or christian charity; which is the sweetest and most benevolent thing that can be, in the heart of man or angel. Zeal is the fervour of this flame, as it ardently and vigorously goes out towards the good that is its object; and so consequently in opposition to the evil that is contrary to, and impedes it. There is indeed opposition, vigorous opposition, that is an attendant of it; but it is against things, and not persons. Bitterness against the persons of men is no part of, but is contrary to it; insomuch that the warmer true zeal is, and the higher it is raised, so much the further are persons from such bitterness, and so much fuller of love both to the evil and to the good. It is no other, in its very nature and essence, than the fervour of christian love. And as to what opposition there is in it to things, it is firstly and chiefly against the evil things in the person himself who has this zeal; against the enemies of God and holiness in his own heart; (as these are most in his view, and what he has most to do with;) and but secondarily against the sins of others. And therefore there is nothing in a true christian zeal contrary to the spirit of meekness, gentleness, and love; the spirit of a little child, a lamb and dove, that has been spoken of; but is entirely agreeable to, and tends to promote it.[66]

---

[66] Edwards, Vol 1, p305-306

Acknowledgements

I was converted in November 1976 in Cape Town, South Africa, and within a month became a regular at St James Church, Kenilworth, where Frank Retief was rector and Barry van Eyssen was pastoral assistant. Both were models of boldness, Frank by his Holy-Spirit-empowered preaching and Barry by his personal evangelism. More than any other these men have been examples to me.

I would like to thank my wife Glenda for her support throughout this project and Patrick Fung, OMF General Director and other colleagues in OMF International for their helpful comments on the manuscript. Christopher Ash of Proclamation Trust and Ray Porter of Oak Hill Theological College gave advice at the early stages of writing which set me on the right track.

We are blessed to have scores of supporters throughout the world and hundreds of prayer partners: without them this work would not have been possible.

Literature Cited

Alexander, J.A. 1857 A Commentary on the Acts of the Apostles, The Banner of Truth Trust, Edinburgh & Carlisle pp 498

Bonhoeffer, Dietrich 1943 Letters and Papers from Prison, Fortress Press, Minneapolis, pp614

Bridges, Charles 1849, The Christian Ministry: With An Inquiry Into The Causes Of Its Inefficiency 8th Ed., L. Seeley, London, pp551

Bunyan, John 1678, The Pilgrim's Progress, Airmont Publishing, New York, pp283

Bruce, F.F. 1968 This is That: The New Testament development of some Old Testament themes. Exeter: Paternoster Press, pp122

Calvin, John 1550 The Golden Booklet of the True Christian Life, Baker Book House, Grand Rapids pp96

Calvin, John 1553 Commentary on the Gospel of John, Christian Classics Ethereal Library

Calvin, John 1562 John Calvin's Sermons on Ephesians, The Banner of Truth Trust, Edinburgh & Carlisle pp705

Carmichael, Amy 1953 If Christian Literature Crusade (1999), Fort Washington, Pennsylvania 19034, This Edition Styled by The Radia Bible Collaborative, http://steppinginthelight.com/wp-content/uploads/2013/03/if-amy-carmichael.pdf

Cormack, Don, 2009, Killing Fields, Living Fields:The

Unfinished Portrait of the Cambodian Church, OMF/Christian Focus, Sevenoaks and Fearn pp 450

Cunnington, Ralph 2015. Preaching with Spiritual Power; Calvin's Understanding of Word and Spirit in Preaching. Christian Focus pp126

Dallimore, Arnold A. 1970, George Whitefield: The Life and Times of the Great Evangelist of the Eighteenth-Century Revival - Volume I, The Banner of Truth Trust, Edinburgh and Carlisle, pp598

Dalrymple, William 2006 The Last Mughal, The Fall of A Dynasty, Delhi, 1857 Penguin Books, New Delhi pp578

Edwards, Jonathan 1742, Some Thoughts Concerning The Present Revival Of Religion In New England, And The Way In Which It Ought To Be Acknowledged And Promoted. Humbly Offered To The Public, In A Treatise On That Subject. in The Works of Jonathan Edwards Vol 1, The Banner of Truth Trust, Edinburgh and Carlisle, pp 691

Edwards, Jonathan, 1746 A Treatise Concerning Religious Affections In Three Parts The Works of Jonathan Edwards Vol 1The Banner of Truth Trust, Edinburgh and Carlisle, pp691

Edwards, Jonathan, 1749 Christ the Example of Ministers in The Works of Jonathan Edwards Vol 2, The Banner of Truth Trust, Edinburgh and Carlisle, pp969

Gurnall, William 1662-65, The Christian in Complete Armour, The Banner of Truth Trust, Edinburgh and Carlisle, pp 1189

Haldane, Robert 1835 republished 1958 An Exposition of the Epistle to the Romans, MacDonald Publishing Company, MacLean, Illinois, p660

Literature Cited

Henry, Matthew 1710 Commentary on the Whole Bible, Zondervan, Grand Rapids pp1986

Hunter, George 2010, The Celtic Way of Evangelism, How Christianity Can Reach the West . . .Again. Abingdon Press; 10th Revised edition, pp 114

Keane, Fergal 2010 Road of Bones - the Epic Siege of Kohima 1944 Harper Press, London pp 550

Keddie, Gordon 2016 'You are the Son of God', Evangelical Times July 2016

Livingstone, W. P. 1915 Mary Slessor of Calabar: Pioneer Missionary, Project Gutenberg, EBook, pp242

Kourdakov, Sergei 1975, Forgive Me, Natasha, Marshall Pickering, London pp201

Leupold, H.C. 1949 Exposition of Daniel, Baker Book House, Grand Rapids, pp 549

Lloyd-Jones, David Martyn 1964, Spiritual Depression: Its Causes and Cure William B. Eerdmans Publishing Company pp300

MacArthur, John F. 2008 The Jesus You Can't Ignore: What You Must Learn from the Bold Confrontations of Christ, Thomas Nelson, Nashville. eBook

Martis, V & Desai, M. B. 1999 Burnt Alive: The Staines and the God They Loved, GLS Publishing pp 215

Olyott, Stuart, 2004 Dare To Stand Alone - Daniel Simply Explained: Read and Enjoy the Book of Daniel (Welwyn Commentary) Evangelical Press pp168

Packer, JI 1973 Knowing God, Hodder and Stoughton, London. pp317

Pink, A.W. 1956 The Life of Elijah, The Banner of Truth Trust, Edinburgh and Carlisle, pp320

Piper, John 2011 Desiring God: Meditations of a Christian Hedonist Inter-Varsity Press, pp368

Rattenbury, J. Ernest 1932 Evangelism: Its Shame and Glory: Epworth Press pp143

Ryle, J. C, (1898). Light from Old Times, Thynne, London 2nd Edition P165, 163 pp456

Sargent, Tony 1994 The Sacred Anointing. The Preaching of Martyn Lloyd-Jones, Hodder and Stoughton, London pp 362

Sibbes, Richard, 1630 The Bruised Reed, The Banner of Truth Trust, Edinburgh and Carlisle, pp128

Stevens, John, blog post, Unexpected Evangelism Training: Discerning The Fine Balance Between Being Bold And Inappropriate In Sharing The Gospel in www.john-stevens.com/2015/11/unexpected-evangelism-training.html

Spurgeon, Charles Haddon 1903 The Soul Winner, Passmore & Alabaster pp170 pdf version

Storms, Sam 2013, Kingdom Come, The Amillennial Alternative, Mentor, pp 592

Stott, John 1986 The Cross of Christ, Inter-varsity Press pp460

Stott, John 1990 The Spirit, the Church and the World: The Message of Acts, Inter-varsity Press pp428

Literature Cited

Thompson, J.A 1980 The Book of Jeremiah, The New International Commentary on the Old Testament, Eerdmans, Grand Rapid, pp819

Ward, Timothy 2009 Words of Life: Scripture as the living and active word of God IVP Nottingham pp186

Ware, Bruce A. 2013 The Man Christ Jesus, Theological Reflections on the Humanity of Christ, Crossway, Wheaton, pp156

Welch, Ed, 1997 When People Are Big and God is Small: Overcoming Peer Pressure, Codependency, and the Fear of Man, P & R Publishing, pp256

Wesley, Charles, The Journal of Charles Wesley, http://wesley.nnu.edu/charles-wesley/the-journal-of-charles-wesley-1707-1788/

Witherington, Ben, 1997 The Acts of the Apostles: A Socio-Rhetorical Commentary (New Testament Commentary), Eerdmans Pub Co, pp874

Young, Edward J. A 1949 A Commentary on Daniel, The Banner of Truth Trust, Edinburgh & Carlisle pp330

Printed in Great Britain
by Amazon